THE ALLYN AND BACON GUIDE TO PEER TUTORING

SECOND EDITION

Paula Gillespie
Marquette University

Neal Lerner
Massachusetts Institute of Technology

PEARSON
Longman

New York San Francisco Boston
London Toronto Sydney Tokyo Singapore Madrid
Mexico City Paris Munich Cape Town Hong Kong Montreal

Senior Vice President and Publisher: Joe Opiela
Vice President and Publisher: Eben W. Ludlow
Executive Marketing Manager: Ann Stypuloski
Production Manager: Charles Annis
Project Coordination, Text Design, and Electronic Page Makeup: Pre-Press Co., Inc.
Cover Design Manager: Nancy Danahy
Cover Designer: Keithley Associates
Cover Photo: Michael J. Gryniewicz, reproduced through the courtesy of Marquette Univeristy
Manufacturing Manager: Dennis J. Para
Printer and Binder: Courier Corporation
Cover Printer: Coral Graphic Services, Inc.

Library of Congress Catologing-in-Publication Data

Gillespie, Paula
   The Allyn and Bacon guide to peer tutoring / Paula Gillespie, Neal Lerner.—
2nd ed.
      p. cm.
   Includes biographical references (p.) and index.
   ISBN 0-321-18283-9 (pbk.)
    1. Peer-group tutoring of students. 2. Tutors and tutoring. 3. Writing centers.
I. Title: Guide to peer tutoring. II. Lerner, Neal. III. Title.

   LB1031.5.G55   2003
   371.39'4—dc21   2003047504

Between the time web site information is gathered and published, some sites may have closed. Also, the transcription of URLs can result in typographical errors. The publisher would appreciate notification where these occur so that they may be corrected in subsequent editions.

Please visit our Web site at http://www.ablongman.com

Printed in the United States of America

3 4 5 6 7 8 9 BKM BKM   0 9 8 7 6 5 4

CONTENTS

PREFACE TO THE SECOND EDITION

Like many writing projects, this book grew out of conversations that we've had over the years, either on the phone, in front of computer screens, or face-to-face. When the subject of those conversations was tutor training, we agreed that our contribution to the field would be marked by the presence of tutors, whether through reflective papers, tutoring journals, or session transcripts. It seems unfortunately trite to say that we've learned amazing amounts from those tutors we've worked with or directly trained, as well as from the many, many writers we've had the good fortune to meet in writing center work. But it's true—those tutors and writers have been among our greatest teachers, and we knew that a tutor-training book should be steeped in their accounts.

We also feel that the structure of our text should mirror the structure of tutor training, starting with overviews of the writing and tutoring processes (Chapters 2 and 3), followed by some self-examination of what one brings to tutoring (Chapter 4), then concrete instruction in observing (Chapter 5), practicing with essays (Chapter 6), and making sense of those first tutoring experiences (Chapter 7). We also felt that we should support our readers' study of tutoring with more depth on specialized topics: reading in the writing center (Chapter 8), working with nonnative English speakers (Chapter 9), conducting writing center research (Chapter 10), understanding the foundations of writing center history, theory, and practice (Chapter 11), and considering the special requirements of tutoring in a writing-across-the-curriculum (WAC) program (Chapter 12). Finally, we also felt that any guide needed to anticipate common scenarios and offer some general advice in how to deal with those potential challenges (Chapter 13).

While there's certainly a sequence to these chapters, we also intend any single chapter to stand alone and allow our readers to pick and choose depending on their particular needs. Along those lines, rather than include readings that might reflect *our* particular needs, we've instead included a list of recommended readings, as well as a list of works cited.

NEW TO THE SECOND EDITION

We have received a great deal of helpful feedback since publishing the first edition of *The Allyn & Bacon Guide to Peer Tutoring*, and we hope that this second edition reflects those voices of writing center directors and tutors.

Additions

We have added two new chapters to the second edition: Chapter 11, "Writing Centers: Historical and Theoretical Contexts" and Chapter 12, "Interdisciplinary and On-line Tutoring." The foundations chapter provides background on writing center history, theory, and practice suitable for undergraduates and graduate students interested in learning about the larger contexts for writing center work. Chapter 12 is geared specifically to the tutoring being done as part of the growing number of WAC programs; it equips tutors with the concepts behind writing-to-learn and some specific strategies they'll need to work with students, whether face-to-face or on-line, from a wide variety of academic disciplines.

Alterations, Eliminations

The chapter on Discourse Analysis has been retitled "Writing Center Research" and includes additional material on the variety of research activities for which the writing center provides fertile ground. Also, we have cut out three chapters from the first edition: "The Mock Tutorial," "On-Line Tutoring," and "Writing Center Ethics." However, we have folded the most important materials from these chapters into existing chapters (particularly into Chapter 3, "The Tutoring Process," Chapter 6, "Tutoring Practice," and Chapter 13, "What If . . ."). Finally, we have expanded and updated the Recommended Readings to include the large number of writing center–related texts that have appeared in the last several years and a comprehensive list of dissertations that have been written on the subject of writing centers.

These are exciting times for us in the writing center field. A thriving international organization and a publishing house, two journals dedicated to our scholarship, a growing number of regional organizations, and a host of new publications—all are evidence of the increasing recognition of the power of the one-to-one teaching of writing. As writing centers grow at all instructional levels, so does the need to have skilled, prepared tutors. We hope that this guide can contribute to that end.

ACKNOWLEDGMENTS

We both wish to thank Eben Ludlow of Longman for his never-wavering support of this project from its earliest, sketchiest form to the latest edition. Editorial Assistant Tania Sanchez provided her able assistance to the first edition, and Bill Russo smoothly stepped in for the second. Additionally, we're indebted to the reviewers of our original proposal for this book and the reviewers of drafts of the first edition—Albert C. DeCiccio, Rivier College; Muriel Harris, Purdue University; James C. McDonald, University of Southwestern Louisiana; Jon Olson, Pennsylvania State University; and Bruce Pegg, Syracuse University. Their thoughtful and helpful comments allowed us to reimagine just what this book could be and for whom. Many thanks too to those reviewers who gave us much to think about as we prepared this second edition: Debra Dew, University of Colorado at Colorado Springs; Michele Eodice, University of Kansas; Francie Jeffery, University of Central Arkansas; Carol Mattingly, University of Louisville; and Howard Tinberg, Bristol Community College. We'd also like to thank the many contributors to the Internet listserv WCenter over the last several years. Many of our ideas for tutor training were gleaned and refined from that discussion list, and it continues to be a vital source of support, encouragement, and collegiality. Bobbie Silk, Jon Olson, Katie Fischer, and Stephen Newmann continue to be our vital support system; this book would not have been possible without them.

Neal would like to thank Nicole Kelley and Anne Ellen Geller for their helpful feedback, and the staffs of the writing centers at San Jose State University, Boston University, the Massachusetts Institute of Technology, and the Massachusetts College of Pharmacy and Health Sciences for all they have taught him about tutoring and teaching. He is also indebted to Tania Baker for her never-wavering support, Hannah Baker-Lerner for her sweet presence, and Clay Baker-Lerner for the sheer joy of his smile.

Paula would like to thank all of the tutors at the Ott Memorial Writing Center; they enrich her life and work. Thanks to Tim Machan of the Department of English, Kris Ratcliffe, Harvey Kail, Brad Hughes, Carl Glover, Joyce Steward, Virginia Chappell, Lori Baker, Alice Gillam, and CJ Hribal. Her family, Michael, Karen, Leigh, Torrey, and Ann, have been wonderfully encouraging and supportive. Deepest gratitude to the family of Norman H. Ott for its generous support of the Writing Center and to the John P. Raynor, S.J. Library for welcoming our presence in their beautiful new building.

ABOUT THE AUTHORS

In the chapters that follow, we offer advice to deal with the complexities of tutoring. However, we don't want to obscure the joy that writing center work will bring you. Instead, we want to open this textbook by giving you a sense of our experience and of the joy that we have found in writing center work. We want you to know how we came to this point as writing center directors and textbook writers.

First, Paula:

I'd tutored in what used to be called the Writing Lab at the University of Wisconsin, Madison when I was a graduate student back in the 70s, and I'd enjoyed it. We went far beyond the drill-and-kill centers you sometimes read about in the literature of that era because the director, Joyce Steward, was ahead of her time, really breaking ground for writing centers. But when I left Madison, my writing center work ended for a few years.

I taught part-time for a while at Marquette, had a baby, and finished up my exams and courses for my doctorate. The Marquette writing center hummed along just down the hall from me, and I referred my students there as I taught sections of first-year comp and sophomore literature.

But then things changed at Marquette. They put into place an innovative writing program that changed the focus from classical rhetoric and the modes of discourse to the process of writing. This program was similar to the one I'd been trained in at Madison when I taught developmental writers there, so when a new full-time job opened, I applied for it and got it. My duties eventually included directing the writing center.

I had never envisioned myself as a writing center director before, but I began reading everything I could get my hands on, and I was sent to spend a few days in New York City with Lil Brannon, who directed the writing center at NYU. A few years earlier, Lil had started up a writing center in a closet—literally in a closet—because she believed so strongly in collaborative learning and in the power of tutoring. She established and edited the Writing Center Journal, *and she had a busy and exciting writing center. She made me feel optimistic not only about directing a center but about the goals and possibilities of tutoring.*

I began tutoring alongside the new graduate student tutors rather than just directing the center, and I found that our common ground made me a better director for being part of the tutoring. But it was more than that: I found that I really, really enjoyed tutoring.

My favorite tutoring experiences came when writers would stay with me through their four years of college. I remember Jane, an older student who struggled to pass her writing courses at first, but who grew in her mastery of writing as the years and courses came and went. She'd never been taught to write essays or to document sources, and she struggled to make her verbs agree with the subjects so that she met the requirements of academic discourse. We spent a lot of time looking at her verbs, but after some time she was finding them herself and fixing them on her own. And with her leaps-and-bounds improvements in grammar and correctness came an increasingly sophisticated ability to read and interpret texts. I don't know what caused what, but I know that her self-respect grew along with her writing ability.

And I remember Tahseena, who came to this country from Pakistan without having studied English, and who also struggled, but wanted to be a philosophy major because a course had made her catch fire. My favorite meeting with her took place outdoors rather than in the writing center where we'd worked together. One day she passed me on campus, waving a philosophy paper in the air. "I got an AB on it! And I did it all by myself!" She didn't need me any more; that's a sad but delicious experience.

Other sad but delicious experiences happen every spring when a class of tutors graduates and takes off for graduate school, law school, jobs of all kinds. A recent research project has involved my colleagues and friends, Harvey Kail and Brad Hughes, and me in looking into the long- and short-term effects of tutoring on the tutors themselves. Pilot studies and focus groups we've done in preparation for the longer study show striking benefits for tutors, as they imagine themselves in professions, as they talk about their abilities and demonstrate those skills in job interviews, and as they use their skills on the job. But most dramatic for me is the way they talk about the way some values they held were furthered and deepened by their training and work experience—values of respect for others and for their work; their pride in their ability to listen, to be attentive to others, to be patient with them, to put others' needs and goals and

priorities before their own agendas, to be capable and confident communica-
tors. These values carry over, they say, into their personal and family relation-
ships. We don't promise transformation in writing center work, but we have
seen amazing things happen. That makes this the best work I can think of.

Next, Neal's story:

My teaching career started with writing center work. After an uneven career
as an undergraduate English major and after several years of working in the
computer industry, I enrolled in a graduate English/Creative Writing program
at San Jose State University, pursuing my master's degree. My short-term
goal was to write fiction and live off student loans (I don't think I had any
long-term goals). However, I soon found that I needed additional work to pay
my rent and buy the occasional sandwich. In the fall of the first year, I applied
to work in the SJSU Writing Center. I hadn't had any experience as a writing
teacher (and thus couldn't secure a coveted teaching assistant position), but I
had taken a seminar course in my first semester on "Practical Approaches to
Composition." In that course, I became intrigued by the study of the writing
process and the challenge of teaching others to write. The application process
for the SJSU Writing Center involved responding to a student's text and com-
pleting a short-answer grammar exam. I did fine with the text response but
bombed the exam (despite having written a great deal since my undergraduate
days, at that time I couldn't tell you the difference between a noun modifier
and burnt toast). For some reason, the director of the writing center saw some
potential and agreed to hire me, provided that at the same time I would enroll
in a class on English grammar and usage.

I loved tutoring from the very first. I was working primarily with students
in basic writing courses or those who had been in a non-college-level track in
high school and found themselves unprepared for college-level work. Many of
the students were of Asian or Latino descent, were anxious to claim their share
of the American Dream, and were frustrated over how their language profi-
ciency was holding them back. But they were also grateful to be getting the at-
tention and instruction that the Writing Center could provide. As far as the
grammar class went, I even found that work to be enjoyable after a while, once
I had broken the secret code of grammar terminology.

After getting my MA and then a high-school teaching credential, I worked
as an adjunct English teacher at a variety of places across the country. But one-
to-one instruction, whether in a writing center or in private, was a constant
thread. By the time I found myself in Boston, in a doctorate of Education pro-
gram at Boston University, writing center work provided several important di-
rections. One was to give me a chance to return to the teaching of writing at
the Boston University Writing Center after several semesters of teaching foun-
dations of education. The other was to give me a dissertation topic when I em-

barked on a two-year study of the tutors and writers who used one particular writing center. I was fascinated (and still am) by the experiences and expectations that tutors and writers bring to their sessions, and how those notions translate into the language each participant uses. Near the end of my program, I also started tutoring at the Massachusetts Institute of Technology Writing Center, working with a steady stream of technically-minded undergraduates and graduate students, all trying to make meaning of and seeking help in that pursuit.

In 1996, I was hired to start a writing center and teach composition at the Massachusetts College of Pharmacy and Health Sciences in Boston, and I worked at MCPHS for six years. Students at MCPHS take required first-year composition and also have other courses and professional tasks with a strong writing component. One feature of the students who visited the writing center was that over 60 percent identified themselves as ESL, compared with 30 percent of the student population who were identified as ESL. Thus, my staff, a mix of professional and undergraduate peer consultants, were always challenged to understand and refine their practice in light of students with a wide range of preparation and skill.

In the fall of 2002, I left MCPHS for a position at MIT; however, rather than work in the writing center, my task now is to work with a rapidly expanding WAC program, part of MIT's new Communication-Intensive Requirement (all undergraduates need to take four courses designated as "communications intensive," and two of those courses must be in their majors). This semester, I'm teaching a writing course that's part of a sophomore molecular biology laboratory class, and I'm working with students, teaching assistants, and faculty in a management class and an architectural history class. It's exciting work, quite different from what I have done previously, but I am finding that my writing center background serves me well. A great deal of my teaching is now done one-to-one. Interesting, of course, that giving up the directing of a writing center—where my administrative work increasingly distanced me from day-to-day tutoring—has given me more opportunity to teach in a writing-centered way. And as I work with disciplines far removed from English, I see even more the power of writing and the necessity for writing tutors. The stakes are high when a biology student is trying to communicate her experimental results, particularly if it is her hope to be a research scientist some day. Those communicative acts take place in a variety of professional and teaching contexts, and all are marked by an attention to the student's writing, her promise as a scientist often determined by her ability to communicate the results of her experiments and argue for her interpretation of those results. Important stuff and a great opportunity for writing instruction.

While I'm not currently involved in the day-to-day running of a writing center, my professional life is still steeped in many things writing centered. Along with Beth Boquet, I am now coeditor of The Writing Center Journal *and have that vantage point to support new and existing scholars in our field. My interest in the history of writing centers has also become an obsession of sorts since Paula and I wrote the first edition of this book. My current project is to reclaim the "idea of a writing laboratory," a wide-ranging work that will include a history of early writing laboratories, including the University of Minnesota General College writing laboratory, founded in 1932; a study of how undergraduates learn to write in a scientific research laboratory; a history of scientific laboratory instruction in American colleges and universities; and, finally, a call to return to the exploratory and progressive notions of writing as a laboratory subject. The one-to-one teaching of writing has had a hold on me for a while now, and I gladly meet its embrace.*

1

WHY WE TUTOR

This is a book about tutoring writing. You'll read about the techniques of tutoring, the theoretical and practical background that you'll need to be successful, and the specific issues that make writing center work both challenging and rewarding.

To introduce you to tutoring writing and to how we hope this book will help you, we want to start at the beginning. Why do we tutor? The answer to that question forms, for us, the foundation upon which our own lives as tutors and writing center directors are based, and informs each chapter of this book.

We'll first explore the question "Why tutor?" by turning to some voices that you'll hear again and again in this book—the trainees in the Marquette University peer tutoring course. Much that is offered here has been tried out on that willing and generous group, and we coauthors have learned a great deal from their experiences. We think you, too, will find much familiarity with the stories they tell, but in particular, in this chapter, they will talk about what they expected tutoring to be like at the beginning of their course and where they believe those expectations came from. We believe that learning anything new starts with thinking about what you already know and then building upon that knowledge. As you read these responses, think about the experiences that you bring to tutoring writing.

From Jessi:

> I remember when I was in fourth grade, I was singled out (I hate when teachers do that) to help a slow kid named Peter with his reading. We sat down during "quiet time" and I helped him go over the lesson we

had learned earlier that day. Each day when we were done, the teacher would give me a sticker, I assume as a reward, that I had to wear on the front of my Catholic school uniform. She never gave Peter a sticker.

Today I am still undecided as to why I was chosen to help Peter. Was it because I have always been good at matters pertaining to English? Did the teacher think Peter would benefit more from my help as a peer? Or was she just lazy and preferred to have "quiet time" to herself? I guess I don't expect a sticker at the end of each of my tutoring sessions these days. I do expect tutoring to be a fulfilling experience for both myself and my students/classmates. I hope to give them something they can walk away with and apply later on, whether it be on that paper or a future one. I hope I can take something I have learned and help them use that knowledge to become better writers.

From Paul:

In my high school, being a tutor meant being a really good speller and knowing MLA style. In fact I remember one of my sophomore year English teachers saying to class one day that with computers being able to spell check and grammar check, proof readers won't be necessary anymore. Now I took this little "gem" of knowledge to mean that tutors were going to be obsolete. Why go and get your writing checked when the computer does it for you? The answer came my freshman year when I went to the writing center. I don't remember my tutor's name. All I remember was he did not care one ounce about my spelling. He wanted to make sure that the paper "flowed." I was dumbfounded; I had no idea what he was talking about. In fact, I didn't even follow his suggestions because anything he said went against the Introduction-Three-Paragraph-Conclusion format I had learned in high school. Well, Dr. Miller gave me a D. I rewrote the paper with the suggestions that my tutor gave me. I got a B.

I learned (the hard way) that tutoring is more than just proofreading. It's about getting the person to realize that there is always more than one set way to go about writing a paper.

From Aesha:

For most of my career as a student, I basically wanted to please my teachers. I was concerned about getting a smiley face on my paper or having my teacher read my paper aloud as an example of what to do for an "A." Therefore, if there was something wrong with my writing that my teachers didn't like, I changed it, even if I liked it. Somehow, I equated an "A" in English from my fifth-grade teacher to mean that she liked me as a person. It wasn't until I came to college that these expectations changed. My English 001 professor, Dr. Gervasi, challenged me to examine my thought processes. If my paper was not "A" material on the first draft, it did not necessarily mean that I was somehow not good enough. Dr. Gervasi showed me this by not being so excited about my hurried grammatical changes (my grade reflected this) as he was about the way I strengthened my support of opinions or even when I changed my mind.

In other words, I don't want the tutee to think that I am somehow judging his/her personality when we are in a session. I want it to be clear that my suggestions, etc. are not the last word, but that he/she must decide what works.

From Megan:

I was a junior in high school, and never having struggled with a class, I was forced by my parental units to seek out a tutor in order to find success in physics. As I knew physics would not play a very important part in my future, I needed not to "understand" but rather to pull out of the class having created the idea that I was physics-minded. Mr. Martinson came highly recommended by a number of my friends. Soon, I found out why. We met at the library for our one-hour session. I would hand him my book and my assignment, and he would proceed to complete each problem, showing his work clearly, and usually with a diagram. I would then take the work home, having been "tutored," and I would copy it, memorize it, and give it to any of my friends who also were struggling. I passed physics, and well too, but in retrospect I know that I have little idea what speed two tennis balls shot from opposite sides of the room would have to be thrown in order for them to meet exactly in the middle of the room.

So this being my experience when I became a peer tutor my senior year, I knew what not to do. Don't do their work. Try to simplify the problem. Have the other person explain what they think they are doing wrong. These were the steps I would take.

As a tutor in the writing center, I can see how easy it would be to get "Mr. Martinson Syndrome": to take the dreaded red pen to a paper and edit and rewrite. But I know this is highly ineffective. So to sum it all up: I think my preconceptions about tutoring are only that I am not here to do the work but to help someone else be proud of the work that they have done without feeling that unnecessary struggle is required.

From Adele:

When I was in high school, I started my freshman year out in "honors" English. After that first year, I was asked to move down to regular

English because good ol' Mrs. Johnson thought I could "handle" it better. That ruined most of my aspirations for writing. I accepted C's because I figured I just wasn't a good writer. God must have given me some other talent, and I tried to find it.

It wasn't until sophomore year of college that I found writing again. Thanks to Dr. McBride's English Lit class, I figured out how to write for myself. Prior to this, I never saw the point in tutoring because I always viewed it as a bashing session by "Mrs. Johnson." And Lord knows we all get defensive when our work is torn to shreds by some dominant little know-it-all. So, anyway, I went to talk to McBride about my first analytical paper, expecting him to scrape up all the little lost pieces. I was desperate. But I was totally thrown off by our meeting. The head of the department wanted to know what I thought; HE was the expert! But that session taught me that the writer is the expert. It was MY damn paper, and I had to learn how to write it.

From Sara:

Most of my experiences with tutoring in high school left a bad taste in my mouth. Because I was a good student and a fairly good writer for a high school student, my teachers would often ask me to work with other students who were struggling. Or my friends, who knew that I got good grades, would come to me with questions about homework assignments. A lot of my study halls would get eaten up by answering questions about subjects from chemistry to English. I enjoyed helping people and didn't mind the time I spent with them, but many times I would end up feeling used. I would get sick of working on assignments with people who just wanted to get to the bottom line, but who didn't care about the whole process behind getting there. Looking back on those experiences after our discussions and readings, I see now that I wanted to be a "minimalist" tutor who caused others to think about their writing or other assignments, but I didn't know how to do that.

Since high school, I have worked at the Educational Opportunity Program over in Marquette Hall as a tutor for the Upward Bound program. My experiences there have been a lot better than those in high school. I haven't ever tutored writing, but I learned by working there that the student learns best when he or she does the work. I, as a tutor, am not there to solve their every problem with the assignment, but to help them think through how they can solve those problems on their own. In some ways, I think the goal of a tutor should be to make yourself obsolete. I hope that all of the students I worked with at EOP learned to problem solve on their own. Like Paula said in class—it's okay that the freshmen didn't come back to the writing center after their first time, so long as they were equipped the first time with the tools to successfully critique their own writing.

As you read these accounts, you might have noticed several common themes. Almost all had their expectations of tutoring formed by being put in a "teacherly" position or by being tutored themselves. And almost all of these writers didn't like the position of being a know-it-all; instead, they have learned that tutoring involves helping someone become a better writer, not handing out vocabulary words or cleaning up someone else's paper (and we'll talk much more about the differences between tutoring and editing in Chapter 3). As Sara wrote, "I, as a tutor, am not there to solve [writers'] every problem with the assignment, but to help them think through how they can solve those problems on their own." So, how do you do that?

CONTRASTING CONCEPTS

One other theme from the tutor stories is that many concepts that surround tutoring writing seem to be in opposition—tutor/editor, novice/expert, process/product, control/flexibility, tutor/teacher. These contrasts frame many of the minute-by-minute decisions we make as tutors. In this book we will expand on each of these contrasts, showing how experienced tutors don't simply reject one concept in favor of its opposite, but instead adjust their actions by being sensitive to a writer's needs and the context of any individual tutoring session. In other words, each of these contrasts exists as ends of a continuum, and any place on that scale contains qualities of both extremes. As an analogy, imagine a color scale with blue on one end and yellow on the other. The exact middle of that scale is green—a fifty-fifty blending of blue and yellow—but as you get closer to the blue end, that green becomes bluer and bluer, and when you get closer to the yellow end, that green begins to pale. In this text we'll often refer to concepts that aren't either/or choices (for example, we won't claim that writing center work is *either* challenging *or* rewarding—it's both!), but instead we'll invoke these contrasts to attest to the complexity of the work you are about to enter. You'll often find yourself closer to one end of the continuum than the other, sometimes in the middle, sometimes at several places over the course of any given session. If this technique sounds active and responsive, well, those are two qualities that experienced tutors often display.

One additional contrast is the prescriptive/descriptive continuum. In this book, we don't want necessarily to *prescribe* what we think an effective tutor should do (after all, there's no way we can anticipate every situation you'll be in), nor do we think that the best way for you to learn is for us to *tell* you what you should be doing. Instead, we'll mainly *describe,* allowing new and experienced tutors to do much of the talking, whether that's in the form of first-person accounts, essays, or transcripts from actual sessions. Although some of the advice we give might come off as more telling than showing, our ultimate goal for you is to use this book in order to become a more strategic tutor, to have a variety of resources you can call on to help you succeed in any tutoring situation, and to pose questions so that you can learn from your experiences. We know what has worked for us as tutors, and we'll share that advice (as well as that of many peer tutors), but you'll have to adapt that advice to your contexts, your individual style, and your needs. In jazz improvisation, learning a new sequence often starts with copying someone else's spontaneous riff; after a while, you make that riff your own, adding shading, tone, or sounds that are unique to you. So it goes with tutoring writing. We hope our book can contribute to that development.

THE WRITING CENTER AND THE WRITING PROCESS

In the next chapter we'll delve more deeply into the writing process and what it means for you both personally and as a tutor. First, however, we want you to consider both the role of the writing center in the ways that writers approach an assignment and how you as a tutor will represent the writing center. The following are two undergraduate writers' descriptions of their writing processes.

Dyana, a sophomore English major:

> Traditionally when I hear about a paper usually it's two weeks in advance till the due date, and I usually put it off for about a day or two, and then I go and do some research regardless of what the paper is. I always do library research just to get a better feel for what I'm doing. And then I jot down some ideas and then usually walk away from it for about a day. And then a lot of times I'll go to the writing center without anything, without having anything really except notes written and just say, "Okay this is what I need to do," because I really need to talk through my ideas to actually develop them. I can sit there and think about them, but they won't come into words unless I talk through them. And so I kind of just go there a lot of times to bounce things off of [my tutor], and she gives me a lot of insight, too. But then I usually write like two, sometimes if I'm feeling very ambitious, three drafts. That's about my whole process.

Yu, a School of Management freshman:

> I will first read the [assignment]. And then after that I try to think about
> what I can do without reading [the assigned text]. And then I start read-
> ing [the assigned text] for the first time, without taking notes. And after
> that I just throw the [readings] away for awhile. And I go back and then
> take notes like I'm marking what's important. And I try to keep think-
> ing [about] what I should write between the time that I decided to write
> and the time I finish my reading. Before I start writing I would nor-
> mally read an editorial in the newspaper where I will just pick it up and
> read it and then I will do my writing for the first time. I think [an] edito-
> rial provides background, and also it's just weird that I think it gets me
> started.

You might see familiarities in these descriptions, as well as distinct differences from the writing processes you use. Such is the idiosyncratic nature of
writing.

From Dyana's description, you can see that some writers know well
how the writing center can help. For others, particularly for writers who
are required to meet with you, it might not be so obvious. As a representative of the writing center, you have a chance to help writers understand
just how useful you can be. Ideally, a writer will meet with you several
times over the course of completing any writing task: when the paper is
first assigned so that together you can clarify the assignment and brainstorm initial ideas; after the writer has done some drafting so that you
can discuss points of development or possible ways of structuring the
ideas; while the writer is revising so that you can guide him or her to focus on the higher-order concerns and put aside editing/proofreading until the very end; and at that very end so that you can help the writer become a more detailed reader of his or her own work. Overall, you can
help writers learn how to learn, an idea that we'll discuss in the next two
chapters.

We bring up this topic because it might happen that you see writers
whose understanding of the writing tutor's role is that of proofreader or
cleaner of texts—more contrasts that complicate our work. Just as less-
experienced writers exhibit less-developed strategies when they write, they
also do not fully appreciate the collaborative nature of writing and how important a writing tutor can be at any point in the process. Once again, you
have an opportunity not only to increase a writer's strategic repertoire, but
to stress the role the writing center can play. Muriel Harris has noted that
"all writers need writing tutors," and this is the foundation upon which
modern writing centers are based.

IT'S A MATTER OF TRUST

You might have noticed that we use the term *writer* to refer to those folks whom we work with in our writing centers. We've chosen this term with specific purpose. While *student, tutee, client,* or *respondent* all are accurate descriptions to a degree, we truly believe that it's important for you to see the people you work with as writers, just as you are. Of course, writers are at various levels of accomplishment and experience, but all deserve the opportunity to find meaning in what they write and to share that meaning with others. All writers deserve our trust.

Trust is essential to the writing processes. Above all, writers need to trust themselves. That trust may help writers have the patience to wade through pages of a truly rough draft, the kind of writing they wouldn't dare show anyone else (as the early versions of this book were). And it may help them to know that they can turn that rough writing into polished prose. Writers also need to trust their readers (whether real or imagined). Readers will do what the writer asks, at least initially: accept the premises of the argument if it's logical, follow the thread of a narrative if it's entertaining, and picture the details of a description if it's well rendered. So many *ifs*, it seems. Perhaps that's why the writing process is such a complicated act, one seemingly both social and individual, public and private at the same time. You might be writing away in your room, on a park bench, or in your backyard, feeling isolated or at least oblivious to the immediate world around you. Yet, at the same time, you're in a social world, one that involves you, your reader, and your content. Even if you're writing fiction, you're creating a social world; in many kinds of nonfiction, you're re-creating a world in order to render it faithfully to your reader.

Trust is no less important in the relationship between tutors and writers. It's one thing to know and to trust the ways that work best for you as a writer. It's an entirely different thing to consider the ways that the writing center tutor functions within students' writing processes. As a student and a successful writer, you have great insight to share. As a writing center tutor, you'll create an atmosphere of trust for the writers who seek your help. In that environment, you and the writers with whom you meet can accomplish truly important work.

It's also essential that you trust yourself—as a tutor and as a peer. You have the unique opportunity to accomplish work that most teachers cannot do: You're not going to give a grade to a writer's essay, you have great insight into what it means to be a student, and you'll have many things in common with many of the writers you meet. You need to trust these great advantages. The rapport that you can create with writers is one of your best assets as a tutor.

So why do we tutor? Well, what we have learned is that tutoring allows us to connect, whether it's with writers' ideas, with writers' struggle to make meaning, or simply with writers as fellow human beings sitting beside us in the writing center.

We hope the chapters in this book help you gain an understanding of why you tutor, both now and by the time you are an old hand at helping student writers. You'll learn about the writing process and the tutoring process, and you'll spend more time thinking about the expectations you bring to tutoring. You'll also have concrete guidance in taking your first steps toward observing, participating in, and then analyzing your writing center sessions. Finally, we'll focus on specific kinds of challenges you'll encounter: writers with reading difficulties, ESL writers, and writers who present a variety of ethical and practical dilemmas.

Most important, we want to welcome you to an experience that can change your life if you allow it to, just as it has done for us. That's a grand promise, we know, but we don't make it lightly. We offer that promise as an invitation—to come explore the work of tutoring writing. We hope that this book can act as a trustworthy guide in that exploration.

2

THE WRITING PROCESS

You're considering becoming a writing tutor or are already tutoring because you've had some success as a writer yourself. That's no small feat. Writing is one of the most difficult—and most rewarding—things anyone can do. And perhaps your motive for tutoring is to pass on to others what you know how to do well. For someone who likes to write, the opportunity to talk with others about writing and then get paid for it (or receive course credit) is quite a good deal. You'll find many others like you in the writing center field who love talking about language, writing, and helping others use language in important ways.

Keep in mind that talking about writing is perhaps the most important thing you will do as a tutor, and contrast that talk with what's often seen as teaching. Teaching any subject is sometimes narrowly perceived to be the passing on of knowledge from an expert to a novice. You can probably remember many schooling experiences that consisted of teachers (and textbooks) holding those "right" answers and waiting for you to guess what was in their heads and pages—answering you with their subsequent approval or dismissal of your answer. Critics such as Paolo Freire refer to this method as the "banking model" of education in which information is held like a valuable commodity by the teacher, passed to students through lectures and textbooks, and then redeposited by students on multiple-choice and short-answer exams.

So what does this have to do with the writing process and tutoring? Well, writing is unique in how it functions. It fundamentally changes our relationship to whatever we are learning. Consider that the act of writing itself is often a process of discovery or of making meaning or, quite simply, of learning. The answers aren't predetermined by the teacher (at least not a good teacher) and cannot be corrected by running your paper through a computer program. The concept of writing as a means of learning is fundamental to the writing process—and to writing centers. Thus, it is important that you be reflective about your own writing process and understand the role of the tutor in writers' processes. These are some of the issues we'll address in this chapter.

WRITERS AND THE WRITING PROCESS

A bit of history: In the teaching of writing early in this century, students frequently wrote what were called *themes*. The instructor wrote a topic on the blackboard and students dutifully went to work, crafting as carefully as they could an essay in response. These themes were collected, corrected (in red pen, of course), and returned. The expectation was that students would learn from daily practice and from the corrections their instructor made. Did students learn to write well from these methods? Perhaps some did, but not enough; this led the popular and academic press at the time to declare a crisis in students' communicative skills. As C. S. Duncan of Ohio State University wrote in 1914, "There is a spirit of unrest, a feeling of dissatisfaction in educational circles over the poor work done by students in English composition" (154). Blame was placed on teachers, families, and, most strongly, on the students themselves (particularly since such crises often coincidee with increasing numbers of nonmainstream students coming to higher education). One solution at the time was to reconceive the teaching of writing as a laboratory course, akin to the scientific laboratory. Just as chemistry students conducted experiments in order to learn and apply the principles of chemistry, writing students would write in conditions that emphasized practice, guidance, and feedback (whether from peers or their teachers). Of course, much of this practice was in the service of having students make fewer mechanical errors (as early as 1895, John Franklin Genung of Amherst College described composition at his institution as "a veritable workshop, wherein, by systemized daily drill, details are mastered one by one" [174]), but the idea began to take hold that writing was an act that required practice and feedback, not simply the display of information in predetermined forms.

Fast-forward fifty years or so (oftentimes ideas take hold slowly in higher education). By the 1970s, the idea of writing as a process took on a renewed importance as teachers and writers such as Peter Elbow, Janet Emig, Ken Macrorie, and Donald Murray became influential. In a time when the function of schooling was called into question (along with a host of other societal institutions), writing was rediscovered in a way, particularly as a way of making sense of one's experience and as a way of controlling one's own learning (or for "writing without teachers," as Peter Elbow told us in his influential book of the same name). Also around this time, educational psychology influenced the teaching of writing, as researchers began to study the cognitive processes involved when one writes. Rather than just examining the habits of novelists and successful professional writers, researchers such as Janet Emig, Nancy Sommers, James Britton, Linda Flower, and John Hayes studied the ways that *students* wrote and described writing as a "recursive" act.[1] An additional strand was to reintroduce ideas from classical rhetoric and to look at the act of writing in terms of its rhetorical components, particularly the relationship between purpose, audience, and content. The confluence of these various movements turned into what Maxine Hairston has called "a paradigm shift," a virtual revolution in the way writing was conceived of and taught (albeit a revolution that was fomenting for 70 years or so!).

So what does this all mean for you as a writer and tutor? No doubt, in high school and college English classes, you've been exposed to notions of stages or steps in the writing process, whether called prewriting/writing/rewriting, or gathering/drafting/revising (or a host of other labels and stages). Most important, we believe writing is a process, not a one-shot deal in a theme book, and we understand that a goal for any writer is to control his or her own process and to develop flexibility for approaching any writing task. These two notions—control and flexibility—seem to be opposites but are, in fact, important contrasts, as we described in Chapter 1, and in a bit we will expand on each. Further, writing is now recognized as a social act; it isn't learned merely through drill-and-practice (which James Berlin calls the "current-traditional" approach to teaching writing); writing isn't completed in isolation by individual geniuses or used mainly to discover personal insight (the expressivist theory of writing); instead, writing and learning to write require us to interact with others (often called the social-epistemic or social constructivist theory of writing). As writing center theorist Andrea Lunsford writes, we need to view "knowledge and reality as mediated by or constructed through language in social use, as socially constructed, contextualized, as, in short, the product of *collaboration*" (4). Writing centers, therefore, are key components in this social view, as tutors

---

[1]Sondra Perl describes recursiveness: "Throughout the process of writing, writers return to substrands of the overall process, or subroutines (short successions of stops that yield results on which the writer draws in taking the next set of steps); writers use these to keep the process moving forward. In other words, recursiveness implies that there is a forward-moving action that exists by virtue of a backward-moving action." She says that writers might reread little bits of their writing, might return to a key word or topic, or might further pause and "look to their felt experience and [wait] for an image, a word, a phrase to emerge that captures the sense they embody." "Understanding Composing," *The Writing Teacher's Sourcebook, 3rd ed.* ed. Gary Tate, Edward P. J. Corbett, Nancy Myers, 150–51.

and writers engage in one of the most powerful means of helping writers find and share meaning—collaborative talk.

Given that background, we now need to lay out some essentials of the writing process, ones that will probably seem quite familiar.

A Model of the Writing Process

For several reasons, we want to provide you with a model of the writing process. As a writer, you can consider this model in light of how to approach any writing task. As a tutor, you can help writers by intervening in their writing processes, providing specific strategies, or helping them to refine the strategies they already use.

However, several caveats are needed. First, models aren't intended to mirror reality. Instead, models are devices that begin to help us sketch a phenomenon, trace its rough edges, or simply begin to ask important questions. Second, the model we'll describe is quite general—and a weakness of many models is that their generality obscures the importance of individual differences. That leads to our third caveat, one that's particularly important for the tutoring of writing: The writing process is an extremely idiosyncratic act. What works for you won't necessarily work for your closest friend or for a writer you're working with. The goal in applying our model is to develop control and flexibility—those two contrasting notions we mentioned previously. Finally, in the model, we'll describe a variety of strategies that you can both use as a writer and recommend as a tutor; however, in no way have we been exhaustive in our list of strategies. We do recommend that you find out more by consulting your writing center's handouts or the many complete texts on various writing strategies.

Our model of the writing process is based on the kinds of questions writers ask themselves at various points in the completion of any writing task and the strategies they might use to investigate those questions. We use three episodes in the writing process—planning, drafting, and revising—plus a fourth episode, proofreading/editing, more for simplicity's sake than anything else, but it's important to keep in mind the nonlinear shape of the writing process (one that's quite hard to render on paper). In other words, rather than steps or stages that one goes through one at a time, we conceive of the writing process as cyclical (or perhaps a vortex that sucks up all of your free time?!). You will often revisit the questions you first pose and the strategies you use to pursue them. Additionally, many things can influence the relative importance you attach to the various stages. For instance, writing a shopping list will require far less revising than writing a letter to the editor. And writing an essay analyzing an assigned reading you're not sure you even liked will take far more planning than a letter to a friend. Overall, we need to stress that context is everything. But first, let's finally describe the model. As you read this description, think about how closely it aligns to the process you use for school-based tasks:

Episode 1: Planning
Questions you might ask:

- What do I know about my topic?
- What is my purpose for writing?
- Who are my intended readers, and how much do they know about my topic?
- How is this task like others I have had before?
- What structure will work best for my topic?

Strategies you might use to investigate these questions (not an exhaustive list!):

- Clustering: a visual representation of your thoughts on the topic, usually starting with a single word that invokes word associations, which you write around that first word, drawing a circle around each association and continually building until you've drawn a "cluster" of words (as conceived by Gabriel Rico).
- Freewriting: quick and exhaustive writing on the topic, often with a timed goal ("I'll write for five minutes without stopping") and, as Peter Elbow tells us, likely to turn off your overwrought editor and tap into the generating portions of your brain.
- Conversation, either in class or with friends.
- Brainstorming: unstructured exploration of your ideas.
- Reading and research on your topic.

Overall, in this episode you're *trying* to answer the planning questions, not necessarily finding answers, and using the strategies that you feel will work best for your topic and task. Consider that a grocery list might come with a quick brainstorm or a conversation with a roommate or spouse, but an essay on the factors that contribute to the destruction of the Amazon rainforest might require far more careful, extensive, and multistrategied planning.

Episode 2: Drafting
Questions you might ask:

- What do I know about my topic?
- What is my purpose for writing?
- Who are my intended readers, and how much do they know about my topic?
- How is this task like others I have had before?
- What structure will work best for my topic?

Yes, we know, the questions are the same as for the first episode. That's our way of saying that, throughout your writing, you are working toward answering these questions. That is also why you might reuse the strategies we described earlier. However, we feel there is one component in drafting that might not be as fully formed during planning—your *intention* or the feeling you get when you are trying to render on paper an idea or image or argument. You have an intention, usually quite out of focus in the early stages. Composition researchers Lil Brannon and Cy Knoblauch call this intention the "ideal text," as if you have a finished copy of your essay locked somewhere in your mind, and the point of this early writing is to find which strategy is the key to free that ideal text so that your rough drafts (your real text) will closely match the ideal. Brannon and Knoblauch are suspicious about this idea, particularly because ideal texts are often presented as absolutes by teachers or authority figures, with little room for students to challenge those ideas. We prefer to imagine that your intention as a writer and just how you'll go about putting that intention into words aren't necessarily complete in your mind. Instead, you need to use writing and language to bring a shape to your intentions. This is perhaps why it just feels so darn good to get something right, to find the words to express your meaning. Thus, in the drafting episode of the composing process, you're doing some writing, perhaps lots of it, as you attempt to render your intentions on the page (or computer screen).

Strategies you might use when drafting:

- Any or all of those you used for planning.
- Outlining: Creating an outline can be particularly useful if you feel a strong loss of control—you have lots and lots to say, but need to figure out how you will present that material. However, outlines need to be flexible, not individual cages out of which your writing can never escape.
- Visual representations of your topic: We mentioned clustering as a planning strategy, but it's worth repeating here that if you have a strong sense of what you want to say, but not a clear sense of how all of those ideas will fit together, visually representing your work can be powerful. Sketch pads, black- or whiteboards, floors filled with arranged piles of readings or notecards—anything that enables you to think visually can work here.

Episode 3: Revising
Questions you might ask:

- What do I know about my topic?
- What is my purpose for writing?
- Who are my intended readers, and how much do they know about my topic?

- How is this task like others I have had before?
- What structure will work best for my topic?

Yes, at the risk of badgering, we know that we've repeated the questions again, but we want to emphasize the recursive nature of the writing process. By this episode, you have perhaps become satisfied with some of your answers to these questions. However, some might still remain under-explored. Revising is a vital episode for many reasons. First, some researchers (e.g., Beach; Faigley and Witte; Flower et al.; Sommers) have shown that revising is a crucial factor that separates successful writers from less successful ones. More significant, it has been our own experience that students often confuse revising with editing, our final episode. When you revise, you are making changes on a large scale, dealing with what Thomas Reigstad and Donald McAndrew call "higher-order concerns." This is when you realize that the "real" start of your essay is on page 3 and that you're better off saving the first two pages for another day. This is also when you realize that you've been repeating yourself on pages 2 and 4 and can perhaps group those parts together. And, finally, this is when you realize (and all of these realizations might come from your own reading of your drafts, a friend or peer's reading, or a writing center tutor's questions) that you simply need to develop one of your points more fully or flesh out a description or make much clearer just what your point is (and thus return to some planning strategies). Dealing with higher-order concerns is often what makes your writing go from good to great.

Contrast the moves above with what we'll call *later-order concerns*,[2] things such as fiddling with your wording, checking your spelling, making sure you've used *you're* instead of *your*. These sorts of sentence-level fixes should come later in the process (though we won't claim that all writers don't fiddle with words and sentences as they draft; for less-experienced writers, however, the fiddling can subsume getting any real writing done). Also, sentence-level fixes are much more the province of editing than revising. They are certainly important and shouldn't be neglected, but an obsession with error should be avoided at all costs.

Strategies you might use when revising:

- Any or all of those you used for planning and drafting.
- Seeking feedback: We won't necessarily assume that, because you're learning to be a writing center tutor, you were a dutiful user of writing center services yourself (though we do hope so). Nevertheless, seeking

---

[2]Reigstad and McAndrew call these *lower order concerns*; however, we'll call them *later-order concerns* because we think that correctness is pretty important, especially to writers and often to instructors.

feedback at any episode in the writing process is valuable, and revising is perhaps the point at which most writers seek feedback. Rather than imagine an intended reader, why not seek out a real one and find out if you're getting your point across?

- Glossing your text: An effective revising strategy we've found is to go back over our drafts, writing in the margins a brief (just a couple of words) description of each paragraph's content (we sometimes call this writing an outline in reverse). When you look at your descriptions, you can detect whether you've been repeating yourself. If your descriptions are difficult to write, you have an indication that your paragraph is un-focused or consists of too many topics. Your marginalia can also include not just the content of your paragraphs, but their function within sections or the essay as a whole. Now is the time you can discover that the paragraph you've marked "conclusion" contains an entirely new topic or that you're spending too much time on a single idea that's not central to your main point.

The Final Episode: Editing/Proofreading

Having made mention of later-order concerns, we would be remiss not to suggest some strategies for approaching editing/proofreading (and keep in mind that we'll discuss the important differences between editors and tutors in Chapter 3). Perhaps the best bit of advice we can offer is to edit in several passes with a different focus on each pass. For instance, you might read your text once just looking for spelling mistakes (and reading backwards—from the end to the beginning—can force you to see each word in isolation). And then you might read your text looking only to shorten sentences and paragraphs, cutting out excess words. And then you might read focusing on the kinds of homonyms that have given you trouble (the find/replace function of your word-processing software is great for this strategy).

One other strategy we offer writers in the writing center is to have them read their drafts aloud, if not to their tutors, then simply to themselves. Reading aloud forces you to *hear* your language and see errors that your eyes glossed over previously. Overall, the idea in editing/proofreading is to create some distance between yourself and your text or, more accurately, between what you've said and how you've said it. If you're still clarifying the point you are trying to make, you are revising. If you put that content aside and focus on the mechanics of your language, you are editing. This distinction is why we caution student writers to save editing for the very end of their process. Why fiddle with your mechanics when you might strike that entire sentence or paragraph in the service of clarifying your point?

TUTORS AND THE WRITING PROCESS

In no way have we been exhaustive in our list of strategies during each episode in the process (we encourage you to refer to the many books on these topics). One thing we do want to point out, however, comes back to the ideas of control and flexibility, one of those contrasts central to writing and to tutoring. Writers need to develop control of these strategies, and this control includes not simply knowing what strategies might be available, but knowing how to use a strategy. And then not just knowing what and how, but knowing when the use of a strategy would be appropriate (this strategic knowledge concept comes from reading researchers Scott Paris, Margerie Lipson, and Karen Wixson). Our previous example of outlining is a case in point. For years and years and still today in many textbooks, writing seemed to be a relatively simple process that started with choosing a topic and then writing an outline. However, we've worked with many frustrated writers in the writing center who told us, "I just cannot seem to come up with my thesis and outline." Well, that's not a surprise since they haven't created any material yet to find a focus or to organize into an outline. They simply didn't yet know what they wanted to say (content), much less how they would say it (structure). Applying the strategy of outlining at this point for these writers will lead to nothing but frustration. Instead, you can help these writers generate material in order to find a central focus. Brainstorming, mapping, clustering, or any of the strategies we described in Episode 1 would be useful. Once again, in terms of strategies, writers need to know the what, how, and when; they need to be flexible and adjust the way they work, depending upon a host of factors—the writing task itself, the conditions under which they are writing, the point of the process that they need to emphasize at that moment, and countless other things that make writing such a complex act.

Flexibility and control can be tied to an important concept that has grown out of work in cognitive psychology—the idea of metacognition or thinking about thinking. Consider how aware you are of your writing process. Do you need to think about how to get started when you're given a writing task? Do you consider the various prewriting strategies at your disposal and the appropriateness of each for what you are facing? No doubt, as a successful writer, you've given some thought to these questions, though you've probably internalized the answers to some degree. But in our work with less-successful writers, we've seen that issues of how well they know and can control the processes they use to write can be problematic. Thus, a goal for every writer is to develop strategic knowledge about each phase of the writing process; writing center tutors can be a vital element in helping writers learn metacognitive control.

Perhaps the most important thing we can say about the writing process and your work as a tutor is this: Avoid creating clones of yourself, and avoid teaching *your* processes as if they are the tried and true methods of approaching any writing task. Sure, they've worked for you as an English major (or sociology or business or biology or undeclared major), but that doesn't mean they'll necessarily work for another. Instead, as a tutor, you should help writers develop control of and flexibility with their writing processes.

One clarification: We are not saying that you should never bring up the strategies you feel have been helpful to you. Remember that writers need to know *what* strategies are available. If you're a big fan of clustering and the writer has never tried it, pull out those big pieces of paper and have the writer cluster away. The same goes for any strategy. What's important is not to offer the strategy as a sure-fire solution; instead, you are helping writers develop their strategic repertoires. You can increase writers' options, teaching them what strategies are available, how to use those strategies, and the most appropriate time to apply a given strategy.

We've slipped somewhat into lecture mode here, but that's because the teaching of writing is fraught with instances of well-intentioned individuals simply applying the "teaching" methods that worked best for them (we've particularly seen this phenomenon when it comes to the teaching of grammar; "but *I* learned by diagramming sentences," they say). This tendency is difficult to avoid, and that is one of the important reasons why you need to reflect deeply upon your own writing processes. Oftentimes, we aren't even aware of how prescriptive and controlling our teaching behaviors can be. Keep in mind that your goal is to create options for writers, not cut them off. And one of the many joys of tutoring is that *you* will learn, from writers, strategies that you had never considered before. Thus, an important line of inquiry that you can pursue in any tutoring session is to ask, "So, how did you go about writing this?"

One last point: Many writers don't necessarily ply their trade in response to assigned topics and in exchange for a grade or class credit. Those conditions are unique to writing in academic settings. And it is in those settings that the writing process and the tutor's role in that process need special consideration.

WRITING IN ACADEMIC SETTINGS

We've made the point a couple of times in this chapter that the writing process model that we offer is idealized. This quality is perhaps most true when it comes to the application of the model to writing in academic settings. Consider the questions about purpose and audience ("What is my purpose for writing? Who are my intended readers, and how much do they know about my topic?"). If you are writing a paper for a class, obviously your purpose is to complete an assigned task and your audience is your instructor. Of course, you might say that your purpose is to convince your reader of your point of view and your audience consists of your peers. However, in most instances, this audience won't be giving you a grade or sending your name in to the registrar at the end of the term in order for you to receive credit for the course. Most writing assignments are quite artificial, and your audience—your instructor—holds tremendous evaluative authority. These elements cannot help but powerfully affect the writing done in academic settings.

What we are addressing here is the relationship between the writer, the instructor, and the writer's text. We hope that you have been lucky enough to feel empowered by the writing you have done and that your instructors haven't made the writing they've required merely a test of how well you've mastered the course content (not that there isn't a role for this sort of writing, but it's certainly a limited role). Instead, you've been able to use writing to make meaning, whether that means discovering and communicating how you feel about a significant event in your life, an important reading, or a topic you feel strongly about. And you've not just found meaning through writing, but you're able to share that meaning with others (your readers, of course)—connections that remind us how much we depend upon human fellowship.

However, some writers you might work with in the writing center won't be coming from such positive experiences. They fully realize that the purpose of their essay is to get a grade and eventually course credit and that their audience is their powerful instructor. Thus, their expectation is that you help them figure out just what it is their instructor wants and how they can go about getting a decent grade.

Other writers, both native and nonnative English speakers, will seemingly be at a "cultural divide" from their instructors, their writing tasks, and, often, from you. Differences and cultural expectations due to language, ethnicity, gender, race, and class can often manifest themselves in something as "simple" as a paper due for a class. For instance, some students' writing closely resembles their speaking, and if these students speak with accents or in nonprivileged form, such as Black English, you might be put into the position of defending the implied values of academic writing—values that stem from largely Western, male, and Caucasian influences. Before you know it, you will be assuming a "regulatory role," as Nancy Grimm calls the function of writing centers, often inadvertently, to manage difference and act as an enforcement mechanism for the status quo.

Now, rather than have you resign your tutoring job before you get started, we want to point out that these dilemmas, while vital and complex, are also best managed by acting in ways that we recommend throughout this book: being sensitive to writers' backgrounds and challenges, asking questions about the writers' tasks and their understanding of those tasks, and working to create options for writers, not to close off those possibilities. Closer investigation of these dilemmas also offers excellent opportunities for writing center research. In Chapter 4, we'll delve more deeply into those often assumed expectations that you and writers will bring to a writing center session and how they can affect your work.

RENT TO OWN

A notion central to writing center work is that writers need to "own" their texts. In Chapter 3, we draw a distinction between editing—something that perhaps many of your classmates have sought from you because they recognized your writing abilities—and tutoring. As we have discussed, many writers might come to the writing center under the impression that a tutor will simply fix their texts. We often call this the dry-cleaner model of writing center and unfortunately have had more than a few writers ask us if they could drop off their papers and then return when they were "done." However, tutors don't fix texts; we teach writers how to fix texts. We don't tell writers what to write; we ask questions about and react as readers to what writers have already written or are thinking of writing. In these ways, writers "own" their texts, and writing center workers respect this ownership just as we would want it for ourselves.

Nevertheless, the student-text-teacher relationship complicates notions of ownership. For many writers, a more accurate concept would be that they "rent" their texts, occupying a topic and content for the length of time specified by the teacher/landlord and thinking little of what they have written once the rental period has ended. This is perhaps why we have had writers tell us flat out in writing center sessions that they plagiarized much of their research papers or that they "hate to write" but know that they need to overcome the "burden" of a required writing course. Writing is not meaningful for these writers because they have never had the experience of its meaning (in school, at least; we've also seen that some of the most reluctant writers in our classes are avid private writers, keeping journals and writing poetry that they would never share). Do these writers "own" the writing they are doing in their classes?

For the writing center tutor, these issues certainly complicate neat renderings of the writing process. At times, writers will position you as proxies for their instructors, expecting an evaluation of their writing. At others, they will put you in the role of coconspirator, especially when they admit plagiarizing or simply not caring about what they're writing. What is important is that you are aware of the writing process—especially the ideas of control and flexibility—and how writing in academic settings affects that process. As a student yourself, you know best what it means to write in academic settings and can best impart to those you work with in the writing center the strategies that are effective.

It is our experience that most writers are eager to find meaning in what they write, even if the task wasn't best designed to achieve that end. And one of the great pleasures in writing center work is helping writers find that meaning. Your knowledge of the writing process will be vital in providing that help.

3

THE TUTORING PROCESS

In this chapter, we want to take you through the entire tutoring process—
from opening a session to closing one—and provide some powerful tutoring strategies. We'll expand on these strategies in subsequent chapters as
we take you from anticipating (Chapter 4), observing (Chapter 5), and then
participating in sessions, first with your fellow trainees (Chapter 6), and
then on your own (Chapter 7). We'll also offer ways to think about specific
situations you'll encounter: helping students with their reading (Chapter 8),
helping nonnative English speakers (Chapter 9), analyzing your sessions
(Chapter 11) and, finally, troubleshooting those many difficult situations
that all tutors encounter (Chapter 13).

We'll frame our overview of the tutoring process by showing how tutors approach each stage of a session and contrast that with what editors
might do in the same situation. As we mentioned in Chapter 1, one of the
most important contrasts in writing center work is the difference between
editing and tutoring. You are probably already a skilled editor, and your
services are in demand from friends and classmates. Also, by no means do
we want to denigrate the good work that many editors do (after all, you
might choose that career); however, writing center work is based on the belief that writers need to do the writing, not their tutors. Like any of the contrasts we presented, the tutor/editor one is on a continuum, and there'll
probably be instances outside of the writing center where you'll be closer to
the editing end (and hopefully be paid for that challenging service). In the
writing center, though, we advise you to tutor, not to edit; after all, it's the
writer whose name is going on that paper, who's paying for those credits,

and who'll be getting the grade. But before we get too strident, we need to define in more detail the differences between editing and tutoring.

When you think of an editor, you might think of a cranky, hard-bitten, cigar-chomping Perry White, calling all the shots and making all the decisions, sending Clark Kent and Lois Lane off on assignments. Or you might think of someone who is responsible for making someone else's good writing perfect—that is, a proofreader. Real editors of various kinds probably wouldn't like these stereotypes of their work, but these descriptions come close to what a lot of friends do when they are asked to look over a paper. That is, your friend hands over the paper, picks up your last slice of pizza, and loses himself in *Days of Our Lives* while you go to work with a pen or a pencil.

You might limit your looking over of the paper to proofreading, and this usually involves making corrections for your friend; it may go beyond proofreading and involve suggesting a better word or a better sentence; it may even involve some advice: "I had a class with her, and she always wants you to . . ." When you do this kind of editing for your friends, you are assuming a large measure of control over their papers (and often they want you to). For tutors, however, this control can squelch any real learning on the writer's part.

THE TUTOR DOES NOT—AND DOES— HAVE TO BE AN EXPERT

An important difference between editors and tutors has to do with the idea of being an expert. Editors are often seen as expert wordsmiths, always knowing the right word, the correct grammatical fix, or the key passage to delete. The writers you work with might indeed put you in this role, just as some of your friends might have, but tutoring expertise is quite different.

As a tutor, you don't have to be an expert on the subject matter of the paper the writer is working on, and you don't even have to be an expert on grammar and correctness—knowing that something isn't right is probably enough (though having a good working knowledge of English grammar and usage can often be helpful, particularly with nonnative English speakers who will know those rules quite well). But you do have to be an expert in some things, each of which we'll explain in more detail in this chapter: knowing how to set a good tone for the conference and making the writer feel comfortable; knowing which kinds of issues to address first; being patient and listening to the entire paper, since it's easy to get hung up on an early section when the real challenge might come later; knowing how to ask questions that are open-ended (not questions that can be answered with a yes or no) and that you really want answers to and don't know already; knowing techniques that let the writer make the decisions; knowing that sometimes our questions take time to answer and having the patience to wait for the writer to come up with a reply; and knowing that when the writer revises, many of the problems with correctness will improve.

As a tutor, rather than as an editor, you'll have to know when more is needed—that is, when there are so many problems that you can't deal with them all in one session—and you'll have to know what to do with students who can't complete everything. You'll have to get a sense that with some writers, you can't address every last problem in the paper, and you'll have to be able to choose one or two to begin with, but then encourage the writer to come for more help. You'll have to know when a writer needs to come back after revision to work on correctness. You'll know that scheduling another appointment at the end of the session is a good way to help the writer stick to her resolve to revise and that the next session should be with you again, if schedules permit. You'll have to be sensitive to due dates; if the writer only has an hour, she may appreciate knowing that she needs to rethink her organization, but chances are she won't be able to do much about it, so you and she can focus on correctness. But you'll also have to know that it's a good idea to invite her back so she'll have a better sense of how to organize and what effect organization has on readers.

All of that is a lot to learn. But as you see, being an expert on grammar didn't even come up. And the writer is responsible for being the expert on her subject matter. If you know the subject well, that's wonderful, but if you don't, it's all right. You can usually still tell what kind of paper is appropriate, whether or not the arguments are well supported, if the organization is clear to you, and whether the audience is being addressed in an effective way.

Nevertheless, we need to mention that there are times that disciplinary expertise will be important. For example, a writing tutor who is a biology major will have much more knowledge of how to approach writing up scientific data than would someone who's never had to approach that task, and a business major will know more about the specifics of writing a business plan than would a theology major. In other words, depending on your major and your experience, you might have specific knowledge about the writing conventions of particular majors or disciplines. Now, this isn't to say that, as a tutor, you'll merely tell the writers, "No, the results of your experiments do not go in your methods section." Instead, you'll have even greater knowledge of the important questions to ask than would a more "general" tutor: "Why did you put your results in the methods section? How have other writers dealt with that placement in some of the research articles you've read?" Your goal is still to let writers control their own work, but your expertise in these matters can be quite valuable. Many writing centers have recognized this value and recruit tutors—often graduate students—from a wide variety of majors, encouraging writers to match up with someone in their discipline. But we also want to repeat a warning: As a tutor, rather than an editor, your job isn't to offer content expertise and launch into a protracted lecture on the roots of the Russian Revolution. You need to respect writers' need to discover—with your help—the information they need to clarify a point or expand an argument.

BREAKING THE ICE

Dawna commented in her tutor-training class one day that her first visit to the writing center a few months before had been a disappointment because of *her* expectations. She'd had a presentation in her literature class by a tutor and had been told about the role of the writing center but still believed that the writing center was a place where experts told you how to fix your paper. She felt that the tutor wasn't doing a good job because he expected her to do all the revising. She asked if there wasn't a good way to let writers know when they first arrive what will happen in the session. As a result, we've started asking writers, "Have you been here before?" If they have, then we can relax and get started. If not, after we ask some initial questions about the assignment and the stage of the project, we give writers a good idea of what will happen and possibly help them to avoid disappointment or frustration.

Writers can come to the writing center with either clear or vague ideas of what will happen, but many come with apprehensions and vulnerabilities. Some see it as a sign that they are not strong writers (it isn't, necessarily). Most are nervous. So taking a few minutes to get to know the writer is really important. Even if you only have a short time to work together, it's important to set a collegial, congenial, friendly tone during those crucial first minutes.

Here are some e-journal entries based on a question about making writers comfortable.

> I think the two main reasons that students are so afraid to come to the WC is because they are afraid to show their work and also because they may not feel as smart as they really are. It boils down to a confidence issue, and I think it is part of the job as a tutor, to help them maintain their confidence.
>
> —Kip

> I think that students feel awkward enough having something as personal as their writing examined and shared with another. . . . It's important to establish a rapport with them that lets them know you're on their level, not this abstract pedestal of English superiority. As a tutor, I think it's important to develop skills that let you gauge and read a per-

son, get a feeling from them. A lot of times, you can just try to be warm and friendly, and humorous. That seems to ease most people. Some writers who are more shy may be scared off by that. In that case, I think it could help just to be more gentle, more reassuring.

—Maggie

In most of my observations, the tutors begin the session by asking the writer what they know about the Writing Center. This allows the tutor to explain why the writer is going to read the paper aloud, which seems to make the writer a bit more comfortable. I've also noticed that the MORE dialogue that takes place before the paper is read, the MORE comfortable the writer seems to feel. It is almost as though the writer needs to establish a "relationship" with you before just diving into the tutoring session.

—Stephanie N

The most effective session I have watched is one in which Katie had an ESL student. I could tell that he was very apprehensive about reading his paper because his English wasn't very good, and here he had two people to read it to. . . . To get the session going, she just asked him about what he was trying to say (it was a personal statement for an application) and then really listened to him tell the story in his own words and then we worked to put that more concisely than he had it.

—Liz K

START WITH QUESTIONS

So, you're on your first shift in the writing center, you've broken the ice, and now you're ready to help that first eager writer, paper clutched in his hand. What do you do? Think about the way you might look over a friend's paper when you are in the role of editor. Chances are, you take the paper and probably go off with it, perhaps somewhere quiet, where you can concentrate.

As a tutor, you're going to do this process differently. We train our tutors to start by asking writers a few basic questions before they even consider the draft:

- What was the assignment?
- What is your central point or main argument? (We don't say "what is your thesis?" or the writer is likely to read us a sentence that won't help us much. When the writer sums the paper up and we write that down,

sometimes the summary is a better thesis than the one in the paper. We can then help the writer see that, so write down the paraphrase for later.)

- What concerns you, or what do you want me to pay careful attention to? (And we write this down, because we'll surely come back to it later and either reassure the writer or address the issue that's raised.)

After you write those answers down, you're ready to work with the writer on the draft.

READING ALOUD

The next step is probably a major shift from what you're used to doing: We recommend that you ask the writer to read the paper aloud to you while you take notes. If you've never done this before, we know that this idea takes some getting used to. But think of the action of taking your friend's paper and going off with it or writing on it. You're in control. You're calling the shots. And the writer in a writing center is probably someone you don't know, someone who doesn't have your pizza to eat and doesn't have a TV handy. If you were to read silently, there would be an awkward moment as he waits for your diagnosis. That metaphor from medicine equating bad writing with sickness or disease comes too easily to mind for this to be a good thing, we think.

When the writer reads the paper, he accomplishes several things, in addition to keeping in control. As you listen, you make a mental note not to interrupt, except to ask him to repeat something you didn't catch, and you listen to the whole paper. Listening to the whole thing from start to finish and taking notes puts you in the role of the learner and the writer in the role of the expert. And our anecdotal evidence is pretty good that the reader is listening, too, to the way the draft is working. Sometimes he'll pause and make a mark in the margin. Sometimes he'll say, "Oh, that sounds bad," and you can say, "Put a checkmark next to it and we'll come back to it." But he's giving his draft a critical reading in ways that will help him revise.

You're taking notes, listening. As we've already pointed out, he's the expert, since it's his paper. We talked about the editor's making all the final decisions, but in a good tutorial, the tutor asks questions, and the writer decides what to do with a draft.

Not all writers benefit equally from the practice of reading aloud, however. Some ESL writers will have great difficulty reading aloud, though their speech will be fine. If writers feel hesitant, don't force the issue. Offer to read for them. TJ writes an e-journal entry that shows how this can work out:

In one session I observed of Paula tutoring, the writer said she really did not want to read the paper, so I read it for her. Throughout the session she became increasingly comfortable and open to discussion. At the end of the discussion, when all the barriers had been knocked down, she confided that she had a learning disability that made reading hard for her. This was unnoticeable by her writing style, but I can only imagine how much more comfortable she must have been when some-one else read for her so she would not have to expose herself before she really wanted to.

—TJ

AN EXAMPLE OF OPENING A TUTORING SESSION

Because what we've described up to this point is so important, we include the following transcript as an example, and we recommend that you read it aloud, preferably with a partner taking the second speaking role. This ex-cerpt comes from the beginning of a session and starts with the writer ask-ing for general feedback on her paper, and then the tutor asks about what the writer is working on:

Writer: This is an analytical paper.

Tutor: Okay.

Writer: It's basically regarding a reading passage assigned in the class, and we're supposed to do a critique on that.

Tutor: Okay. And two things: First, what was the reading passage?

Writer: The reading passage was "The Tourist," by Jamaica Kincaid.

Tutor: Jamaica Kincaid, yeah, I know her, but I don't know that [piece]. Was it an entire essay or just a passage from an essay?

Writer: Actually it was a short essay.

Tutor: Mm, hmm. And when you say critique it, what is your conception of what that involves, what that task involves?

Writer: Well, I'm supposed to take a stand, whether I agree with her or I have a different opinion, and I guess I have a different opinion.

Tutor: Okay. So tell me two things, what was her position?

Writer: She doesn't like tourism . . . because she comes from a different country, I guess.

Tutor: Yeah.

Writer: And she doesn't like tourists going to her country because they exploit her country in such a way.

Tutor: Mm, hmm. That's her main reason?

Writer: Right.

Tutor: Because it constitutes exploitation? And does she give examples of the exploitation, what that might look like?

Writer: Well, in the paper I have some of her viewpoints but, and then basically she says that, at the very end she says that the natives, every native would like to travel, that's for sure, but most of the natives in this world are very poor and so they are not able to, they cannot afford to go to other countries, so they would envy you and the fact that you, as a tourist, come to their country, it makes them jealous more.

Tutor: Mm, hmm. So her audience is, the readers she has in mind, sounds like those who would be tourists?

Writer: Right.

Tutor: I'll tell you what, will you read it to me? Reading's a good way, you can tell me, in a sense, what I should listen for, what your concerns are with this draft. And reading it out loud is a good way for you to get a feel for how it's shaping up, what your language is like.

Writer: Okay.

Notice several things in this excerpt about what the tutor does. He doesn't just ask about what the assignment is (an "analytical paper," according to the writer), but he also probes further by asking questions. What did the writer have to read? (And notice that the tutor immediately acknowledges that he's not familiar with the reading passage, thus putting the writer into the position of teaching him the essay's content.) What is the writer's conception of an analytical paper? And once she describes that task ("I'm supposed to take a stand, whether I agree with her or have a different opinion"), he asks more questions to preview the paper itself: What is the author's position? What evidence does she present to support that position? Who seems to be the author's intended audience—whom is she trying to persuade?

These questions accomplish several things. They probe the writer's understanding of the assigned task and of the reading itself. They also introduce some of the elements of a critique essay: a summary of the author's main claim, a presentation of her evidence, and a sense of her intended audience. Once the writer gives this information, it provides the foundation for what will happen once the writer reads the paper itself, a means of checking back on whether or not the writer has included these elements and is consistent with what she told her tutor, compared with what she wrote.

Notice, too, that the tutor asks the writer to read her work aloud, giving a short justification. Thus, in this passage the tutor establishes his responsibilities: to ask about the task and the context, to help the writer better understand the task, and to evaluate how well the writer fulfills her stated purpose. Overall, he's putting himself in the position of reader of her essay, making as visible as possible what he'll be expecting and listening for as she reads her essay aloud.

Now consider that the dialogue on the previous page took up only about two-and-a-half minutes! The first few minutes of a session are crucial to establish a rapport with the writer, set goals, and lay a foundation for what next occurs. The exchange that time was brief, but what occurred was certainly crucial to the success of the session as a whole.

Here's another way of thinking about the opening of a session. The series of activities we engage in offer the writer repeated opportunities for reflection about the paper and about ways of talking about the draft. Here is a handout we give to tutor trainees at Marquette. We make it clear we don't expect tutors to follow it as a blueprint, but it lays out the various opportunities for the writer to think analytically and critically about a draft they bring.

The First Steps in a Conference Where the Writer Has a Draft

The Activity	*The Purpose/Intent*
Greet the writer and *ask* what he is working on.	Create a friendly relationship or break the ice
Have the writer fill out a writing conference record (WCR—see the example on page 43).	Collect information for our database with an eventual eye to communicating the information to others
	Find out the *due date* of the work
	Learn what the writer defines as the main issue or problem or challenge or goal
	Provide the writer with the opportunity to see how she describes writing tasks
	Provide the writer with an opportunity to reflect on her purpose

The Activity	*The Purpose/Intent*
Look carefully at the WCR.	Determine what, at first, seems to be the writer's goal Create an agenda for the conference and prioritize based upon the writer's needs
Ask: What is your main point or argument? If the writer begins to read the thesis, ask him to look away and paraphrase. Write these words down, to refer to later.	*Provide the writer with a chance to rethink what the argument is or should be* *Show the writer that his ideas are important*
Ask: Would you read your draft aloud? Tell the writer you will take notes on what she says and ask questions afterwards.	*Provide the writer with an opportunity to revisit the draft, rethink it in the light of hearing it* *Provide an attentive reader for the piece* *Assure the writer that what you are writing down is not criticism, but notes and questions*
If the writer feels awkward about reading, offer to read for him. Ask him to note parts he wants to change.	*Show the writer that reading aloud is an important revision strategy* *Give the writer a chance to hear his writing in another voice*
Before the writer reads, ask "What would you like me to listen for?" After the writer reads, ask "Now that you've heard your paper, what do you want to do to revise it?"	*Give the writer a chance to rethink the categories she/he checked on the WCR* *Provide an additional opportunity for the writer to self-assess*

The writer has now experienced incremental opportunities for self assessment.

HIGHER-ORDER CONCERNS COME FIRST

Okay, you've started the session with questions, you've taken notes, and the writer has read her paper aloud. Now what do you do? One way to create the right atmosphere is for you first to comment on something you like in the paper (and this is a major contrast between the work of tutors and what editors do). We all want praise, and the writers with whom you'll work make themselves quite vulnerable by sharing their writing with you. However, don't push it. Writers will know if you're being phony and will feel patronized. But there's generally something good in every piece of writing. Find it. If words fail you, you can comment (if this is true), "Wow. You've really done a lot of work on this." Or "You've really done a good job of finding research sources," or "Great topic." But only say those things if they're true for you.

As we mentioned in talking about the writing process, one of the most important things you can do as a tutor is to deal first with what Thomas Reigstad and Donald MacAndrew call higher-order concerns. As a tutor, you'll save grammar and correctness for later (and, as we noted in Chapter 2, we'll call these matters later-order concerns). Higher-order concerns are the big issues in the paper, ones that aren't addressed by proofreading or editing for grammar and word choice. This isn't to say that proofreading isn't important for writers to learn, but we can tell you that, from our experience, if we help writers proofread first, a lot of writers—especially those who are inexperienced or hesitant—won't want to change anything in their papers, even to make things better, because they feel that once they have their sentences and punctuation right, all will be well with their writing (and perhaps you felt this way as well at some point in your writing history).

When dealing with higher-order concerns, you'll think about such questions as these.

- Is the writer really addressing the assignment and fulfilling its terms?
- Is there a need for a thesis, and if so, is there one?
- Do arguments have the support they need? Is there an organization I can relate to as a reader? Is this piece addressing an audience in an effective way?
- Does the piece show appropriate levels of critical thinking?

In the ideal world (where writing tutors would be out of a job!), we'd answer these questions with yes, yes, yes, yes, yes, and yes. But quite often the answer is no, and then we have a focus for our session.

Let's say the draft has some problems that the questions above will identify. As an editor, you would tell the writer what to do. You'd tell the writer that she needs a thesis, and maybe you'd suggest one to her. You might even write one for her. But that's not necessarily what's best for the writer.

In his well-known essay "The Idea of a Writing Center," Stephen North says, "[I]n a writing center the object is to make sure that writers, and not necessarily their texts, are what get changed. . . . [O]ur job is to produce better writers, not better writing" (438). As we pointed out, you're probably already a good editor and might have lots of good ideas for ways to improve the papers you'll be seeing, but it's better for the writer if she makes the decisions about the paper. Making decisions gives the writer a better sense of ownership of the paper and more pride in it when revisions go well. This emphasis on ownership will prompt us to ask questions not only about the paper in question, but about the writer's processes of composing:

- How many drafts has she written?
- What kind of revising has she done?
- Have any classmates or her teacher read any of the drafts and offered any advice?
- How does she feel about the advice?
- What are her revising strategies? (Does she have any?)

Some students who come to the writing center have never really revised a paper and have no idea how to go about rethinking a subject or even how to move paragraphs around. You need to find out how comfortable the writer is with these moves. Sometimes it's good to save the questions about revising for the end of the session when the writer has a better sense that she may need to make some sweeping changes.

If we see an organization that seems odd to us, we might ask the writer, "What made you put this section on X right here between this section on A and this one on B?" When we ask such questions, we're showing the writer that we trust her decisions. Maybe there's a connection that we didn't see. If we didn't see it, and the writer explains it, we can ask if some sort of explanation or clarification belongs in the draft, or what's more likely, the writer will say, "Oh, I need to make that clear, don't I?"

There are lots of good questions we can keep handy for tutorials. One of the best ones was a suggestion of one of our tutors, Dan Giard. Dan always likes to ask, right after the writer has read the draft, "Now that you hear it again, what do you want to do with it next?" This keeps the writer in the role of expert (and after all, she's likely to have done plenty of research on her topic; if not, and if it's needed, you need to ask more questions about the content). Another good question starts with a thumbnail sketch of the organization of the essay as you heard it and as you took notes about it. Then, the question is simply, "Is this what you wanted me to get out of your paper?"

These questions show that we trust the writer and the writer's decisions. We're not trying to take over the writing process. We're trying to help the writer see what kinds of questions she should be asking of her own paper. If we model these questions for the writer, then it's our hope that next time, she will ask them herself.

ANOTHER CONTRAST: CONVERSATION AND QUESTIONS

What does the ideal session, the totally textbook session look like? It would look like two peers having *a conversation* about writing, where each is equally likely to ask a question, move the conversation forward or point out his or her confusion as a reader. (We'll accept that these two peers are unequal in their expertise, but that's probably true in most conversations.) The tutor might be asking questions but not in the role of the teacher drawing the right answers out of the writer. Muriel Harris says of conferences with teachers, "When a student in a writing conference mistakenly thinks the teacher has the answers, all real thought ceases while the student begins searching or guessing for answers the teacher will accept" (62). We believe this is often the case with tutors as well. Nick Carbone sums this up well in a discussion on WCenter, a computer listserv for writing center directors and tutors:

> Question-asking the wrong way can become a kind of inquisition. Very often tutors ask questions in the hopes of leading the writer to some "right" answer. . . . But some tutors are just really good at question placement in the context of conversation. So there are the get-to-know/ice-breaker/context questions . . . : about the assignment, dates due, purpose of the essay, and so on (and you don't always need to ask these up front, it can trickle in as needed). But the real trick is moving to a conversation about the writing, where as a tutor you can talk to the writer, be a good listener, hear the ideas, ask questions about those the way an interested friend will ask questions about some event you're telling them about. Part of that means talking with the writer about the idea, sharing opinions, disagreeing, agreeing, thinking of examples, the way people do when they get together and talk about things.

So what are the right and wrong ways of asking questions? Ask questions only if you really want to know the answer. This might mean letting go of an answer you may *think* you know and trusting the writer to know a good answer. You may ask, "Why did you choose to put this section here?" The writer is still going to hear this question as "This doesn't belong here." She may ask, "Should I move it?" You can then rephrase the question: "Is there a good reason why it belongs here?" That allows her to assert that indeed it does but that maybe she needs to show the reader why.

There are all kinds of questions that work well and that don't have canned answers. Content-clarifying questions can be important: "What does this term mean?" "What is this paragraph's function?" Overall, avoid questions that put the writer in the position of trying to guess the answer that's in your head; those sorts of closed questions are usually not at all productive.

Sometimes, though, questions are not the best route. Let's imagine that you see a major weakness in a paper; for example, the paper is not fulfilling the requirements of the assignment. This is probably not a good time to ask a question. You might ask to see the assignment sheet again, and in a way this is a kind of question that indicates your concern. But there's no law against saying, "I'm concerned about the way your paper addresses the assignment." This kind of statement puts you in a position of expert, but at the same time shows the writer honest respect. There might be all kinds of leading questions that might get the writer to see this problem himself, but those kinds of questions would be somewhat transparent or might seem manipulative and might erode the trust you build with the writer when you withhold expert knowledge. Instead, you and the writer could get right to work on that most pressing problem. Then new questions will move the session forward.

WHAT IF THERE'S NO ESSAY?

If you've had any experience with a writing center (maybe you've visited yours as a writer already), you know that not all sessions start with a draft of a paper. Writing center directors do a lot of public relations trying to let writers know that the earlier in the process they come in, the better they are helped. You probably know from your own experience how helpful it is to talk over your assignments with your friends, classmates, or instructors before you ever do any writing. And once you start writing, you know how your ideas can take shape if you just take time to talk them over again. This is another kind of help we offer as tutors and that contrasts with the work of editors.

A good way to begin such a session as this is to have the writer paraphrase the assignment for you. This will give you a good sense of how well he knows what's expected of him. If he's stumbling around and pulls out an assignment sheet, that could mean he's having a hard time just understanding what's expected. You can help here, looking over the sheet with him, asking questions about the assignment, and encouraging him to clarify any ambiguous points with his instructor.

You know from your own experience that you'll write the best papers on topics you care about, so it's good to help the writer identify parts of the assignment that are meaningful or that draw from his life experiences in some way or that touch on subjects he may be interested in as he plans his career. Sometimes writers find topics that simply fascinate them, and they will write well about them, because they want to know more and because they want to share what they know.

Sometimes writers come to us with a lack of trust in their own perceptions of things. Many schools begin with an assignment that asks them to relate their experiences, giving such directions as "Write about a time when writing went really well for you" or "Describe an experience that changed you." Inexperienced writers can be very uncomfortable with those assignments, because many of them have been taught "Never use first person," or "Never give your opinion. Just the facts." They have to unlearn these rules, and talking about the assignment can help them warm up to these writing tasks. The research paper will come soon enough in most schools.

As we pointed out in Chapter 2, there are many ways that you can help writers generate material or figure out what it is they want to say. We like to help writers get their first thoughts and preconceptions out of the way by writing them down. (Peter Elbow and Pat Belanoff call this Loop Writing.[1]) Now you can point your questions toward refinements of those first thoughts. Lots of beginning writers will go with those first thoughts and use them for a paper topic; however, for most college assignments, this won't be good enough. They will probably be common knowledge, certain to put the instructor to sleep. As a tutor, you can ask the writer what interests him most about those ideas he's generated already. What would he like to know more about? Does he know how to find good research sources? Or does the assignment call for him to write about his own experiences?

HELPING WITH LATER-ORDER CONCERNS

Imagine that all those higher-order concerns are fine in a writer's draft, but there are some errors. Or imagine that you've already spent a session or two on the higher-order concerns and can now address later-order concerns. How do you know there are errors if you've only listened to the writer read the paper? Chances are that you don't, unless you heard some awkward

---

[1]They then have writers develop either moments, stories, or portraits, then generate some dialogue; then they have them vary their audience or chronology; and then they have them think of lies, errors, or sayings about the topic. Some of these techniques will be more valuable than others, depending on the assignment.

sentences (the ones that just didn't make sense to you) and unless you heard the writer misuse some words. To address later-order concerns, you have to *see* the paper. We suggest that you sit next to the writer for this process, and *you're* going to reread the essay, perhaps now reading one sentence or paragraph at a time. Once again, we're going to trust the writer. Maybe this time you'll read the paper aloud as you both look it over, but instead of going all the way through it, you'll stop when you spot an error or think you do. In your editor role, you'd have corrected the error. But tutors have better ways of helping students, ways that make them better writers.

Many sentence-level problems are not the result of a writer's carelessness or lack of understanding about correctness. All of us will often write confusing sentences when we're trying to convey ideas that are particularly complex or only partially formed in our minds, or when we're writing in ways that we're really not familiar with (as in writers who tell us, "I've never written a critique essay and have no idea how to approach it"). Few writers get it right the first time, but many have the capability to correct their sentence-level problems with your help; rather than acting as an editor, you'll be teaching writers techniques so they can become good editors. An example of this technique is to say, "There's a sentence in the middle, in that paragraph about . . . that confuses me. Could you paraphrase it for me?" Write down what the writer says. Chances are that the paraphrase will be clear, because there's a clear context for it and a specific audience (you) that makes it easier for the writer. Then you can give feedback: "I really understood what you just said." Show the writer what you wrote down—and be sure not to correct or to add your own words to it, but keep it in the writer's own words. You might ask about the writing process at this stage and see if the writer can reflect a bit on what was going on during the composition of the unclear sentence. Sometimes she will be able to see what she needs to do to make things clearer.

For a writer whose entire paper was full of unclear sentences, we've tape-recorded the entire tutoring session. She'd read a sentence, paraphrase it, and move on quickly, and we then loaned her the tape. Writers are very grateful for that kind of help.

ERROR ANALYSIS

We often find that new tutors are most terrified by the idea of a writer's paper that is just full of errors. Where do you start? Well, as we've emphasized, you start with higher-order concerns, but there will come a time when you'll need to help writers work to correct those repeated errors and become better editors of their own work. Composition researchers such as Mina Shaughnessy and David Bartholomae have given us a great deal of insight into the study of errors that writers make. Most important, you need to view errors not as manifestations of carelessness or sloth or stupidity but instead as stages in any writer's development. So what does this mean for you as a tutor? Well, trying to understand the logic behind a writer's errors is perhaps the most important help you can offer. While editors wield red pens and circle errors like stains on the page, tutors try to get at the reasons why writers made the choices they did. This process isn't particularly different from the way you addressed higher-order concerns. You asked what the writer already knew about the sort of essay she had to write or you asked about why she ordered the paragraphs in the manner she did or chose particular details, and then you tried to build upon that prior knowledge. With error analysis, you'll take the same approach to comma use or subject-verb agreement or sentence boundaries. Your most powerful question for the writer is, "Why did you make that choice?"

One other important strategy in error analysis is to look for patterns. As you read through the essay, perhaps a paragraph at a time, you can look for certain types of errors that the writer makes repeatedly. A common example is a comma splice or two independent clauses joined with only a comma (and we've also found that writers are often quite aware of the types of errors they make since they've been told repeatedly that they have that problem but often aren't shown how to correct it). Imagine that you are reading the paragraph and see several instances of comma splices. Your best bet is to ask the writer, "Why did you put this comma here?" While this is sort of a leading question (and most writers will reply, "Is that wrong?"), many will explain a logic behind the comma placement, perhaps that they felt that the clauses on each side of the comma were short or closely related or that they heard a pause at that spot and thought the rule with commas was to put one wherever they paused in their writing. Sometimes a writer will have memorized rules that are wrong.

At that point, you would tell him that it's an error, let's say, to put a comma alone between independent clauses. You may need to explain the idea of the independent clause to him, perhaps looking the concept up in the handbook that your writing center most commonly uses. Referring to the handbook is a good idea if you know something is wrong but don't have the answer at your fingertips, and it also models a behavior we want writers to imitate: to go for the handbook and look up the rule.

In more step-by-step form, error analysis looks like the following:

1. You see an error. First, you want to know if the writer spots it and can correct it. So you ask, "Do you see an error in this sentence?" Chances are that the writer will find and correct it without any problem. But let's say that the writer doesn't see it. Then we get to the next step.

2.   Talk about the general class of errors, saying, "The problem is with your verb, " or "There's a punctuation error." Give the writer time to spot it, and if he still doesn't see it, it is time for the next step.

3.   Point out the error to him. "The problem is with this comma." Ask about the writer's logic behind making the error. See if he knows how to fix it. If not, ask him what rule he used to decide to put a comma where he did. As we noted above, writers often misinterpret or misapply rules. If the writer still hasn't made the correction, proceed to the next step.

4.   Explain the specific rule (and refer to the handbook, as we pointed out), and have the writer apply it to his error. Help him make the fix if you need to, but explain as thoroughly as you can why you're making the choices that you made.

5.   Go on to the next example of this error, but try to have the writer apply what you've taught in the previous example. And then treat each error in this fashion. For many writers, you'll soon not need even to point out the problem—they will recognize and fix the error on their own.

As you can see, error analysis can be a slow process and completely different from telling the writer what to do (as an editor would). As an effective tutor, you're having the writer do as much of the work as possible and teaching the writer the ways to correct errors. If you've noted patterns of errors, we advise you not to deal with more than three different types in a single tutoring session. That's all you'll have time and energy for, and it's all most writers can learn to correct in one session.

Another important role you can play in error analysis is not to focus just on errors but to find and point out instances where the writer has made correct choices. For instance, in the case of a writer who has a few comma splices, like the one we described previously, you then see that there is a sentence where he has punctuated two independent clauses correctly. Point it out to him. It's a process of giving positive reinforcement, not just of finding errors, and you want to maintain the good rapport you have established with the writer, not come across as a representative of the grammar police.

ENDING THE SESSION

A good session will fly by, so you'll have to be aware of time. If there's no clock where you tutor, have a watch handy. It's often a good idea to offer the writer something such as, "We have ten minutes left; do you still want to talk about the five pages we haven't looked at or is there another priority we should address?" When the time is almost up, it's a good idea to get a sense of what the writer got out of the session. "What do you plan to do

---

Writing Conference Record

Phone Number: _____ College: _____ Student ID:_____

Year in School (Circle) HS 1 2 3 4 5 G Other   Is English your first language?   Y N

E-mail: _____

Date: _____ Name: _____

First visit this year? Y N   Circle: Fall/Spring

Course (e.g. Engl 001): _____ Due Date? _____

Instructor: _____

What are you working on?

_____

_____

_____

What do you want to work on in this session? (check all that apply)

- ☐ Discuss an assignment
- ☐ Choose a topic
- ☐ Get feedback on a draft
- ☐ Check for development/support
- ☐ Check for organization/coherence/transitions
- ☐ Check research/citations
- ☐ Other:

What are your plans for revision?

_____

_____

_____

Tutor's name: _____

Tutor's comments: _____

_____

_____

---

next?" is a good question to ask. As the writer tells you, you can encourage him to write those plans down. If a lot more remains to be done, you'll want to schedule another appointment, or maybe even two, if your center allows that. Schedule those appointments with you if at all possible, because you know the assignment, you know the writer's revision plans (and you'll keep a record of that), and you'll be able to jump right into the session without a lot of explanations. You're also building a relationship with the writer, and you want him to feel comfortable about coming back to you with this or other writing projects.

AFTER THE SESSION

Most writing centers ask you to write down some notes on the session you've just completed. Sometimes this is a note for instructors, and sometimes it's just a memo for the next tutor this writer may work with ("We worked on a paper on jet lag. We looked at his organization and he clarified for me how he meant it to be set up. He'll reorganize it, get more research, and come back on Wednesday"). Always be aware of your audience with these notes. If the writer has any access to them, be sure there are no notes you'd be embarrassed to have him see. You'll have to be sure you leave time to do this between sessions, because believe it or not, after three sessions with writers, you're likely to have forgotten a lot about the first two.

WRITING CENTER ETHICS

To sum up this chapter, we want to point out that while its content comes from our own experiences as writers, tutors, and writing center directors, it also comes from our ethics of tutoring. We don't use the word *ethics* lightly. Ethics are usually associated with values and morals, a sense of right and wrong, a framework for behavior. In tutoring writing, ethics are synonymous with responsible conduct. For instance, as a tutor you're responsible to yourself, to the writers with whom you work, to your tutor colleagues, to your writing center director or equivalent, to your writing center itself, to your school, and even to the writing center field. Your conduct in any single session can have an impact on these various interested parties. For instance, showing up late to your tutoring shift can affect your own standing in the eyes of your director and of the writer signed up to meet with you, your colleagues' opinion of you, and your writing center's reputation. As a tutor, your responsible conduct has a ripple effect, demonstrating to all parties with a stake in the matter that the work you do is meaningful.

Your responsible conduct also has larger meaning, particularly in the contrast between tutors and editors. When we remind you that writers should own their texts or that tutors shouldn't simply clean up writers' texts and then hand them back as if they were dry cleaners, we show certain values and responsibilities that imbue writing center work. Your work as a tutor will require an ethical code, a conscious system of behavior that is reasoned, thoughtful, and responsible. And this code includes not only local responsibilities (for instance, treating all writers and colleagues with respect, fulfilling your job's duties, not using the writing center as a dating service!), but responsibilities that you now bear as a member of the writing center field. After all, we want our work to be taken seriously by those outside of our field. Responsible conduct—and continual discussion and examination of those responsibilities—is essential to this goal.

EDITORS VERSUS TUTORS—A SUMMARY

What we've described about the tutoring process is very different from what went on in the TV lounge of your residence hall as those friendly neighborhood editors went about their business. We'll end by summarizing the contrast between tutors and editors:

Editors	*Tutors*
Focus on the text	Focus on the writer's development and establish rapport
Take ownership of the text	Make sure the writer takes ownership
Proofread	Start with higher-order concerns and worry about correctness last
Give advice	Ask questions
Read silently	Ask the writer to read aloud
Look mainly for things to improve	Comment on things that are working well
Work with an ideal text	Trust the writer's idea of a text
Make corrections on the page	Keep hands off and let writers make corrections; help them learn correctness
Tell writers what to do	Ask them their plans for revision

4

EXAMINING EXPECTATIONS

When you attend a class, what do you consider to be your responsibilities? To arrive on time? To be prepared? To take notes in response to what your teacher says or writes? And what do you consider to be your teacher's responsibilities—also to arrive on time and be prepared? To stimulate learning? To respect you and your fellow students? Where do you believe your expectations for these responsibilities come from?

Just as in classrooms, in writing center sessions, you and the writers with whom you'll work bring expectations about each of your responsibilities, and each of you will also bring goals for the session. When goals and expectations reasonably agree, the work of the tutorial can go on relatively smoothly. When the goals and expectations clash, however, you're left feeling pretty awful. Something didn't work. Was it your fault? The writer's fault?

In this chapter, we focus on the goals and expectations that you will undoubtedly bring to your tutoring (and to your observation of others' tutoring) and how your preconceived notions about many of the contrasts that define tutoring—tutor versus editor, peer versus teacher, writer versus writing—are powerful influences that you and writers might not even be aware of. We'll discuss how those expectations might have been formed and why it's necessary to reflect deeply on what has shaped your expectations for behavior. In particular, we'll focus on two powerful influences: (1) your culturally based expectations for the rules of communication and (2) your influential teaching/learning experiences. We will also introduce you to Adria, a graduate student in applied linguistics and a writing center tutor. We'll describe how Adria's expectations for effective tutoring—largely the result of her student experiences—manifested themselves in her sessions as a fairly nonflexible approach and became a source of nonproductive tutoring.

We need to stress that it is perfectly natural for your experiences to guide the expectations you'll bring to tutoring. This is a key process in learning. Here's how linguist Deborah Tannen puts it:

> The only way we can make sense of the world is to see the connections between things, and between present things and things we have experienced before or heard about. These vital connections are learned as we grow up and live in a given culture. (14)

However, it would not be ideal for your connection between old and new to turn into inflexible rules and summary judgments; rather, you can listen, observe, and reflect thoughtfully about the contrast. Our goal in this chapter is for you to develop control and flexibility, that important contrast we described in regard to your writing process. Becoming an effective tutor will often mean transcending your expectations and opening up communication so that you and the writer have a clear sense of what you both can accomplish in a session, as well as how and why.

COMMUNICATION BREAKDOWN

We all have cultural expectations for behavior, particularly those that have to do with communication (and we use culture here to refer to those influences based on race, ethnicity, religion, gender, sexual orientation, and class). It is quite likely that many writers you'll work with will not share your cultural experiences or will attach different value than you do to certain kinds of behavior. Whether this means a writer who refuses to make eye contact or one who sits closer than is comfortable for you, it is essential that you not condemn these behaviors simply because they are different from what you value. Instead, you need to reflect upon what you're observing and why you're making certain interpretations and judgments.

Observation and reflection are not the only things tutoring requires, however. After all, you will be a participant in the activity that occurs. You will be enacting the social rules that govern all interaction. As an example, consider a conversation you've had recently with a friend. Both you and your friend have internalized the various rules each of you follows to ensure that your conversation flows along, isn't too awkward, and achieves the goals each of you has (for example, to learn or shape some new information or to solidify your friendship). These rules include those involving turn-taking (and you probably have had conversations where two people spoke at once—not very productive!) and maintaining the topic or at least moving on to tangents with some sense of agreement. Consider the verbal cues you or your friend might have used to signal that the other should keep talking ("Uh huh," "Yeah," "I know what you mean") and the verbal signals to indicate it's the other person's turn to speak ("That reminds me of something I needed to tell you," "What do you think of that?"). Many years of conversations within particular cultures have made these rules something you don't even think about—except when they are violated.

In a tutoring session, social rules for the interaction apply just as much as for conversations (and we'll supply much more depth on how to analyze the discourse of a session in Chapter 10). As a tutor, you need to pay particular attention to the rules of behavior that you and the writer seem to be relying upon. For writers new to the writing center, meeting with a tutor might be more like meeting with a classroom teacher than with a peer, and their behaviors might position you as much more of an authority figure than you might expect. Or, perhaps, the opposite might occur, and the writer might approach your session much more casually than you would wish. In either case, both you and the writer have certain expectations for behavior, expectations that arise out of your experiences with similar situations.

Instances of cross-cultural communication can particularly mark clashes between expectations for social rules. After all, your notions of the right way to act in a social situation are largely products of your culture, and you won't always share cultural expectations with writers. That does not mean that your tutorial with a writer from a culture different from your own will be marked by awkwardness, confusion, and frustration. Instead, our point is that as an effective tutor, you need to try to understand why some interactions simply do not feel right—including sessions you just observe and those you play a part in. When you hear a fellow tutor come out of a writing center session saying, "That really didn't go well. We just didn't click," think about the sort of clues—both verbal and physical—that you could observe to explain that feeling. Just as in conversation, a host of other factors play an important role in tutoring sessions, such as who speaks when and who controls the topic, how you and the writer sit in relation to one another, where the writer's paper is positioned, and the noise level in the room.

A QUESTION OF GOALS

Expectations for the rules of interaction are just one influence on the outcome of your sessions. You and the writers will also bring goals for your sessions, and one of the many tricky parts of tutoring is not only uncovering your own goals (which aren't always as visible as you think), but negotiating with the writer on a mutually agreeable goal. This agenda setting during the first five minutes of a session is perhaps the most crucial of all. A typical clash of goals occurs when the writer is interested primarily in getting his paper fixed (and, after all, who can blame writers for wanting better papers to be the result of their writing center sessions? After all, that's primarily how they're being graded in their classes!). The tutor, on the other hand, is primarily interested in improving the student as a *writer,* with less of an emphasis on the *writing,* as Stephen North told us a while back. Yes, it's that editor versus tutor contrast again.

Consider the writer's perspective. If his main goal were to improve his paper, then his expectations for what you might do as tutor would be to make the corrections. After all, you're the writing expert, and the end result would be much better if he were able to have you don your scrubs and perform a quick surgery on his ailing prose. However, as we have stressed up to this point, writing centers are not about editing. We are about teaching and maintaining a much larger view than correcting the immediate paper; our goals for sessions are to help the writer learn the skills needed to improve not just this paper but subsequent papers. So, do our long-term, process-oriented goals clash with writers' short-term, product-oriented goals? At times, yes, and one of your frequent tasks as a tutor will be to teach writers just what the writing center does and why a long-term view makes sense.

One important word about goals, however: It won't always be clear what a writer's goals are, and you will need to work toward clarification. Consider the following list of actual requests writers issued at the start of sessions, often in response to the tutor's questions, "What can I help you with?" or "Why don't you tell me what you're working on?"

> "Well, I'm doing this paper on the construction of the pyramids for my archeology class, and basically I wrote it, and I guess my grammar and my word structure is not good enough. So I need a proofreader, and they advised me to come [here]."

> "If you could check the grammar?"

> "Basically, [focus on] the usage of words or idioms. Also, I have difficulty using the definite article *the,* also some other articles, *a* or *the.*"

> "Well, just go through it, and, I mean, for punctuation. You don't have to correct it; just point out whether it's, like, punctuation mistakes but mainly both grammatical and sentence structure."

> "Look for grammar and misspellings, but see if you understand what I'm trying to say."

> "I want to know about the overall organization and maybe some expressions that I may not have used correctly in this paper."

"I want to see what flows."

"I wanted to see what you think."

"One of the things that I'm having a problem with is writing a book review; I've never really done a book review. I've also been under some personal issues I've been dealing with and trying to write this at the same time. I'm concerned about just the overall clarity and construction . . . and also if there happens to be grammatic stuff going on."

"I don't know how this works, so you should tell me how it works and then I'll just follow your lead because I've never been here before."

What would your reply be to these varied requests? After all, writers don't necessarily know the vocabulary of tutoring, and a grammar check request might mean a host of agenda items. Our point here is for you to be aware of the goals you and writers bring to tutoring sessions, to think about where the expectations for those goals might come from, and to scrutinize the language used to express those goals.

TAKING RESPONSIBILITY

Whatever your goals might be for a session, you have some expectations for what your responsibilities are to achieve those goals. In time, these expectations will come from study and practice into the art of tutoring writing, but before you're able to have those experiences, your expectations might be informed by factors you're not even quite aware of. We discussed cultural issues previously, and in the next section we present the powerful influence of your learning experiences. One factor related to both of these influences has to do with your perception of the relationship between tutors and writers. Who should be in control of the agenda? Who should be asking the questions? Who should control the flow of the session and be attentive to time and topic? Your answers to these questions all come from some source, some expectation for who should do what in a tutoring session. Literacy theorist James Gee and his colleagues believe that face-to-face interactions such as tutoring can be controlled by the participants' "ideologies" or "largely unconscious values and viewpoints within social activities that have implications for the distribution of power" (238). Being "largely unconscious," these ideologies are rarely critiqued; instead, many of us just express certain beliefs as the right way to do things. In tutoring, your attitudes toward the distribution of power will have a great influence on what occurs in your sessions.

Perhaps those power relationships are most clearly manifested through your beliefs about who is responsible for what in a session. Here's how some of the tutor trainees at Marquette answered the question, "In a tutoring session, what are the responsibilities of writers?" As you read these responses, consider not only which you agree with, but more important, why.

From Jessica:

> Writers should be attentive, open to new ideas, be willing to change and establish new habits. They must be sincere in their intentions. Writers as well as tutors must be good listeners.

From Adele:

> The writer has the responsibilities of being a critical thinker and an honest person. If either tutor or writer does not understand something, then they [should] ask. Honesty and clarity are what makes the whole equation work. The writer also must be open-minded, as well as the tutor, and willing to consider different approaches to writing.

From Kristina:

> The writer is responsible for making the paper what he or she wants to make it. He or she accomplishes this by engaging in conversation with the tutor about the paper. Answering the questions the tutor asks, critically thinking about the paper as the discussion moves along, and writing things down along the way.

From Angela:

> The students should not totally rely on the tutors to get the wheels churning in their minds. Students should come with their best draft, so that progress can be made. Also, they should be able to answer questions [such as] what they like about the paper, what they don't like, etc. This way, even if they don't know exactly what they want to do with the paper, they know what should stay, or what should change.

From Jason:

> The writer must be an active part in the tutoring process. The writer cannot expect to be a "mental sponge" and absorb all the information from the tutor. Instead, the tutor and the writer must work as a team to achieve the desired results (the improvement of the writer).

From Aesha:

> The writer is responsible to utilize the skills already present in him/ herself. He/she must be willing to try something different, move out of the comfort zone. He/she must recognize the fact that the tutor is someone who can help him/her do what he/she already knows how to do and not do it for them.

Each of the trainees describes a fairly active role for the writer, one that reciprocates the hard work that the tutor is demonstrating and one that is in the writer's best interests. However, think in broader terms where these expectations might have come from. Are they products of value systems? Of culture? How are they confounded when a writer has a very different sense of personal distance or politeness or authority, as many writers from countries outside of the United States (or from a different culture than yours) will have? And how empowered are some writers to own their texts in the face of poorly conceived assignments or dull course work? Do many writers have a voice outside of the writing center to register meaningful protest, or is there something about their schooling that they are unhappy with?

Even in the writing center, writers don't necessarily have the same rights and obligations as tutors. We think Andy explained this dilemma well in his response to the question of writers' responsibilities:

> I realize more and more students are aware of the way the writing center works, so their expectations are being met more and more often. However, students are not part of this dialogue about what their responsibilities are, what tutors expect of them, so how can they be prepared to meet expectations?

Andy nicely makes our point here. A variety of influences will determine just what you believe your and the writers' responsibilities are to be. However, it's important that you give writers a voice in determining how a session is run. Certainly, we all cringe at those requests for proofreading or grammar checking, but we caution you to look beyond those convenient labels (or at least investigate why the writers are issuing these sorts of requests).

A March 8, 1996, posting to the Internet discussion list WCenter, read by more than 350 writing center directors and tutors, provides another example for potentially mismatched expectations about responsibilities. Janet Mittendorf proposed the following definition of the effective tutor:

> The effective writing tutor knows how to spot and help improve the most important problems in a written piece, how to keep the conference

focused and productive, how to support the tutee's efforts while indicating areas ripe for improvement in the writing, and how to quickly forge a strong, professional bond with tutees in order to motivate long-term improvements in their writing processes.

At first reading, you'll probably find much of this description quite reasonable. But on closer examination, consider how several of these items could be quite different, depending on one's perspective (and expectations). On one level there would be difficulty in agreeing on the "most important problems in a written piece," in imagining what a "focused and productive" conference would look like, and in describing abstract qualities such as "support" and a "professional bond." On another level, embedded in this definition are expectations for what each of these abstract characteristics might be and expectations for the goals and responsibilities tutors should adhere to in order to achieve this effectiveness.

So have we hopelessly complicated tutoring at this point? We hope not. Instead, we want you to give careful thought to why you feel as you do about what writers and tutors should or should not do. Being reflective is the key here. But before we end, we need to add one more major influence on the expectations you'll bring to tutoring writing.

THE INFLUENCE OF TEACHERS

Consider for a moment who your most influential teachers have been or those particularly powerful teaching/learning scenes that are etched in your memory (and those can be positive and negative). We often remember teachers who convinced us that we had something to say or demanded clearer and clearer prose or who filled our drafts with red ink.

Now think about how you would go about helping someone else learn to write—the advice you would give, the style of feedback, the strategies you'd endorse. In the chapter on the writing process, we cautioned against simply applying what works for you to another's situation. In the same way, we want to caution applying (or immediately avoiding) those teaching and learning experiences that you see so clearly in your mind's eye. Here's how Shantel, a student at Marquette, described how her views of tutoring writing were formed:

I guess I have viewed tutoring in terms of power, that is, the tutor being the authority figure while the tutee submissively sits back watching the red pen marks disfigure his/her creation. This scene always seems to take place in a room with an imposing gray desk cluttered with papers, and for some strange reason *my* paper would always be lost among that heap. I never thought of tutoring defined in the terms of my friend who lived next door to me freshman year, nor did I really have a clue that the writing center tutors would be figures of lesser authority than my high school English teacher—who just happened to be a retired naval officer.

For Shantel, tutoring originally meant teaching in an authoritative, all-controlling way; hence, the contrast between tutors and teachers (or at least stereotypes of teachers!).

We don't mean to cast cynical doubt upon your experiences—after all, they might have been very effective for you. However, to simply apply those techniques in a different context can often be a frustrating experience for you and for the writer. Instead, you need to reflect deeply upon what some of your more influential learning experiences have been and think about the many factors that surrounded your experience and determined success (or failure). Overall, you need to listen and observe in a tutoring session and ask yourself why you're acting in certain ways and where your actions are coming from.

In the same way, the writers with whom you'll work will have expectations for how you should act, expectations that come from *their* influential learning experiences. You will need to counter these expectations, open up lines of communication, and try to understand why writers are positioning you in certain ways.

For an example of the influence of one's learning experiences on her tutoring and the need to develop both control and flexibility as a tutor, we now introduce you to Adria. A writing tutor and a graduate student in applied linguistics, Adria had been an undergraduate dual major in biology and English and also had worked as a peer tutor. As you'll see, Adria has calm control over the writing strategies she passes along and hopes to help writers develop that control as well; however, in terms of flexibility, Adria often dispenses the same strategy to each writer, without regard for the particulars of that writer's process, task, or context for writing. Adria's impulse is good; after all, her goals are to increase a writer's strategic repertoire. However, as you'll see, her technique needs to be refined; there are limits to handing out the same strategies for each writer you encounter.

In a series of interviews, Adria talked about the influence of her student experiences on what she does as a writing tutor: "Some of the most fabulous professors I've had . . . shaped the way I write papers still today and the way that I teach my students to write." While listening to an audiotape of one of her sessions, Adria described that what she does involves "the whole notion of being systematic and explaining how I do these things and pass[ing] them along. That's what my professors have done for me, so I'm trying to do it for the student now."

In tutoring sessions that Adria tape-recorded, her approach often involved dispensing strategies as "hints" and "tricks." Adria would diagnose a problem in the writer's text, tell the writer of a helpful "trick" to fix that problem, and then show the writer how to apply that technique. As she told one writer during a session: "I'll tell you, you've come to the right place. I am Miss Shortcut. If there is a shortcut to be had, I've got it because I like to make things nice and simple." In another session in which a writer was working on a summary of an article, Adria tells her, "Okay, what I'm going to try to do is give you a few really helpful hints to help you make this a lot easier. Don't think that writing a summary should be difficult for somebody, and if I give you these hints, maybe it will be easier to do." When a writer expresses trouble with keeping her tenses consistent, Adria says, "I have a really good clue for that, a nice little trick. I like to do everything in nice little tricks; it makes it nice and easy."

For organizing ideas, Adria often prescribes using "glossing" or margin notes as a reading and revision strategy and writing an outline in order to organize ideas. For example, when giving a writer advice on composing an article summary, Adria tells her, "The best way to take care of this is as you go through each paragraph, jot down little notes in the margin, so when you go back, you don't have to reread the article again."

In the following example, the writer has drafted a memo recommending that a company purchase a piece of machinery. Adria models the margin-note strategy, summing up each paragraph of the writer's memo in a word or two in order to examine its structure. She elicits these summaries by rapidly questioning the writer on his chosen organizational pattern. As you read these transcript excerpts, keep in mind that they are written-down speech; thus, it might be best for you to read them aloud or, even better, read them with a partner, treating them as a script:

Adria: Okay, what did you mean by this part right here?

Writer: That's why the company should purchase the machine.

Adria: Okay, where do you tell the company to purchase the machine?

Writer: Up here.

Adria: Okay, where were you going to put the pros and cons?

Writer: In the middle.

Adria: Okay, why? Aren't they kind of scattered?

Writer: Yeah they are [writer laughs].

Adria: Okay, that's really what the problem is here. I think what you have to do is structure it a little bit more. So in this first part, what do you say?

Writer: Well, I said the company is not in good health.

Adria: Exactly. And you're very clear here. You have your numbers. You have your data and everything. So this is not in good health, we'll put that in the margin. [Adria writes] Okay? Now here, you're saying what? Your recommendation is to buy this machine.

Writer: Yeah.

Adria: Okay, "buy machine" here. And what are you saying down here? They should buy the machine.

Writer: Yeah, they should buy the machine. And in the middle, why they should buy the machine.

Adria: Okay, why they should buy the machine.

Writer: Well, the last one is the conclusion of something in the middle.

Adria: Okay. Where are you going to put the pros and cons? And here is not an option, right? Because you have "you should buy the machine," "why you should buy the machine," and "why you should buy the machine" as the conclusion.

Writer: After that.

Adria: Okay, exactly. So you need a whole new paragraph here.

This excerpt displays Adria's offering and modeling a specific strategy and reinforcing the use of that strategy. She asks for the writer's intentions by questioning and then evaluating the writer's memo with very specific comments ("Aren't they kind of scattered?" "So you need a whole new paragraph here"). Often these techniques will lead to Adria writing an outline or drawing a graphic that she will give writers at the end of the session.

In the next example, Adria is working with a different writer whose task was to summarize an article on funding mechanisms for brain-injured students. At the following point in the session, Adria sums up a series of her questions and the writer answers to discern the gist of the article:

Adria: So let's make up a little trick because this can get kind of confusing. [Adria writes on a separate piece of paper] So because there's no agreement, there is no definition. Because there is no definition, there is no money. And because there is no money, there is no help. So this is kind of what happens. They're trying to tell you, and there's a little bit of a discrepancy here because they're trying to tell you, "Well there's no help because there's no definition," and in reality there's no help because there's no money. And there's no money because there's no definition. So they're leaving that step out. Does that make sense?

Writer: Yeah.

Adria: Because this is all stuff you've told me; I'm just laying it all out for you. Okay, so you want to talk about this whole argument probably. "Well this is a big problem. There is no help. The reason there is no help is because . . . " Does this make sense?

Writer: Mmm, hmm.

Adria: Okay, I'm just recapping everything that you've told me, and I'm just organizing it.

In this exchange Adria plays a directive role in producing a coherent narrative for the writer ("So let's make up a little trick because this can get kind of confusing") while phrasing the results as a joint effort ("I'm just recapping everything that you've told me, and I'm just organizing it") and frequently checking the writer's understanding ("Does this make sense?").

In many ways, Adria's approach seems quite effective. After all, we described in Chapters 2 and 3 many strategies you can use at various points in a session. Doesn't it make sense to pass those strategies along to writers? Isn't increasing a writer's strategic repertoire aligned with the goal of focusing on her as a *writer?*

Well, yes and no. Writing center theorist Andrea Lunsford describes a model of the "Writing Center as Storehouse" which "operates as information stations or storehouses, prescribing and handing out skills and strategies to individual learners" (4). Lunsford is critical of this approach because it sets writers up as autonomous units with similar needs and ignores the collaborative nature of learning. The social nature and complexity of learning to write confound the goal of dispensing hints and tricks.

On a more obvious level, the one-size-fits-all nature of these strategies was not readily accepted by all writers. In an interview with the writer in the excerpt about funding for brain-injured students, she commented upon the usefulness of one strategy Adria endorsed. The purpose of this strategy was to overcome getting stuck while writing by saying, "Wait a minute. I'm stuck. How would I tell this to Adria? What would I say to her?" This writer noted that "I think it was easier said than done. . . . easier for her to say to me, 'Oh, do it like that.' It doesn't always work like that. . . . It's more, it's not as easy, you can't just tell someone and write down what you want to tell them." She wondered if using "the same things per person" might not always work since "you don't know the people."

So is Adria a horrible tutor, one who will besmirch the reputation of the writing center? Certainly not, and we don't mean to bash her here. Adria is a resourceful tutor, one who has expertise in many facets of the tutoring process. However, she has very explicit, if not rigid, ideas of what her goals and responsibilities are in a session, and those ideas stem from how she feels she best learned to write. In many instances, writers gratefully appreciate being shown strategies that they can use on their own. In other instances, however, Adria's lack of flexibility won't be as effective. Adria needs to strike a balance and uncover the writer's needs more fully.

Our point for you here is to reflect on the ways of tutoring that feel right. Where do they come from? How much flows from what worked for you as a writer? Rather than merely transmit strategies or even enact practices that you've seen work in other sessions (whether that means asking questions or having the writer read aloud or any other strategy), the important thing is to approach a session with a curious and open mind and, once again, to develop control of the strategies that you might offer writers and the flexibility to know what's working in a session and what adjustments you need to make. What you'll often find to be your most important resource isn't what you can tell writers, but instead what you do instead of talking. In other words, by listening and observing, by looking at body language and uncovering what the writer is doing and why, you can continue to improve as a tutor.

We'd like you to give careful thought to the role your expectations are playing in what's happening or about to happen. Whether that means negotiating the rules of communication or holding in check the endorsement of an infallible strategy, as an effective tutor you'll need to be a careful observer and a thoughtful communicator. We never said that tutoring would be easy, but in its difficulty and complexity lie great rewards and thought-provoking experiences.

5

OBSERVING IN THE WRITING CENTER

We both learn a great deal from observing our tutors. We're always picking up new, better strategies we wouldn't have thought of on our own, and we admire the way our tutors function in different circumstances. In the same way, tutors—new and experienced—learn from observing one another. Thus, the contrast between novice and expert is blurred, as the writing center becomes a site for collaborative learning, not just for writers, but for the staff as well.

In this chapter, we introduce you to the essentials of observation. In an activity as interactive as tutoring, it might not be obvious just how important effective observing can be. Whether you are observing the sessions of an experienced tutor as you try to learn from the model of others or observing the behaviors a writer displays in your own sessions, observing well is one of the best ways you'll develop as a tutor.

Here's what Caroline Goyette, a peer tutor at Marquette, wrote about the importance of her observation experiences:

> The tutoring sessions which I have observed to date have been quite different from one another in terms of focus, goals, and approach. From them, I believe I have learned much about the manner in which the tutoring methods espoused here may be applied to a wide variety of tutoring needs, as well as the ability of the individual tutor to manipulate these methods to form his/her own unique and effective tutoring style. Above all, however, my observation experience has given me the

confidence to tutor by showing me that there is no trick, no secret method or cryptic agenda to which every tutor must adhere.

In what follows, we first establish some of the essentials to keep in mind when observing the tutoring sessions of another or participating in your own. We'll also give you some advice about how to get the most out of observation, and we'll tell you how we have our tutor trainees learn to observe. Finally, we'll take you through a brief excerpt from an actual tutorial and point out some observations that will help you begin to make sense of the sessions you will see.

GET PERMISSION

Before you observe, it's important to have the cooperation of the director or person who runs your writing center. Let him or her know what you want to do and why, if a process of observation isn't already in place. It's also important that both the tutor *and the writer* feel comfortable being observed. At Marquette, we have an understanding with our experienced tutors that if it's all right with the writer, they could be observed at any session. If they don't feel comfortable with this, they can tell us, and we make sure our trainees know which tutors they can observe and which ones aren't ready for observation yet. To observe a session at Marquette, all tutors need to do is check the schedule (see the example schedule on the following page), find a time when someone is working with a writer, and pencil their names in as observers. If possible, they schedule a session with the tutor immediately afterwards so they can discuss what they saw. This means they'd be signing up for two time slots, one with a writer present, and one for just him or her and the tutor. We recommend one observer to a session to keep writers from feeling overwhelmed.

OBSERVE SEVERAL SESSIONS

Observe as many different tutors as your training program allows, and observe different sessions with the same tutors. You'll see a rich range of tutoring strategies, and you'll see an individual tutor vary his style or approach depending on the writer he gets and the kind of session they have (brainstorming or revising, for example). You'll also see differences based on how well the tutor knows the writer and how many sessions they've had together. A tutor working for a third session with the same writer might just dispense with the early talk and jump right into the session, eager to see the draft. You'll see differences in the comfort level, too, and maybe in levels of formality with these repeat visits.

Tutor
&
Room #

	Week Twelve		Monday, November 16		
	Kelly 467	Stacie 476	(Val 450)	Stewart 432	Crystal 472
9:00	Heather Schmidt ↓ *Andy*	Angela Bohlke ↓ *Brad*			
9:30	332-8864	456-5665			
10:00	Shane Ethan ↓ *Andy*	Gabriel Diques 229-4331 *Brad*	Letitia Gomez ↓ *Sara*		
10:30	933-8910	Brenda Cardenas ↓	229-3992		
11:00	Craig Woytal ↓ *Kristina*	261-3001			
11:30	962-2516	Brad			
12:00					Erica Gumm ↓ *Sheri*
12:30					933-3339
1:00				Lee Kennedy *Shantel*	Sheri
1:30				332-5933	
2:00				Robert Barker *Shantel*	
2:30				592-5993	
3:00					
3:30					
4:00			Emma Baker *Adele*		
4:30			961-4553		

Writer
&
Phone #

Observer

BE ON TIME!

Be sure to show up early for your observation. You don't want to interrupt after the session has started, and observing the tutor from the very start of the session is an important part of what you'll get out of the observation. Either you or the tutor will ask the writer if he or she minds being observed, and if it's okay, then you're set.

RECORD YOUR OBSERVATIONS

Be sure to bring paper and a pencil or pen to take notes. As you observe, you won't get everything written down, but take as many notes as you can. The trainees at Marquette have a log they keep of the sessions they observe and conduct (see the example log on page 69). This log is intended to provide material for reflective papers the trainees write at various times during the semester, but it's also useful for them to see the way they develop both as observers and as tutors.

BE OPEN-MINDED

Consider the following scenarios. Does a writer slumping in her chair mean she's bored? Does a writer rapidly reading from his text, barely allowing the tutor to understand or keep up, indicate he's not crazy about coming to the writing center? Does a writer nodding vigorously to everything the tutor says and indicating with "yes" and "uh huh" mean that she completely agrees?

Certainly these conclusions for the observed behaviors could be true. But alternative explanations could be true as well. Perhaps the slumping writer had a lousy night's sleep? Perhaps the rapid reader just has little practice with reading aloud? And perhaps the eager nodder is thinking about her plans for the upcoming weekend and is simply trying to have the tutor do all the talking!

The bottom line here is that what you observe in a tutoring session can have multiple meanings. That means not only that you have to reserve judgment of what you see until you have as much information as possible (or not make judgments if you can help it), but that you have to increase your powers of observation to notice the subtle clues of behavior that you might ordinarily have missed.

We encourage our tutor trainees to stay as objective as possible, recording what they see. For instance, you may find yourself formulating different questions for the writer, questions that would take the session in a different direction than the questions you hear the tutor asking. Relax about this.

There are many ways to take a session, all of which will help the writer improve. So your role is not to evaluate the tutor, but to look for good qualities you can adopt.

It might be a good idea to jot some of your questions down, however. You never know when a tutor might turn to you and ask if you want to participate.

DISCUSS THE SESSION

With a little luck, you'll have a chance to talk the session over with the tutor. It's also good to talk with someone else who has also been observing sessions, so talking to another trainee is a very good idea. If you have a training class or group that meets, that's another good place to discuss your observation.

REFLECT ON THE SESSION

How, then, can you make sense of what you saw? As you look back at your notes, respond to as many of the following reflective/analytical questions as you can.

- How did the tutor make the writer feel welcome?
- What body language did she use? Did she smile? Make small talk as they got started?
- What questions did the tutor ask about the assignment or paper?
- Were there additional questions you'd have asked?
- How did the tutor use the space available to make the writer feel comfortable?
- Was the tutor a good listener? How could you tell?
- Who did most of the talking?
- Did the tutor seem to respect the writer's work? How did she communicate this?
- Did the tutor address the questions the writer came with?
- If the tutor had a different agenda from the writer, how did she negotiate that?
- Did the writer respond well to the tutor's style? Why do you think so? Or think not?
- What kinds of questions did the tutor ask about the project?
- How do you think the writer responded to those questions?
- How did the tutor make known the responsibilities of tutor and writer in the session? What did she say or do?
- How would you describe the role of the tutor: editor, coach, authority figure, peer?

- If the tutor needed to change the subject or get the session back on track, how did she do that?
- How did the tutor end the session?
- Did you feel that the writer knew what she would do next to revise?
- Did the tutor ask her to return?

As you reflect on what you observed, trust your sense of the session. Did it seem positive? What did the writer seem to get out of the session? Did he or she feel pleased at the end? Did his or her attitude change toward the paper? How could you tell? Was the paper the main subject of the session, or did the session primarily focus on the writer's composing strategies? Most important, what did you get out of the session? What new things did you learn, or what techniques did you spot?

WRITE UP YOUR OBSERVATIONS

As we have mentioned, your observations and reflections can become the source for a reflective essay, a powerful way of using writing to understand how you're developing as a tutor. What follows is one tutor's account of observations, taken from a reflective paper required for the peer tutoring course at Marquette:

> My jaw dropped. Attending my English 192 class for the first time, I was already contemplating my withdrawal from this class. Paula had just informed us that 20 hours of tutoring and observation in the writing center was required to pass the course. This writing center business was most unexpected. Being a very conscientious student, I had registered for English 192 without any idea what it was about. I knew it was a writing class, which is what I required for graduation. Normally, the unknown is a frightening spectre; however, this time I saw a rare opportunity to seek truth in a foreign environment. Little did I realize I would learn a great deal about helping others, about myself, and the power of a chicken sandwich.
>
> I was eager, if a bit apprehensive, to begin observing tutoring sessions in progress. I had never felt the need to spend any time at the writing center prior to this. Due to a combination of shyness, decent writing skills, and what my father would call "bull-headedness," I could never bring myself to ask for help on a paper. Fortunately, the tutors, whom I had encountered at the first writing center staff meeting, seemed friendly and helpful. Naturally, I didn't trust them.
>
> My first session was spent in observation of Crystal, who was working with a female first-year student on a reflective essay about a time when she changed her mind about something. It was their second

session together. They seemed to have a good rapport. Even I felt comfortable, despite the pervasive feeling that I was guilty of a kind of academic voyeurism. The student was very concerned about word choice and "flow." At the tutor's request, the student read her paper aloud. It was about the moment she realized she would not qualify for state in track as a senior in high school. Crystal asked leading questions, forcing the student to think for herself. I felt this was very positive, and began to see where Crystal was heading. Eventually, the student learned what to look for, and was catching problematic phrases before she read them. She revised her descriptions as well, making them more vivid, eye-catching. In this case, the tutor not only helped the student revise a paper, but indirectly taught her to see her paper from a third-person perspective. Impressed, I left the writing center with a renewed hope for mankind, or something like that.

As I walked to my car, I reflected on what I had just witnessed. I began to mentally reenact the session, only with myself as the tutor. Full of confidence, I felt as if there were some things that I would have suggested to make the student's paper greater still. Delusional visions of an "ideal text" filled my head. Deliciously assembled articulations spilled from my brain like something of a spillable consistency. The paper was mine to manipulate, to shape into my own monster (insert evil laughter here).

"Growwwwl," said my stomach, objecting to my ignorance of standard breakfast protocol. It was the occasion of my second observation, and I was hungry for a chicken sandwich. Sarah was seeing a male physics student working on his dissertation. His primary concern was grammar and punctuation. Sarah obligingly pored over each phrase with him, reading silently as the student read aloud. He obviously felt very comfortable with Sarah, as he felt no remorse in asking her opinions on each (real or imagined) transgression he stumbled upon. Like Crystal, Sarah was doing a superior job, making the student feel at home while maintaining a professional distance. I dutifully took notes despite my emaciated state and the haunting image of a chicken sandwich impressed onto my brain. Initially I had felt intimidated about the stature of the assignment at hand. However, as he read, I found that the dissertation actually made sense to me, and I regained my tutorial egotism. Sarah, in a not so subtle attempt to make me feel more useful, asked my opinion on three or four occasions. This unleashed the writer within, determined to create order out of chaos, to impose truth where truth was not necessarily wanted or needed.

As the session wound down and Sarah was taking care of the paper work, I began to compose on the topic of my hunger, just for sport. More precisely, I wove a tapestry of unbridled and powerful prose about the philosophical, aesthetic, and practical importance of the chicken sandwich. Chicken sandwich as the path to nirvana. Chicken sandwich as neo-realist art. Chicken sandwich as paperweight (I had just read Nancy Sommers).[1] Obviously, the hunger was starting to affect my brain. I was so ready for a chicken sandwich at the time, and when I finally got one, it would be the best I ever had. It would have to wait until tomorrow, as I was out of money.

Next, I met with Joe, only this time it was to have him tutor me. Since I scarcely had any real draft, we instead brainstormed on what I might write about regarding my tutoring experiences. It was then that Joe made a statement that has since defined my view of the writing center. "We are not here to write their papers for them. It's not ours, it's theirs, for better or worse, lumps and all. Not every paper is going to change the world."

He was right. I could not hope to guide each student into my view of an ideal text. The best I could hope for is to help them make the best of the paper that they bring in. As I sat down at Boston Market to enjoy my long anticipated chicken sandwich, it hit me. Sometimes, a paper is not going to be the Mona Lisa of English 01 papers. Likewise, sometimes a chicken sandwich is not going to be the Taj Mahal of chicken sandwiches. As I tasted my Holy Quail, I sighed. It was a little dry.

—Daniel Scherrer

Dan first observed Crystal, a graduate student, and then Sarah, a senior. Notice, though, that Sarah is tutoring a graduate student working on a dissertation. She doesn't have to be an expert in physics, though, to tell if his writing is clear and correct.

REFLECT AGAIN

After you've had some tutoring experience of your own, it's a good idea to look over these accounts of the sessions you observed. They will mean different things to you at different points in your training. It might be good for you to write a narrative the way the tutors at Marquette do (though your stomach needn't always play a role in these essays) and send it to *The Writing Lab Newsletter* Tutor's Corner or to the IWCA website where tutor stories are published. These kinds of stories and observations help us all know more, not only about the training process, but about the tutoring process.

---

[1]Dan had just read "Between the Drafts" by Sommers.

English 192 Writing Center Tutoring Log

Name *Adele Smith*

Please draw a line across the page after each session.

Date	Time In	Out	Description of session	Supervisor's Initials
9 - 20	6:30	7:40	Read Ben's paper over on e-mail. He had a lot of really great ideas, but lacked some focus. My main concern was that he did not clearly explain his thesis. The paper was going in a bunch of different directions, it seemed. I asked a number of questions about order & expansion of ideas.	AS
9/23	1:00	1:35	I observed w/ Stewart, tutoring a freshman who had the assignment of writing about a transition & how he changed his view of something significant. Throughout the session Stewart asked the tutee questions, most of which he did not answer, but rather nodded his head & said "Yeah, that's a good idea, that will work." Both Stewart & I attempted to ask leading questions, and a few times we had to say "will you TELL me?" This led to a sort of directive approach by the tutor, but I do think that the tutee walked out with more ideas and he agreed that the session was very helpful.	EW
10/7	10:00	11:00	Andy & Val's session was so awesome. Andy came in with a pretty rough draft - something he had typed very late the night before, but he had some really great ideas - they just needed a lot of explaining. Val asked a bunch of "What do you mean by that" questions. This really got Andy talking about his paper. It was totally textbook and Andy said it helped out a ton. It helped me out a ton too, because I got to see how Andy really improved his thoughtfulness by the end of the session.	VM
10/8	2:00	3:00	This was my session for the reflective essay - and the first time I have gone to the writing center to be tutored. (I loved it - I'm definitely going back with other papers). This was a helpful session because Stewart and I were able to clear up some concerns I had about the explanation of my ideas in my paper. When I write reflectives or analyses, it is easy to confuse the reader (because I know what I am talking about, and I sometimes forget to explain it clearly). It also helped for us to just talk about tutoring because it gave me some good ideas that I might of otherwise looked over.	EW

EXAMPLES FOR OBSERVATION

To help you practice making sense of what you'll observe in live tutoring sessions, we include two transcript excerpts. Both come from the beginning of sessions. With the first, we'll supply some analysis, but we'll leave the second for your comments and scrutiny. As you read these (and we recommend you read each aloud, preferably with a partner taking the second speaking role), picture the scene in your head. Use the reflective questions we posed earlier in this chapter to make sense of what you're seeing.

In this first example, the writer has already told the tutor that she's writing a book review for her graduate education class. The transcript picks up from that point:

Tutor: How do you want to proceed? I'm wondering if I should have you read this to me; yeah, it's only four pages. Will you do that? And that way you can include the comments, or additions, or changes better than I would be able to.

Writer: Okay, personally I find this first paragraph, I know what I'm trying to say and I find this kind of awkward. Okay? And I don't know why.

Tutor: What are you trying to say? Before you read it to me, tell me what you're trying to say, then I can hear it.

Writer: Okay, well what I'd like to discuss is just the . . . I guess to bring the reader of this piece into the idea of my opinion of what Alphabet City, or the place where this book was going to happen, before I even got into the book. I had some biases.

Tutor: Interesting.

Writer: It's a preconceived thing. That's just sort of a way to talk about where this book is taking place. And then get into the book and so that's . . .

Tutor: So in a sense this is your response to the book? You want your reader to know where you started in your response to the book?

Writer: Okay.

Tutor: At what point you were? Is that correct?

Writer: Yeah, I never said it to anyone, I just started trying to write it. Yeah, I guess I'm just trying to set up what my impression was before I picked up the book.

Notice several things in this excerpt about what the tutor does. He asks the writer to read her text aloud, justifying that request ("And that way you can include the comments, or additions, or changes better than I would be able to") by demonstrating that she's the expert, she's the one in control of her paper and will need to be the one to revise. When the writer next expresses disdain for her first paragraph, the tutor asks her to clarify it for him before she reads anything. In that way he probes the clarity of her thoughts, discovering if it's her writing that's unclear or if her understanding of what she's read needs work. Also, notice that after the writer explains her first paragraph, the tutor rephrases her explanation in terms of "a reader" ("You want your reader to know where you started in your response to the book?"). By doing this, he conveys to the writer the need to think in terms of the rhetorical situation, particularly her purpose in her first paragraph and how she's trying to convey that purpose to her reader. Finally, note that the tutor doesn't simply announce his clarifying of the writer's intentions, he asks her to verify ("At what point you were? Is that correct?").

In these moves, the tutor establishes what his role is: to support the writer as *she* clarifies her meaning and to demonstrate how to think about her writing in rhetorical terms. He also establishes the writer's role to convey her interpretation of the book and to make "comments, additions, or changes." Now, consider that this excerpt took only a minute and 15 seconds! Certainly, much of the important work of your sessions will take place at the very beginning.

The next excerpt is for your practice observation. As you read and examine this passage (again, reading aloud if possible), think about the roles that tutor and writer play. What do they seem to convey to each other in terms of their goals and responsibilities? How can you tell? Once again, the following passage comes at the very beginning of the session. Note, too, that dialogue in all capital letters indicates the reading of a text aloud:

Tutor: Since you haven't been here before, could you please fill this out for me, and I'll read over your assignment while you're . . .

Writer: I think the first thing that I want . . . it's for art history. It's about the architectural, the Boston Public Library and the Museum of Fine Arts and I had problems with the first paper. He said to me that he knew that I had a good ideas but he couldn't understand them because they were not well written. So I want you to sort of . . .

Tutor: Look for those things?

Writer: Yes. Look for grammar and misspellings but to see if you understand what I'm trying to say.

Tutor: Okay. Fantastic. Do you have your assignment with you so that I can read what your professor asked for?

Writer: He didn't give us something written. It's just a paper on the additions of the Museum of Fine Arts and the Boston Public Library.

[silence while writer fills out forms]

Tutor: Okay. All set?

Writer: Yeah.

Tutor: How about you read through this out loud and I'll listen, and you might find things yourself as you read along that maybe aren't so clear, and then we can work as we go.

Writer: You read it already?

Tutor: No, I haven't read it already, but it just makes more sense for us to do it this way today.

Writer: Okay. Do you want me to read it?

Tutor: Out loud.

Writer: Out loud?

Tutor: Yeah.

Writer: Oh, okay.

Tutor: Sometimes when you hear things, you pick up, if something's difficult to understand or doesn't quite flow, you'll hear it. Your ears will recognize it before your eyes do sometimes.

Writer: Oh, wow, okay. AN ADDITION TO AN EXISTING CORPUS, IN THIS CASE A LIBRARY AND A MUSEUM, IS A VERY DIFFICULT TASK TO REALIZE FOR AN ARCHITECT. Could you tell me when I'm not saying the words the way I should?

GOOD OBSERVING = GOOD TUTORING

In a session that lasts from 30 to 60 minutes, you'll have plenty to watch for, plenty to record, and plenty to make sense of. It might be difficult at first, but learning to observe takes time and patience. We're convinced that good tutoring starts with good observing, and that as you gain experience, your powers of observation—and your ability to reflect on what you observe—will become some of your greatest assets in your development as a writing tutor.

6

TUTORING PRACTICE

This chapter will give you some guidance about good practices of note-taking, a skill you'll find useful in tutoring, and then offer some guidelines about an exercise that tutors tell us benefits them greatly, the practice tutorial.

TAKING NOTES

Just listening to writers read papers can be a challenge if you're not used to it. Now add to that the tasks of taking notes and formulating questions, all at the same time. These skills take time—and patience with yourself—to develop. We've made practice with note-taking and questioning a regular part of our training, and we offer some examples of how these activities might be done.

First, when listening to writers read their papers aloud, or when reading the papers aloud to the writers, it's vital to listen to the whole paper and not jump into a section before you hear the entire thing. A few years ago, we had a bad experience with a writer, an experience that only came out in our staff meeting when we began discussing it. The writer had a problem in her first few paragraphs, and two different tutors worked with her but stopped her, working on the introduction. When a third tutor listened to the entire paper, she found that the paper's main problem lay in the middle and that the paper didn't really fit the assignment. The first two tutors had gotten hung up on the first problem and hadn't seen the forest for the trees. Once the writer revised, all the problems of the introduction cleared up. So it's important to form an impression of the whole paper.

Taking good notes that you will be able to make sense of later is important to having a good session. All our tutors have their own unique styles of note-taking. The important thing is to be able to refer to specific sections of the paper that need attention and to include your own reactions. Some tutors like to work on a large sheet of newsprint paper that the writer can write on, too. Some simply write their questions down and have a great capacity for holding the paper and its parts in memory. But most people can't remember an entire paper that well. So here is a model for note-taking that works for lots of tutors. At the top of the page, write down the concerns the writer has expressed, the assignment, and the main idea as the writer has expressed it to you. You'll come back to this when you start asking questions.

Draw a line down the page, about two inches from the left margin.

| On the left side, take your own notes: check with a + the things you like. Write down a word or phrase from a sentence you want to return to. Mark with a ? those things you don't quite understand. | At the right of the line, take notes as if you were attending a lecture. These notes will furnish you with a rough outline afterwards, and this outline will allow you to talk about the organization and structure of the paper. Draw lines when you think you hear a paragraph break. You can check with the writer to see if your sense of the organization of the paper matches hers. Get as many details as you can—the more the better. |

It's important to explain to the writer what you're doing when you take notes. You don't want the writer to think that you're writing down criticisms, or she will interpret all your writing as trouble for her. Instead, explain that you are going to take notes on her paper as if you were in class and that when you finish, you should have a rough outline of her paper. This makes it clear to her that she is the expert and that you are learning from her writing. Often writers will ask if they can have your notes, and we always willingly hand them over. Writers seem to appreciate your outline and the comments you might make in the left margin. It takes a while to get the hang of taking complete notes and getting down all the parts of a paper, so don't expect to be perfect at it right away.

We'll show you some of our trainees' first attempts at note-taking from a paper read aloud to them in class. The following paper was written for a first semester first-year composition course. The paper assignment was to do a family history, interviewing family members and relating to a general audience the way in which the family experienced a historical event or period, American or otherwise. Have someone read the following paper to you, so you can practice taking some notes yourself:

The Tale of an Immigrant Farmer

Faith played a larger role in past generations than it does in the present one. In looking over my family history, I found my great-great-great-great grandfather, five generations before me, was a man of strong faith, almost too strong for his own good. His name was Emile Dubois, and the story of his life follows, as well as my reasons for the above claim.

In the mid-nineteenth century, some parts of Europe were quite hellish. Unemployment was a major problem, simply because there were too many people trying to live in the same place at the same time. Due to the population explosion, and a drastic change in the way life from a rural society to a more urban society, land became scarce. Since only one family could be supported by one plot of land, which is relatively small by today's standards, only one child would inherit the entire farm. The other children would have to either marry into a farm, become a migrant worker, or emigrate to the Americas and start from nothing. A young Frenchman by the name of Emile Dubois chose to follow the third option. His father owned a large, four-hundred-year-old farm of thirty-five acres, in Beullot, France; however, the farm could only support his elder sister and her family, so Emile went to join his brother in Illinois. He left in 1846 by way of Le Harve, a major port in Southwestern France, and was fortunate enough to leave before massive emigration took place from that port.

Emile beat the rush and made it to New York with no problem. From New York, Emile joined his younger brother, Modeste, in Lee Center, Illinois, where they both worked in a stone quarry. Between their savings after one year and a loan, the two brothers had enough to buy an eighty-acre farm, at $1.25 an acre, in Bradford, Illinois. The farm was very successful, for after one year, the profits were enough to pay off the mortgage and pay for improvements. One year later, Modeste sold Emile his share of the farm, which by that time had grown into a massive three hundred twenty acres. Illinois has an ideal climate and excellent soil for growing crops, so successful farmers were plentiful, as Modeste displayed when he went on to start his new farm. By the time of his death, Modeste owned fourteen hundred acres of farmland, as well as being the father of fourteen children.

Emile's life after the two brothers split up was a little rougher. He married a young French girl by the name of Sophie Godard, and together they soon had a son, Henry. However, the girl did not like all the hardships the prairie life had to offer, so a little over one year after their marriage, Sophie took Henry and went to live in Chicago. Emile needed a wife and family in order to survive farm life, as my father, Floyd T. Roberts, states in a college essay. He writes, " . . . the family was the operating economic unit. . . .

Continued

The father was the head of the household and its enterprises. He controlled the family's fields . . . The mother's domain was the house, the livestock, and the children. The children in turn contributed to the economic well-being of the family as soon as they were able" (Roberts, 1). So, being left by his wife left Emile in a sticky moral situation. If he did not remarry, he would soon be forced off his farm. However, his strong Roman Catholic faith would not allow him to remarry. Emile made what I am sure was a painful decision, the decision to remarry. He married a local girl, Roberta Danton, and together they had four boys. Unfortunately, Roberta died after the birth of the fourth, which put Emile back in the same situation as he was before. This time, because he had four boys, he had no choice but to remarry. He married Mrs. Harris, a widow with six children, and together they had four more children, the eldest of which is Clementine Maude Dubois, my great-great-great grandmother.

Mrs. Harris died when Maude was twelve, and Emile Dubois never remarried. I cannot say that I blame him: he must have been shell shocked by that time. Clementine Maude, Emile's daughter mentioned above, describes the hardships in an interview with my father before her death in 1972, "Especially after Ma died, Pa was a moody man . . . he would eat supper and then sit staring at the fire for the longest time, not talking to anybody . . . [he was] kind of sad and worn-out like," (Roberts, 5). I would like very much to have talked to him during that stage in his life. What was he thinking? Was he depressed only about his last wife, or about all of them? Perhaps he was in remorse for ever remarrying, and the deaths of his loved ones was part of his punishment from God. If he was so apprehensive of being damned by God about marrying twice, I can imagine that he thought that there was no hope for himself for marrying three times.

Why do past generations seem more devotedly faithful than the present ones? Perhaps it was the hardships they felt and experienced that brought them closer to their faith. Maude stated in the interview with my father, "But it was terrible hard work; sometimes even the women and girls had to work in the fields at harvest time, and keep up with their own chores, too! I wouldn't ever want any of you to have to work as hard as we did then" (Roberts, 6). Why would any man give up a successful future because his faith does not allow it? It would be an interesting perspective, but I can only guess how Emile felt during the remainder of his life.

It is safe to say that past generations were more devotedly faithful than today's society. In a society where a second marriage is as common as a second car, you would have a hard time finding a person in the same situation as Emile. However, due to the drastic change in society and way of life in the past few decades, you cannot go wrong if you are just as moral a person as you can possibly be.

Here were some pages of notes the trainees took.

Sheri's notes:

Assignment: Engl 001—family history interview—communicate how the period was, based on family experiences.

Comments	Text—paraphrasing, etc.
	GGG Grandfather has too much faith for his own good (at times)
+ Good economic explanation	*Emile Dubois—Loans, hard work, farms, etc.*
+ Why farming was a booming industry	*Illinois soil*
– When were they able?	*The children contributed as soon as they were able*
+ Moving quote and insight	*Daughter of Emile: "I wonder what he was feeling."*
Focus ⟶	*Why faithfulness and devotion to spouse was important*

Questions: Why did you bring this up at the end of your paper?
Is this essay about hard work/faith in God/or relationships in the past and present?
This painted a very vivid picture, but I'd like to see more development of one main theme.

Notice that Sheri wrote down the assignment (a very important thing to take down). If this had been a real session, she'd have written down the comments the writer made at the start of the session, and his concerns. She then took the notes from the paper on the right side of the sheet and used the signs +, –, and ? to indicate things she liked, things she didn't like, and questions she had. She would probably have started the session by telling the writer about the things she liked. She might have held off on the section of the paper she didn't like until she saw how the session went. She felt that the paper wandered from topic to topic, so she wrote some questions that she hoped would lead the writer in that direction.

Here are Kristina's notes:

Interview someone from family—interesting about history of family related to history.
Exhibit historical period w/family member.

Tale of an Immigrant Farmer	*Really like the introduction, of talking about*
Grandfather—5 generations before	*faith. Good idea.*
Mid-19th century⟶ *conditions*	
Rural⟶ *urban, land scarce*	*Where?*
Talking about urban life	

Young Frenchmen ——➤ *in France*	
Went to Illinois to join brother	*Modeste: Emile*
Worked in stone quarry	
Bought Farm ——➤ *grew*	*Do not even touch on faith until here.*
Modeste ——➤ *life after farm split up was good*	*Too much listing. Confusion here.*
Emile ——➤ *Bad* ——➤ *need family*	
"sticky moral situation"	
Catholic faith	
Decided to marry	
2nd wife died	*Not clear in this area*
Remarried again had 4 boys	
3rd wife died—did not marry again	*Concentrate on marriages* ——➤ *not clear*
Past generations more faithful	*about faith: moral situation*
	◄—— *Need to focus more on this in the*
Today lots of people have multiple marriages	*body; confusing.*

Questions: What do you want to focus on in the paper? Do you feel you have achieved that focus?
What do you mean by faith?
Why was it a "sticky moral situation"? That was not clear to me.
Look at your conclusion. Do you focus on those things in the body of your paper?

Like Sheri, Kristina wrote down the assignment and added the title. Then she took notes down the left side of the page and wrote her questions and comments in the right margin. She wrote her questions at the end. Like Sheri, she felt that the paper needed more focus, and she urged the writer to define the terms *faith* and *sticky moral situation*. Also, like Sheri, she noticed that the conclusion did not seem to fit well with the body of the paper.

Here are Aesha's questions.

- What is your thesis?
- How do you show that Emile's life is an example of this thesis?
- What is the significance of mentioning Emile's brother? How does he fit in with the thesis?
- What do you think is the moral situation of today?
- How is Emile's time different from today?
- What is faith to you? Religious, faith in self, faith in family?
- How does Emile overcome his "Sticky moral situation" and still hold on to his faith?

Any of these questions would be an excellent way of starting this session and getting the writer thinking about good ways to revise his paper.

Here is another paper—same paper topic, same class. Trainees' notes and questions follow.

Newlyweds at War

The year was 1966. My parents, Donna and Mark Molloy, had just been wed. Mark was in his last year of law school at the University of Minnesota and Donna, at the ripe age of nineteen, was working part time as a lab technician. The newlyweds looked eagerly at their futures together. They planned to travel the world, take time to be together and simply enjoy one another's company. Little did they know, that the Vietnam conflict would disrupt their new found happiness and turn their world upside down.

The R.O.T.C. program put Mark through college. After law school, he was required to fill a two year commitment to the army. His friends from college, on the same program, fulfilled their duties immediately following college. They were assigned to countries like Europe, performing tasks such as couriers. Mark assumed that when his time came to serve he would be doing likewise.

Mark graduated from law school in June of 1967 and proceeded to take the Bar Exam on July 15, 1967. Mark then received notice that he was commissioned to Fort Benning, Georgia on July 28, 1967 to act as a First Lieutenant. The position entailed being an infantry officer with army intelligence and going through eight rigorous weeks of infantry school. The couple uprooted from their St. Paul apartment and landed in a short-time lease, cockroach infested housing project in the humidity of the south. My father was up before the sun, spent hours on end in the fields and rarely returned home before dark. For young Donna, this meant days filled with boredom and loneliness. She met up with other wives in the same position. In their new community, they taught each other craft projects and had solitaire marathons to fill the time.

The eight weeks was nearly over and Donna was thrilled that they would be moving on. Although Vietnam was a realistic threat for my parents, they assumed that my father would only go as far as Washington to serve as an advisor. They did not imagine that he would actually be sent to Vietnam to fight. The mail on September 6 brought a pleasant surprise, Mark had passed the Bar Exam. A prosperous future was in sight. Unfortunately, the very next day's mail was not so kind. Surprisingly, Mark was ordered to Vietnam and Donna was faced with the fact that she would be left alone, thousands of miles from her husband for only one year.

To prepare for the voyage, the couple moved to Baltimore, Maryland. There, at Fort Holabird, Mark and Donna teamed with other lawyers and their wives who were going through the same horrible, but very realistic situation. As the men attended Army Intelligence courses, the women began to form bonds. Luckily, these friendships provided Donna with the strength and support she needed to see her husband off to war.

Time passed quickly and before the couple knew it, they were forced to face December 8, 1967. Mark and Donna exchanged their good byes with thoughts of the future haunting

Continued

their minds. Mark boarded a plane for Saigon and Donna waved good bye with tears welting in her eyes. She stared at his face with a deep fondness, wondering, if God-forbid, she would ever see it again.

In the days that followed, Donna moved back to Minnesota and continued work as a lab technician. She shared an apartment with her cousin, and three friends. The doctor that Donna was working for decided to practice elsewhere, not only did she not have her husband, now she did not have a job. My dad's father felt compassion for his newest daughter and convinced her to move in with their family (the youngest three of seven children were still living at home). They shared the same loneliness as Donna, and together, they worked through Mark's absence.

Mark was living among the Vietnamese, Mekong Delta, serving as an advisor with seven other Americans. He was in charge of intelligence missions. When weapons were confiscated from the enemy, my father was in charge of inspecting them and determining their type. He also flew in helicopters, taking pictures of incoming B-52's.

The mail became vital in keeping communication alive between Mark and the family at home. The news broadcasts would run and the family kept their fingers crossed, waiting for Mark's letters, often delayed by the mail service. My grandfather would send tapes of himself and the family, along with anyone of town members, to Mark. If the weather agreed, Mark would sit on the roof and listen to the familiar voices, over and over and over. In turn, Mark would send slides of Vietnam with a tape to accompany it. In one slide, Mark took a picture of the gate outside his home that had been hit. My grandfather recognized the gate from previous slides and it was times like these that sent the entire family into panic.

In August of 1968, after being separated for eight months, Mark and Donna were given the opportunity to see each other. Mark had been granted a one week "R&R" (rest and relaxation) period. They met in Hawaii with a couple they had met at Fort Holabird. They had seven short days to catch up on all of the events that had passed since Mark's departure. The last day of their vacation came upon them and once again, Donna had to repeat the dreaded good bye at the airport. This time, however, she had hope that she would be seeing him again soon.

Once Mark was back in Vietnam, he had to deal with dysentery. He got the disease from eating the food, cooked by the Vietnamese. Although the bout with sickness put a scare on Mark and the family, they knew the end of Mark's army commitment was in sight. On December 8, 1968, Mark flew home, leaving his memories of war behind. Unfortunately, it was a leap year and it took one day longer for him to return. My grandmother always said that God must have been on their side because not only was December 8 the day her son returned, it was a holy day as well.

One last step had to be taken before the couple could return to normalcy. They were back together, and that was worth anything the last months of my father's commitment required. Once again, it was necessary that they move. This time Mark and Donna wound up at Fort

Lenardward in Missouri, were Mark served as an intelligence officer. He was now a captain and his final duty was to provide security clearance for new recruits.

July of 1969 came along and they were free! Mark and Donna moved to St. Cloud, MN. In September of 1969, Mark was granted a partnership with a local firm. At last, their futures were falling into place. In the fall of 66, they had no idea what was ahead. Their marriage had survived the strain of a war, and they knew now that they had the strength to tackle anything their futures may hold.

Jessi's notes:

Paper topic ——➤ *History paper—historical concept through use of family narrative.*

"Newlyweds at War"
-parents just married in '66—dad was w/ROTC and Nam interrupts marriage.

↓

Sent to Georgia to be lieutenant 8 wks

↓

Passes bar, then ordered to Nam
moved to Baltimore
went to war
Dec 8, 1967 he leaves

↓

Mail as vital communication, tapes of family members—slides sent back home from Nam

↓

In 1968—they met for 1 week of R&R

↓

Dec. he returns home. They move to Missouri

↓

1969 moved to Minnesota—things were back to normal

↓

They can now handle anything.

Notice that Jessi marks the divisions of the paper (as she hears them) with arrows. Later she can use these arrows to ask the writer if these indicate the true paragraph breaks.

A number of trainees wondered what the focus of the paper was and felt ill at ease that the writer depicted the story as such a happy-ever-after sort of tale. Kristina asked some hard questions that might have made the writer deepen her inquiry into her parents' history.

- Did your father suffer from any postwar stress that made returning to the States challenging in some way?

- How did your father feel for the year he was in Vietnam?
- Has he ever given you a vivid description of what things were like in Vietnam?

As the class discussed this paper, we found that we all wondered why this writer chose to depict the war as a scary inconvenience, and we felt that the paper might have benefited from some more details about what else might have been going on during this time: How many from their town died in the war? What were the casualty rates? How lucky was her father, actually? They speculated that the story she told is the story *she* was told and that perhaps all the members of his family might have agreed that this was the story they could live with. They discussed being sensitive to the writer's sensitivities and having respect for family privacy.

Our notes are often our prompts for what kinds of questions to ask. Remember to come back to any concerns the writer had and address them first, either by dealing with them or by assuring the writer that you'll come back to them. When you look at your notes, remember to put higher-order concerns first. Sometimes the first thing you notice on your page of notes is something about a word or expression that sounds wrong to you. Remember to deal with the topic, its suitability to the assignment, the support, and the organization first. Then come back to that word, if it seems appropriate. As you become an experienced tutor, you'll feel good about your ability to take notes on a session, whatever system you develop for it.

THE PRACTICE TUTORIAL

Listening practice and asking theoretical questions are good classroom or training session activities; they allow tutors to compare their questions and notes and get a sense that there are no set responses to a paper. More dramatic, though, is actual tutoring practice. In this exercise, you'll get tutored—and you'll tutor someone else—on a piece of real writing, and something really good can come out of this practice.

There are many reasons why we like to use this exercise in our training.

- As the tutor, you'll get to listen to a text being read aloud and then get to try out note-taking.
- As the tutor, you'll also get to formulate questions about the text you hear.
- As the writer, you'll get tutored on work you really wrote, and you'll even enjoy that process.
- As the writer, you'll get to see how it feels to read aloud and get some, perhaps, unexpected feedback on your work.

- As the observer, you'll get to help the tutor by affirming what she's do-ing well, and you'll also get practice observing and with taking notes on that process.

There are three roles you'll play in this triad: the writer, the tutor, and the observer. As the writer, you'll bring a piece of your own writing, a paper you've handed in and like a lot, one you're working on, or an old one you'd genuinely like to revise. It will help if you're open minded about the ques-tions and comments the tutor makes about your paper. You could learn a lot about your own writing from this.

As a tutor, you'll conduct this as if it were a real session, asking names, getting acquainted, asking about the assignment, asking what the writer likes about it and what he wants to work on. The writer reads the paper as if this were a real session, and the tutor takes notes and then asks questions of the writer and gives feedback.

Meanwhile, the observer is taking notes on what is going on in the ses-sion, and after it's over will answer the following questions.

- What happened?
- What did you see?
- What did the writer get out of the session?
- What was good about the session?

Allow at least a half hour for the whole tutorial: a few minutes for precon-ference talk and questions about the assignment, paper, and so forth; about seven minutes to read the paper aloud (assuming it's about five pages); a few minutes for the tutor to gather her thoughts; about ten minutes of good questions; and then about five to ten minutes for the observer to comment. If a class of tutors can break into groups and do this, then it's good to com-pare notes at the end and see what came out of it for the entire class.

A SAMPLE SESSION

In the following session, Adele was the writer, Aesha was the tutor, and Sheri was the observer. Adele agreed to read a paper she'd written in her first-year composition class, one that had earned a good grade. However, she still had some unresolved feelings about it and felt it should have been better, but the teacher's comments didn't help her to see how. You might want to read this paper aloud and formulate your own questions about it; then read the dia-logue below that Adele had with Aesha. After some introductory talk and a description of the assignment (a paper written to other students trying to convince them of something), Adele read the following:

On November 3rd I attended the men's basketball game. On November 9th, yet another. On November 7th, a girl's basketball game. Did anyone want to join me? Because when I asked people if they went to the game, I got a lot of "Well, no. I had a lot to do." Hey, I had a lot to do too! The funny thing is that most of the people I had asked to go to the game were also Fanatic Club members. I say that if you are going to spend that much money on season tickets, you might as well attend the games. The T-shirts you get aren't all that great, so what motivated these students to purchase tickets? Who knows! But I do know that this season is bringing another display of Marquette's lack of school spirit.

What is so darn important about school spirit, you ask? Let's concentrate on athletics. Marquette is a Division 1 school, our men's basketball team is the defending Conference-USA Champion, our women's track members are the defending Conference-USA Champions, our men's soccer team is going to the finals, our women's soccer team finished their home season undefeated and second in the C-USA Conference. I'd say we have a pretty strong athletic program here at Marquette. So what is stopping you from displaying some enthusiasm about it? You can't do homework all the time. And even if you do, there needs to be a balance in your life between recreation and studying. Take a break! The games are only a couple hours long. And trust me—you will certainly be refreshed when the game is over.

So are we just scared to be enthusiastic? I don't think we are, at least we shouldn't be. If you love something enough to be a part of it, as you are of Marquette, then show it! There must be some reason you chose this school. Show people how proud you are to be a Golden Eagle. Attend a basketball game or two, or ten if you want to. (Support your soccer teams, too. The Fall Festival had a pathetic attendance.) And since you're there, you might as well cheer for your team. And don't just cheer at the Cincinnati or Louisville games. I'm pretty sure that the players would like to hear some screaming at all of their games. Losing against Dayton can be just as detrimental to their season as losing against Cincinnati.

Going to games also gives you a great opportunity to get involved socially by meeting people other than those in your classes or at parties. Most of the students sit in the same section, so all of your friends are going to be right there with you. The games provide a chance for you to let loose, scream a little, and just to have a great time.

I don't know if you all watched or went to the University of Wisconsin–Madison game, but you could have learned a valuable lesson on school spirit from them. They actually stood up and cheered when their team scored, and even more so when their team was down.

They seemed to be having so much fun. For a second I almost wanted to go over and sit with them just because our own student section was so downbeat. But I am dedicated to Marquette, and to creating a spirit like so many other colleges have.

I need your help though. It takes more than just twenty people at the games. Do you laugh at the schools that get all dressed up and paint their faces, and make signs for games? Call it stupid? I call it spirit. And that is what we need. We are a university. Have you ever really looked at the word "university"? Do you see the word *unity* in there some-where? Do you see how we should support our fellow students, and our entire school to defend our unity?

So get up and say for once "this reading can wait." None of us can study all the time, and if you really do, then take a break! Go out and do something important to you and to your university. Offer the encour-agement to our students that the Marquette Jesuit tradition is "famous" for. Don't be the student that walks away from college having only studied and partied. You are only in college for a few short years, but if you get involved, you become a part of your university, making memo-ries and leaving your mark forever.

Aesha asked Adele: What were your main reasons in support of going to the games?

Adele: We should be willing to support our sports program because we have really good teams. Going to games is a way to get involved. We should have more team spirit.

Aesha: How did you support your claims?

Adele: I felt I was really critical of other students and of our school. Does it sound too critical of the people I was trying to persuade?

Aesha: If you were reading it, would you be offended? (Lots of laughing)

Adele: I'd really like to change the tone. It's too much like a slap in the face. I think I did too much accusing. I'd like to suggest a course of action instead.

Aesha asked a series of questions:
- "What do you think is the problem? Why don't people go to the games?"
- "How can you persuade people who don't want to go to attend?"
- "What makes *you* want to go?"
- "What course of action would you want to propose?"
- "What are other people's views on the subject?"

These questions led Adele to think of a section she could have added to the paper to suggest ways to get students more interested in showing school spirit by attending games. She also noted that she hadn't included any opposition in her paper, something she would add if she revised it. By the end of the tutorial, Adele had a very good sense of how she would revise the paper and how she would improve it.

THE OBSERVATION

If you were the observer, what would you point out? During this practice tutorial session, Sheri noted that Aesha was not condescending and seemed interested, that she listened and smiled during the discussion. She liked the way Aesha let Adele say what she really thought; she felt the good questions allowed that to happen. She complimented Aesha on the way she let the writer come up with the answers.

Sara, another student in the class, reflects on the process:

> I have found the practice tutorials to be a big help. I can hear about something in class and read about it in a textbook, but it usually doesn't click for me until I have to apply it myself.
>
> I have to admit that I was a little nervous about playing the tutor. I wasn't sure if I would be able to do it. I had this horrible vision of me listening to the student read her paper and then either having nothing to say or having so much to say that I had no idea where to start. I was afraid of being utterly clueless. Actually doing a tutorial in class has helped me to see that I'm a lot better at it than I thought I would be. Not that I'm perfect by any means, but at least I know that I won't fall flat on my face! I think that our exercises in class have done a lot to boost my confidence level.
>
> Also, during my tutorial with Kristina I learned that listening, being patient, and being able to ask good questions are more important than "having all the answers" about a particular subject. I knew nothing about what she was writing about—an autobiographical essay on her life for grad school—but by asking broad questions on her experiences, I think I was able to help her brainstorm about where to go next with her paper. As far as patience goes, I learned that sometimes you need to be comfortable with silence while the student thinks about what she would like to say next. It was tempting for me to jump in at

one point, but I needed to let her think before she responded to a question I had asked.

—Sara

We think that there are so many good questions to ask a writer that you'll never come up empty. It's always a good idea to ask the writer, "Now that you've read the paper, what do you want to do with it to revise?" That gives you a breather while the writer gets warmed up talking about revision.

We also believe in the power of silence. It's surprising to notice how little time some professors give students to reply to questions in class before they give out the "right" answer. But sometimes it takes a minute to process a good question and think of a good answer, so give the writer a minute and don't consider all silences awkward.

It's not unusual to feel daunted about starting on your own. But keep in mind that if you had to be thrown into a tutoring situation today and if you didn't have all your skills in place, you'd still do the writer a lot of good, even if all you did was listen to the paper and ask how the writer planned to revise.

You'll know as you try these practice tutorials that they're not like the real thing, exactly, because the person you tutor will be anxious to make the tutorial work. But even though there is an air of artificiality, the act of formulating good questions and the satisfaction the writer feels at the end are genuine. Enjoy this process. Your fun is just beginning.

7

REFLECTING ON THE
FIRST SESSION

Sometimes our first tutoring sessions come before we really feel ready for them. Sara, a trainee, was in the writing center observing a session. Just as the session was ending, Craig, a first-year student, showed up and just wanted someone to spend five minutes with him as he got ready to write his first lab report. All the experienced tutors were busy, but Sara had just finished observing a session. Craig just wanted to talk to anyone about this assignment, and in fact, he said that if no one was available, he'd just go to his dorm and ask for help, because lots of sophomores lived there.

It was still fairly early in Sara's training, but she felt all right about just answering five minutes' worth of questions. Craig needed to know about finding and citing on-line sources, and Sara was able to answer his questions well. He said he'd be coming in a lot with his papers, and Sara ended her first session feeling confident.

ANXIETIES

Sometimes trainees feel hesitant to dive in, and if they have a choice, some will put off their first solo sessions. Stewart discusses this anxious feeling in a reflective paper.

> When I first started in English 192 [the Marquette training course], I ea-gerly awaited the delivery of the "formula." I became convinced that there was indeed a formula when I read a letter from an English 192

student from last year, and it advised me not to worry about learning the formula because there is none. (What a way to throw me off!) I expected that sometime around the sixth week of the term, the instructor would come and say, "Okay, now that we've rooted out all the losers, here is the super-secret formula for successfully tutoring anybody in any situation." I imagined that this formula would come in the form of a five-page handout and that these few sheets of paper would hold an algorithm with which I could successfully conduct any tutoring situation from freshman English to doctoral dissertations and that it would require almost no thinking. The semester wore on, and we did read lots of different books and dozens of articles about tutoring, but none came close to unlocking the mysteries of tutoring or the greater mysteries of writing. No formula! (Not even from Jeff Brooks!)

If you've done some practice tutorials and if you've observed some sessions, you probably wonder if you'll ask the right questions or if you're ready or good enough. You're ready and you're good enough if you respect the writer and are willing to let the writer do the work. If you let the writer read the paper to you, and if you start the session by asking the writer, "All right, now that you've read it to me, what do you want to do next?" then you've got the session off to a good start.

Donald Murray, in an article called "The Listening Eye," talks about asking his students the following questions and then just sitting back, putting his feet on his desk, and waiting for answers.

- What did you learn from this piece of writing?
- What do you intend to do in the next draft?
- What surprised you in the draft?
- Where is the piece of writing taking you?
- What do you like best in the piece of writing?
- What questions do you have of me?

If you think it will give you confidence, feel free to write these questions down and keep them with you, but we believe that you'll know some good questions to ask on your own.

FIRST SOLO FLIGHTS

First tutoring experiences range from wonderful to scary. Here are two accounts of first-time tutoring experiences.

My first session was with an 001 student who was working on the fourth paper assignment, which focused upon the presentation of a persuasive argument. I felt that we established a good rapport right from the beginning. In fact, we caught the same elevator up to the fourth floor of Monitor Hall, and had talked about the fact that this was her first visit to the writing center, that she was a first-year student and volleyball player and so forth; we did not discover that we would be working together until I consulted the appointment book. The fact that we had already engaged in some initial conversation and felt comfortable with each other made the situation ideal for a tutoring session (especially for my first one: I was nervous anyway, and it was nice to be able to work with someone that I knew—however briefly—in some other context).

The student had chosen a topic for her paper (the possible health benefits of marijuana for patients with terminal illnesses), had done a great deal of research, and had done a lot of writing. The problem was that although she had written out her three main arguments, and constructed passages anticipating and refuting possible counterarguments, she didn't know how to organize the paper. Accordingly, she did not have a cohesive rough draft, but instead several pieces of paper detailing her various points, all of which were well-written but not in any way connected to each other.

At first I was a little baffled as to how to proceed. I started out by having her tell me what she thought her thesis statement and her three main points were, and writing them all down. Then I had her read me the different portions of her paper so I could get a better idea of how she had planned to argue her points.

While I was listening to the student read, an enormous sense of responsibility for her and her paper hit me. What if I gave her bad advice? What if my advice resulted in her getting a bad grade? What made me an authority on any of this? Upon reflection, I think the reason for these anxieties lay in the fact that I myself have often had difficulties with organization. When the student told me at the beginning of the session that she had a clear idea of what she wanted to say but was having a hard time finding a logical way of organizing her points, since they all seemed interrelated, I saw myself in her confusion. Initially, then, instead of making me more confident to tutor someone having this problem, the fact that I had experienced a similar difficulty in writing made me think that, because I myself hadn't found a solution, I couldn't begin to advise others on how to do it.

Time ran out on my agonizing, however, when she finished reading the paper and looked expectantly at me. Forced to say something, anything, I looked back down at my notes and asked the first question that came to mind, about whether some information that she had included under one point might really work better to support another. That first question, and her ready, engaged response, was all it took, and soon we both were able to discuss ways in which she could make her three points distinct from each other, but simultaneously in support of one thesis. We also talked about smooth transitions between her arguments, and tried to think of ways in which one of the arguments could be seen as providing a different angle on another, which would allow her to move from one focus to the other with ease.

When the session ended, the student told me, "This was fun," and said that what had helped more than anything was just being able to talk about her ideas, and thereby see the connections between them, as well as possible ways of organizing them. I, too, left the session feeling I had gained something: a positive first tutoring experience, and insight into my own processes as a writer. By seeing another person's struggles with organization, and helping her to work through them, I was able to recognize the same problem in myself and (hopefully) bolster my own confidence for dealing with the problem—a gain which would be tested by my next essay assignment.

—Caroline Goyette

Caroline could relate well to the writer she worked with, and her session went very well. Sometimes it can be reassuring to the writers if we tell them that we struggle with the same things they do—anything from procrastination to dangling modifiers—and that, like them, we are working on our own writing. You'll know from the context of the session whether this is the right thing to do or not.

Not all first sessions go as well or give such good insights, and we have to go easy on ourselves if our first session isn't all we hope it will be. This reflective essay tells the story of Stephanie's first independent session:

Last night was one of those impending deadline panic nights. Tonight is another. It's one of those weeks when there is a test on Tuesday and a paper due every other day of the week (and that's not including this one) . . . In some ways, nights like tonight comfort me in my struggle to understand the tutoring process. After all, I *am* those students I will be tutoring. I'm panicked, full of coffee, and searching for clarity. I'm trying to take notice of and discover my "felt sense."[1] In other ways, nights like these instill a sense of anxiety about tutoring because I am truly the students' peer. How can I help another when I have trouble with my own papers—when I can't decide if a semicolon goes here or there?

I think these feelings of confidence and anxiety manifested themselves in my first tutoring session. When I was asked to tutor the stu-

---

[1]Stephanie's "felt sense" is a reference to Sondra Perl's essay, "Understanding Composing," from *College Composition and Communication* 31 (December 1980): 363–69.

dent, I accepted with little concern. My reasoning was that I've helped all my friends with papers at some point and I usually succeed in my own essay endeavors, so why should I worry about my first tutoring session?

I was knowledgeable about the writing center philosophy of letting the students help themselves. I knew that my job was to listen and address the text in terms of the assignment and higher-order concerns. Then I would slowly work my way down to things like grammar. I was not to mark on the paper, only question and lead the student to discover and interpret his or her own mistakes and shortcomings. I had observed only an hour of tutoring previously and it appeared simple enough. The question is, simple enough for what?

I soon discovered that it was simple enough to understand, but not simple enough to practice immediately. As the student I was tutoring began to read aloud, it occurred to me that not being able to read the essay myself was going to make concentrating difficult. I couldn't pick out many points to question her about. The paper was definitely not a disaster, but it did need some work. I missed some content in my determination to catch grammatical errors and found myself mentally scurrying for generic questions to ask in hopes that they would lead to more specific questions.

The assignment was the "changing your mind" paper.[2] I asked what she liked about the paper and what she wanted specific help with. She told me that she liked the topic of the paper (how a friend's tragic car accident helped her find God) and wanted help with grammar and "making it clearer." The clearer part I could handle. We discussed the "before the change" aspect of the paper. She had written well about "during the change" and "after the change," but really hadn't established herself before the incident. I think that she found this discussion helpful. Then we moved on to grammar.

We moved our chairs closer together and began to go through the paper page by page. She asked me a lot of questions like "Does this go here?" and "Can I put this comma outside the quotation marks?" This segment of the tutoring session really made me sweat. I noticed a few things that didn't look quite right, but I couldn't figure out if they were awkward or incorrect. I pointed them out to her and said I wasn't sure if it was incorrect and that she should check her handbook. She then asked a tricky question about whether she should put her own thoughts in

---

[2]All first-year students were working on this topic, based on Chapter 7 of *The Allyn and Bacon Guide to Writing,* 2nd ed., by John D. Ramage and John C. Bean. Here was the way this assignment was described by one instructor: "Write a brief autobiographical narrative shaped by contrary experiences or opposing tensions in which you tell the readers about a time when you changed your mind about something significant."

quotes. I found some spots where quotation marks weren't necessary. She looked relieved and our time was up.

I went back to the main office, filled out the summary of our session and picked up a grammar handbook to double-check any advice I had given her. Everything looked okay except one of my quotation comments. It looked like she should have put quotes around one of the thought statements—where I thought quotes were unnecessary. I began to become really anxious. What did I tell her? Did I say something that was going to get her paper marked down?

I worried the whole walk home. Finally, when I reached my apartment, I couldn't stand it any longer and called information to get her telephone number. She was home and I told her that I had looked in the handbook and maybe she should take another glance at the one sentence. She thanked me for taking time to call and then we hung up. As I put the receiver down, I was overwhelmed with a feeling of incompetence.

For the past couple of weeks, I've been observing more tutoring sessions. I feel like I need it to gain more confidence. I know that my grammar in essays is often correct, but it has been a real struggle for me. I've learned that I can apply certain grammatical concepts correctly simply because I use them over and over. They fit my style of writing. What surprises me about tutoring is the number of grammatical conventions students use that I don't understand simply because I *don't* use them. There is a lot of variety at my disposal that I never really noticed until I started observing/tutoring at the writing center.

All of this information has started to move my own writing process. Nights like tonight and last night have been more challenging. I revised one of my papers as if I were in a tutoring session. Surprisingly, it was easy to look at my own work objectively. I found sections to question and rework. Tonight when I revised my philosophy paper, I discovered a sentence with a grammar mistake. I started to rearrange it into two correct sentences, when I realized that I was doing what I always did. I was reworking it into my grammar comfort zone. I decided that just this one time, I would expand my horizons. I got out my freshman grammar handbook and looked my sentence up. I'm proud to say that, earlier tonight, I used my first semicolon.

—Stephanie Wankum

Don't be afraid to take a handbook off the shelf and say, "Let's look this up." We have copies of the first-year students' required handbook in every tutoring office to help them get the idea that they can use the handbook on their own and that they will find good things there. We also feel free to admit to writers that we don't know exactly what's wrong with a given sentence but that we know it needs revision. Until you know more about grammar (and nothing will teach you about grammar the way tutoring does), it's good enough.

You might try this with other tutor trainees: In the tutor training course at Marquette, the trainees teach grammar to one another. We make up a list of common errors. Some of these errors are pretty simple, and we can feel comfortable just reading the rules for them. But some are confusing, and it would help us help students if we knew more about how to punctuate conjunctive adverbs, when to use commas with restrictive and nonrestrictive elements, when to use *which* and when to use *that*, when to put commas between coordinate adjectives. These terms take most of us way outside our grammar comfort zones, but if you teach one another, somehow, good learning takes place. We come to class with a stack of grammar handbooks, and groups of trainees look up these concepts in all of them. They decide on a topic and design a handout. Then, over several class days, they teach one another. Last year, for the rest of the semester, trainees joked about knowing what a conjunctive adverb was (*however* or *nevertheless*, among others), but they were glad when they had to explain how to punctuate one. And the work with handbooks makes the trainees familiar and comfortable with them.

SELF-ASSESSMENT

After your first session is over, you can do some self-assessment. Sometimes you'll feel like Stephanie, full of doubts about parts of the session, and sometimes you'll feel like Caroline, happy to have helped. (And clearly, Stephanie helped, too, since the part of the session where they dealt with higher-order concerns went well; that would often be as far as the session got.)

After your first session is over, try to be as respectful to yourself as you have been to the writers you've worked with. You realize that sometimes when they are making mistakes, it means they are trying out new things, and they just simply have to have enough opportunities to try them out before they'll get them right. Sometimes when writers discover the beauty of the semicolon, for example, they overuse it and get it wrong. They'll get it right eventually, if they have the right kind of feedback.

So you need the right kind of feedback, too. You need feedback from the writer, so don't hesitate to ask for it. "Did this session help you?" (And believe it: You'll know when *not* to ask that question.) Chances are the writer will grin and tell you, yes. Then you need to do your own self-assessment. Ask yourself these questions.

TUTORING SELF-ASSESSMENT QUESTIONS

1. What type of tutoring went on in the session? (Brainstorming, work on a first draft, final draft, or what?)
2. Was the writer able to articulate the kinds of help he or she needed before the session began? or during the session?
3. Did you and the writer establish a good rapport?
4. What is the proportion of tutor talk? What kind of talking did you do?
    - Interpretive paraphrase?
    - Directive questions?
    - Open-ended questions?
    - Advisory directives?
    - Content-clarifying questions?
    - Opposition-based questions?
    - Other? (What?)
5. Was the writer asking good questions of the text, too?
6. Did you ever find yourself interrupting the writer, or did you listen and then wait a second before joining in?
7. Did you encourage and/or praise the writer's work?
8. Did you allow digressions when appropriate? Were you able to get the discussion back on track? Did you finish the session on time?
9. Was the writer critical of the instructor or the assignment? Grades? What kind of tone did you and the writer set for this discussion?
10. Did the writer try to get you to do the writing? How did you get around that?
11. Did the writer seem to be able to step outside the paper and analyze it (the structure, for example, or the audience or the purpose)? Did you model that kind of analysis?
12. Afterwards, did you help the writer to see what had gone on in the session? Did you ask what his or her plans were for moving the project forward?
13. What do you think the writer got out of the session?
14. What was most positive for you in the session?
15. What would you do differently if you had more time?[3]

Write some notes in your tutoring log (see the example in Chapter 5). Seek out someone to discuss the session with. Talking it over will help you think productively about it.

---

[3]This list of questions was modified from a list developed by Peter Carino, "Posing Questions for Collaborative Evaluation of Audio Taped Tutorials," *The Writing Lab Newsletter* 14 (Sept. 1989): 11–13. Modifications were made with Jon Olson for "Tutor Training," *The Writing Center Resource Manual,* ed. Bobbie Bayliss Silk (NWCA Press, 1998).

Remember the sessions you observed, and remember that everyone, even the most seasoned veteran tutor, has awkward or poor sessions, encounters a writer who may have been made to come and doesn't want help, or wonders where to begin a session after listening to a seriously flawed paper. Recently, one of our veteran tutors was at his wits' end because a writer seemed indifferent, was shoving peanuts into her mouth while reading, and didn't really want to change her draft. Those sessions happen to everyone once in a while. And if your first session has even one or two areas where you feel you helped the writer well, it will have been worth his or her while to be tutored.

It may help to read Andy's account of having been tutored. Andy was one of our trainees who, as part of his training, was required to be tutored on a reflective paper.

Last Sunday, I was walking across campus, trying to think of a central idea around which to focus my reflection paper for this class, when I had a burst of inspiration. It was a windy day, and I saw the way the shadows of the tree branches danced on the ground as the wind blew through the leaves. I thought about how, in the Biblical story of creation, God separated light and dark on the first day. I thought of God's separation of light and dark as the simplest distinction between light and dark and a beginning. Interactions between light and dark have become infinitely more complex since the original separation. People have learned to control light and shadow and have used this knowledge to produce great works of art.

I saw the increasing complexity of interactions between light and dark as a great metaphor for learning how to be a writing center tutor. I thought that I could describe how our class began with the idea of nondirective tutoring as our light, separated from the darkness of directive tutoring, and that the idea would just snowball from there. I thought, "Great! Now that I have this killer metaphor, I can write this paper in an hour or two. Everything will just fall into place around this metaphor." This was a great relief to me because I had a busy week and knew I would not have much time to devote to writing this paper before getting tutored on it. I thought when I got tutored on the paper, I would impress the tutor with my incredible metaphor (maybe even make her reconsider the way she thought about tutoring), and she would help me with a few passages that were not clear. I would fix those sections in an hour or two on Thursday, in time to go out Thursday night.

I started writing my paper Tuesday night at midnight, and my tutoring session was the next morning. I worked until two and was really frustrated. The paper was not writing itself the way I thought that it would. I realized that I had a lot of thinking to do about what I actually thought about tutoring. I wasn't too worried, though. I still had my great metaphor that was going to make this paper work and wow my tutor. I could fill in more details about tutoring by Friday.

I went to the session the next morning and was pretty confident. Val was tutoring me, and I had observed her before. I told her before I read the paper that I had written it quickly late the night before, so it needed quite a bit of work. Then I began to read my paper. As I read it, my stomach began to get a bit queasy. I noticed that I described increasingly complex interactions of light and dark in my first paragraph. In the next paragraph, I described my reactions to learning about nondirective tutoring during the first week of class. I referred back to my metaphor vaguely in the last sentence of the paragraph. I then vaguely described the first tutoring session I had observed and, again, referred back to my metaphor in the last sentence of the paragraph. I thought, "God this paper sucks!" I knew I was going to admit there were a lot of problems in my paper, so I redefined my goals for the session. My goal became to save my metaphor. I finally finished reading the paper, not even really hearing what I read in the last couple of paragraphs.

Val asked me the standard question after I read my paper: "Now that you've read your paper what did you think of it?" I stumbled verbally around words for awhile before slowly stating, "I thought that my examples were really unclear. I have to put more concrete facts in my paper about what really happened in those sessions." Val had me reread the passages in which I described my reactions to things the class had discussed and tutoring sessions I had observed. She asked me about things that happened. I knew that she was drawing good material out of me for my paper, and I appreciated her doing this for me, but I was stunned to find that I was being tutored.

After we discussed passages, Val asked me what I was trying to accomplish by using my metaphor. I described to her what I explained in the first paragraphs of this paper. She asked me if I ever had said that in the paper. I reluctantly answered, "No."

I became more shocked the more things we talked about in my paper, and the more I realized I was being tutored in an actual nondirective session. I realized I was not prepared for the questions Val asked. I thought I asked myself these questions as I wrote, and that was enough. Despite what we learned in class, I thought tutoring was for less-developed writers who did not know how to ask themselves these questions while they were revising their own papers.

Finally, after I had described my metaphor and tried to tie it more closely to the details of the process of learning to become a tutor, Val asked me again why I was using this metaphor. I explained to her the great inspiration I had been blessed with the previous Sunday. Then she asked the question I was afraid to hear all session. "Do you think you're letting your metaphor control your writing?" I knew the answer. I knew it was. I had to admit that I had to get rid of my metaphor, or it would ruin my paper. I could not admit to her that I was going to give up my metaphor, so I quickly answered yes to her question and changed the subject. We talked a bit about things not related to my paper, and I left more than a little bit dazed by what I had just experienced.

Before the session, I was still quite skeptical about nondirective tutoring of writing. I had observed three sessions with freshman writers. The common factor I observed across sessions was that both the tutor and writer looked somewhat tired and frustrated by the end of the sessions. I questioned whether there was a more efficient, less-taxing way of helping people become good writers. I also did not know whether the students would improve their papers, because they did not leave with fixed papers. They left with "things to work on." I understood that there were things I realized about my writing during the session that I could not articulate and did not have to for the session to be successful.

Before Wednesday, I believed I knew enough about my own writing so that I would never need a real tutoring session. I expected to just go through the motions of being a tutee in a tutoring session. Experiencing a successful tutoring session as a tutee made me realize the true value of tutoring, and it was the most valuable experience I have had in learning to become a tutor. It was not easy for me to be tutored through a successful session. It was humbling and thought-provoking, but it was extremely helpful. When I finished my session, I felt like I had the look of fatigue on my face that I had seen on the faces of students when they were finished. I think now that the look was not a look of frustration because the session went poorly, but a look of realization that they had some further thinking to do about their writing, and that they may not get out until an hour later than they thought they would on Thursday because they were going to spend that time becoming better writers.

—Andrew Helminiak

HAVE I TALKED TOO MUCH?

We want to end this chapter by sharing some tips for talking and listening that Carol Kaufman, Trissa Luzzi, Libby Miles, and Christine Fox Volpe from the University of Rhode Island gathered from the Internet listserv

WCenter (and generously allow us to reprint here). In your first sessions on your own, one of your main concerns will probably be, "Did I talk too much?" Here are some of the ways you might find out, and, more important, how you might counter the tendency to talk too much.

Techniques for Judging How Much Tutor Talk Is Too Much

- If you are hoarse at the end of a shift, you are talking too much.
- Shoot for no more than 50 percent of the talking, unless the situation really warrants more.
- Tape (audio or video) your own sessions and judge for yourself.
- Observe other tutors and provide descriptive feedback to each other.

Methods for Self-Monitoring Your Talk During a Session

Attitudinal Shifts for Tutors

- Assume the role of the writer's audience, rather than the role of a writing expert.
- Periodically ask yourself whether or not you are talking too much, just to raise your own level of awareness.

Behavioral Techniques for Turning the Session Over to the Writer

- Ask the writer to read the paper aloud (rather than reading it aloud yourself) so that the writer gets comfortable using his or her own voice.
- Give the writer time and space to enact the revision principles you've discussed by leaving the tutoring space for a little while (get a handout, look something up, print something out, or just make up an excuse to leave the student alone a bit).
- If you are modeling in the session, do it once, then ask the writer to try the next one. Follow up by asking the writer to describe what he or she did.
- If the writer seems to want the tutor to do all the work (and talk), ask him or her to walk you through the paper, explaining what has been attempted with each paragraph.
- Ask follow-up questions such as "How else might you say this?" or "What do you think?" or "What did you mean by that?"
- Ask descriptive meta-analysis questions such as "What have you done when you've encountered this problem in the past?" or "What do you think your strengths are as a writer?" or "What kinds of comments do you hear about your writing?" or "What do you know about yourself as a writer?"
- Ask speculative questions such as "What would happen if . . . ?" or "How do you think your teacher might respond to . . . ?"

- Always offer multiple alternatives when modeling revisions or word choice for writers. Afterwards, ask the writer to make a choice and explain why a particular option was picked. See if he or she can add more to the list of possibilities.
- When you ask questions, wait for the answer. Be patient. When you think you've waited long enough, wait that amount of time again. In other words, wait twice as long as you think you need to before stepping back in. You'll probably find that the writer was really thinking during those moments and not just staring into space.
- Make sure the writer gets the last word. At the end of the session, ask the student to summarize what happened. You may need to prompt with such questions as "What writing issues emerged as we worked together?" Next, follow up by asking the writer to describe the strategies you developed together for attacking or sidestepping the problem. Finally, ask what the writer plans to do next to continue the revision. The idea here is for the writer to have the last word.
- Build regular reflective moments into your day (between sessions, before tutoring for a shift, after a couple of sessions, on a day off) to stop and ask, "What else might I do to encourage the writer to talk more?"

8

READING IN THE WRITING CENTER

We start this chapter by asking you to consider the following question: What do you do when you read?

Your answer might focus on the perfect environment that you seek out when you read or perhaps on the specific strategies you use to engage with a text. Here's how students in the peer tutoring course at Marquette responded to the question.

From Sheri:

> When I am reading for class, for starters I make sure that I have all of my reading supplies. These include my glasses, a highlighter, pencil, blue pen, notebook paper, dictionary, and a quiet place to read, which has a desk or table (It also has to be cold!). Before I read for class or for research purposes I always look over chapter headings or bold print words and then formulate questions based on these. When I do this it helps me to become more interested in the text I am reading because I am now looking for answers.
>
> Also, if there are study guide questions, I will look them over so that I have a basic idea of what to look for. I will then read the text all the way through, find the answers to my questions, and underline all of the study guide answers in pencil.
>
> When I read for fun it's a whole other story! I always take off my shoes and sit on the floor/ground or in a very comfortable chair. I always prefer to read in natural light and preferably fresh air. I just read and relax and totally immerse myself in the story or article or whatever!

From Sara:

> When I read for class, I always have a pen or pencil in hand to write down observations, underline important info, and so forth. When I was in high school, I had a teacher who wanted us to keep logs of what we read, and when I read something that is especially important, I try to do that. Most of the time I have too much reading to do that very often though. Also, I prefer to read for class in a quiet place, but I'm pretty good at focusing even when there is a lot of noise. I rode the bus to school in junior high and high school for over two hours a day, and I learned to concentrate and do homework in the middle of the craziness of that environment.
>
> I liked the idea about taking a nap before reading boring material. A lot of times I'll be reading something and get so sleepy. If that happens, I usually just let myself nap for awhile, but it might help if I went into the reading fresh.

From Aesha:

> Usually when I read, I need a quiet spot so that I can concentrate. My bedroom does not count, because there is a bed and a chance that I might find myself on it with my book as a pillow. I also need to form a visual image of whatever it is I am reading; otherwise, it won't make sense to me. I've tried writing marginal notes and underlining, but I'm not too consistent with that (something I need to work on). With the really difficult stuff, I have to read out loud. It helps me to concentrate and it keeps my mind from wandering too much. One thing that I have found that I have liked is reading with someone. My boyfriend reads aloud with me on occasion. When we do this, we each have to summarize the portion that we read to the person who is listening. This helps with my listening skills, too.

From Susan:

> I'm what some people call a close-reader. It's reminiscent of the Seinfeld "close-talker"—but not exactly the same. . . . I sit with my pen in my hand and plod along, reading every last word, circling, underlining, and writing little notes to myself. Evelyn Wood I am not. Sometimes I wonder about the time invested in this style of reading. I mean, I've been known to write marginal comments in *newspapers!* So much of what I read, I'll never read again. But, then, something happens like the little surprise exercise that we did in class today, and I'm

darn glad that I have my thoughts all gathered in scribbles at the end of the page!

These responses might seem quite familiar to you; after all, if you have achieved success as a writer, it's quite likely that you're also a successful reader. We hope that you enjoy reading, that you find yourself catching chapters of paperbacks while waiting for the bus or between classes, or that you regularly comb used bookstores in search of treasures. Many writers you'll meet in the writing center, however, won't be either as skilled readers or as fond of engaging with their texts as you. In fact, reading and writing are inextricably linked, intertwined in ways that make it difficult to determine whether a writer's difficulty with a writing task is a problem with his or her reading or writing or both. As a writing center tutor, you'll encounter many clients who are writing from sources, and those sources span the disciplines and genres—from literature and poetry, to essays and editorials, to primary research, to textbooks, to newspaper articles, to advertisements. And in the service of helping students become more skilled writers, you'll need to know some of what they are facing as readers. How can you help them become more strategic readers, developing control and flexibility, just as was your goal for them as writers? How can you work with writers who are reading texts far outside your major? And how can you avoid being positioned as a content expert when writers are reading texts with which you're familiar—in a sense, how can you avoid being positioned as an editor/interpreter rather than as a tutor? These are some of the questions we address in this chapter on reading in the writing center.

DEVELOPING STRATEGIC READERS

In looking at the research on the relationship between reading and writing, Robert Tierney and Timothy Shanahan come to the following conclusion: "What has emerged from this research is a consistent finding: Writing prompts readers to engage in the thoughtful exploration of issues, whether it be in the context of studying science, social studies, or literature" (268).

As the movements to incorporate writing across the curriculum (WAC) or writing in the disciplines (WID) flourish, more and more students come to our writing centers having written in response to something they are reading. At times this writing is simply to make sense of what they are reading; at others, it's to analyze or evaluate, and still at other times it could be to present that reading as a background for the writer's own research. As you surely know from your life as a student, the kind of writing tasks you'll engage with will be varied, and this variation has much to do with the kinds of texts you are reading. Ultimately, as a writing center tutor, you'll be encountering writers who are grappling with texts. At times, you'll be frustrated because the dilemma isn't a problem with the writer's processes for writing or even command of mechanical issues (though some reading problems sometimes manifest themselves this way). Instead, the problem is with a writer's understanding of what he has read. "He just isn't getting it," you think. "How can I help?"

One source of help is to understand some of the processes of reading. When you considered the question "What do you do when you read?" you might have thought of specific strategies you used to engage with your texts. Now consider the question "What do you do when you read something you don't understand?" Do you picture the writer and try to figure out what his or her intention was? Do you make associations with the text? Do you gloss the text, making notes in the margins, asking questions, underlining and highlighting what you believe to be important? You probably have a variety of strategies that you have found essential to your reading. Here's a list of strategies that workshop participants at Bristol Community College's 12th Annual Conference on the Teaching of Writing came up with in response to "What do you do when you read something you don't understand?"

- Reread
- Look up words
- Take notes on content
- Write summaries
- Question oneself
- Take breaks
- Change environment
- Just keep going
- Check understanding word-by-word
- Imagine the writer
- Discuss with another
- Get frustrated
- Break sentences down into manageable parts
- Read out loud
- Give up
- Speed up
- Ignore it

Unlike this rich variety of strategies, poor readers have a limited repertoire and little conscious control of and flexibility with the strategies they do possess. For example, one of the frequent strategies poor readers employ is simply to reread something they don't understand. However, rereading won't be of much help if the vocabulary is unclear or if there's background information that the reader is missing or if the text is structured in a way that's unfamiliar to the reader.

In our chapter on the writing process, we stressed the idea of metacognition or awareness of one's own learning process. When it comes to reading, metacognition is equally, if not more, important. In fact, one concept we introduced—levels of strategic knowledge—comes from research on reading. Scott Paris, Margerie Lipson, and Karen Wixson believe that the goal for readers is to develop three levels of strategic or metacognitive knowledge: (1) declarative knowledge or knowing what strategies are available, (2) procedural knowledge or knowing how to use a strategy, and (3) conditional knowledge or knowing why and when to use a strategy. Successful readers have a strategic repertoire that they consciously control; poor readers often do not.

Reading researcher Ruth Garner views a reader's metacognitive knowledge as having three components: (1) knowledge of self or of one's own abilities, (2) knowledge of the task itself, and (3) knowledge about specific strategies to approach the reading task. Each of these components plays an important role in determining whether readers will have successful encounters with their texts. As a reader, your goal is to develop control and flexibility.

So what does this mean for you as a writing tutor? Well, your goal as a reading tutor is to help develop writers' control of and flexibility with reading processes. There are several ways you can do that.

- Ask the writers you're working with about their reading strategies. In posing this question, you help them first become aware of their thought processes, and then you can comment upon the appropriateness of that strategy or suggest refinements.
- Talk about the reading strategies that *you* find successful. Show the writer a text you've marked up, explaining why you made the comments you did and how your notes, underlining, or highlighting are intended to help you understand and respond to the text.
- Model the reading strategies that work for you. Read a text aloud, vocalizing the thoughts that are occurring to you as you read. In this way, you are making your thinking visible for the writer. Or co-read a passage with the writer, comparing your thoughts, comments, and strategies with his or hers.

In addition to these methods, you can help writers learn how to use three common strategies of successful readers: (1) looking up words they don't understand, (2) identifying the text's main ideas, and (3) asking questions about what will happen next in the reading (Cole and Griffin). For the first strategy, you might show a writer how to use a dictionary (not everyone will know how to do this well). For the second, you can use the writing of summaries as a way of increasing the writer's reading comprehension. Behrens and Rosen break summary writing down into several useful procedures.

- Read the text carefully first.
- Reread the text, dividing it into sections or stages of thought. Then label these sections with a few descriptive words.
- Write one-sentence summaries of each stage of thought.
- Write a one- or two-sentence summary of the entire text (the writer's thesis for the summary).
- Write the summary itself.

Have writers summarize their text by following these procedures, and then you can tutor them on the summary itself. Thus, you'll be helping them with their reading *and* their writing.

For the strategy of asking questions about what will happen to the text, we recommend you demonstrate for writers a procedure known as SQ3R (Vacca and Vacca). This acronym stands for:

Survey: Have the writer preview the text to get a general sense of what it's about, making note of subject headings, indentations, underlining, and boldface or other means of placing emphasis on certain parts of the text. Ask the writer how this text is like or unlike others she's read before and have her make guesses about what she will read based on the title, headings, subject matter, assignment, and the like.

Question: Based on the survey, have the writer ask questions (and write those down) that she feels the text will answer. Help model some of these questions if the writer is stuck.

Read: Have the writer read the text (reading aloud will give you an idea if her difficulties are a matter of vocabulary), searching for answers raised in the previous step.

Recite: In this step, the writer reads aloud or writes down the answers to the preview questions. You might try to answer some of her questions as well and then compare your responses to hers.

Review: Have the writer reread certain portions of the text in order to reach clarity on the answers to the questions raised.

Certainly, these strategies won't necessarily work for everyone. Once again, as a tutor, you need to be flexible about what to use in specific situations. What is important is that you make writers more aware of their reading strengths and weaknesses and that you help them rely on their strengths and overcome their weaknesses.

Overall, your job isn't to explain the meaning of a text to a writer who is confused; instead, you want to help the writer discover that meaning, not just of that particular text but of future readings. When Stephen North said, "Our job is to help students become better writers," he certainly could have added, "and better readers, too."

EXAMPLES OF READING IN THE WRITING CENTER

We want to give you some examples from actual tutoring sessions that show just how complicated it can be to deal with reading in the writing center. The tutor's and writer's familiarity with the reading itself and the writer's understanding of the assignment and the task, among other factors, can greatly affect what happens in writing center sessions. Your overall goal should be to help the student become a better reader and writer, but as the following examples show, at times this goal is easier to accomplish than at others.

Example 1—Co-constructing Confusion

In our first example, the tutor is a graduate student in sociology who has a professed dislike for working with writers on literary analysis. The writer is an undergraduate in first-year composition whose task is to write an essay after reading *Howard's End*. Here's how the session begins:

Tutor: Okay, why don't you tell me a little something about the assignment.

Writer: I'm supposed to read this, *Howard's End*, the first three chapters. And I'm supposed to figure out . . . there's like two parts to this. The first part where there are the letters. That's Chapter 1. Then Chapter 2 and Chapter 3 is like the actual story. And then we're supposed to say how the letters that were written about some of the characters . . . well, the character I did was Charles Wilcox. We're supposed to see how the letters in the first chapter show what kind of person he is and demonstrate what kind of person he is in the second and third chapters.

Tutor: Okay, so it's basically describing Wilcox, right, in the context of the novel?

Writer: Yeah.

Tutor: Okay. So why don't you tell me a little something about what you've written.

Writer: This guy, Charles Wilcox, is basically like a really masculine person. He's really kind of authoritative in a way. He's like his father, similar to his father. I wrote how he's similar to his father. There's stuff inside the story, and I just read that and relate it to the second chapter.

Tutor: Okay. I'm sort of digging back now because I remember seeing this movie. Did you see this movie?

Writer: I haven't seen the movie, and I haven't read the book except those chapters.

Tutor: Yeah, it's a good movie. Okay.

If red flags are waving in your tutor-mind's eye, you're developing strong sensibilities for detecting trouble. The tutor here is unfamiliar with the book (though he's seen the movie) and is thus dependent upon the writer to teach him the book's content (or at least the content of the chapters in question). But the writer's brief recapitulation of what he's written ("There's stuff inside the story, and I just read that and relate it to the second chapter") sounds awfully vague, the first sign that he perhaps didn't understand what he had read well enough to write a character analysis.

   Later in this session, the tutor is reading the writer's paper aloud (indicated by all capital letters in the transcript) but comes to a passage that he finds confusing:

Tutor: HELEN SAYS THAT THIS MORNING IS "NOT LIFE BUT A PLAY." SHE WAS AMUSED TO WATCH THE WILCOXES THAT TUESDAY MORNING. THE WILCOXES SEEMED COMICAL BECAUSE ALL OF THEM ARE ILL. MRS. WILCOX WAS WATERING THE GARDENS . . . Okay, I don't really get that.

Student: Yeah.

Tutor: Why is that comical and amusing?

Student: The ones on the hill are the ones that are working out. Like, Evie was working out on like a tree or something, and both the Wilcoxes have been playing croquet or something, and Helen was amused.

Tutor: Oh, I see. Okay, so you need to put that in to show what's amusing, right? And Mrs. Wilcox is not ill, and she's watering the garden. Is she aware of the others or is she just more self-absorbed?

Student: It seems like she's more self-absorbed. She's just paying attention to herself and the flowers and just watching them at 7 a.m. in the morning.

Tutor: So what you're going to want to do is to interpret this to show why they would seem comical. This sounds strange when you say, "They seem comical because they're ill." You don't normally say that about someone who's ill but if they are, you know, they're not seriously ill right but they're just like constantly sneezing.

Student: Right, I should say they're sickly?

Tutor: If you say they're sick, it's the same thing but . . .

Student: I can't seem to get it in my head how to reword it. Can you think of a word?

Tutor: The thing to try to do is to try to look at this family, the Wilcoxes, from Helen's point of view, right? Because Helen is probably seeing things about them that they don't even see themselves, right? . . . To try to get into her head in a sense. And that's what literary analysis often is. It's getting into the mind of the character. And in this case it's getting into the mind of Helen and seeing why she'd be interested in this family and these characters.

Student: So I should write "the Wilcoxes seem comical to Helen because they're all so active, uh, and they're all sick." That seems, I don't know . . .

Tutor: [Sighs loudly] Does that make sense? [long pause] Maybe just do this then, all right? "She was amused to watch the Wilcoxes that Tuesday morning. The Wilcoxes seemed somehow comical to her." Just take this out. [loud crossing out sounds] This is not helping this at all. [more sounds of crossing out]

Student: Okay.

In this excerpt, the focus is on one word, *ill*, but it's indicative of the tutor struggling to understand the writer's presentation of these characters. The tutor offers a possible way of approaching the task, couching his advice in disciplinary terms ("And that's what literary analysis often is. It's getting into the mind of the character"). However, the writer continues to focus on the rewording of a small part, ultimately leading the tutor to a frustrated crossing out of the writer's work. It's hard to imagine that either participant emerged from this session feeling that his or her goals were met.

Example 2—Crossing the Line

In some sessions, you will know well the reading that the writer is trying to understand, or you'll have a strong interpretation of that text's meaning. In these instances, the temptation is strong to simply dole out your understanding or interpretation to the writer, who will eagerly accept your words of wisdom. If you feel this temptation, ask yourself if it is in the service of developing the writer. Sure, you might have had teachers in the past who stood up in front of the room and announced the correct meaning of a story or essay, but did you learn anything in those instances (anything positive, that is)? And is the meaning of texts so fixed and stable that we can simply dump it from our heads into the writer's?

In the following example, we believe the tutor, a graduate student in applied linguistics, crossed the line. The undergraduate writer here has the task of responding to a short quote from Henry David Thoreau's *Walden*. The tutor is first reading aloud from the writer's text (indicated by all capital letters) and then reads part of the Thoreau quote before she begins asking the writer questions:

Tutor: THOREAU EXPLAINS THE SIMILARITIES THAT HE SEES BETWEEN ANTS AND HUMANS. And then he writes "WATCHED A COUPLE THAT WERE FAST LOCKED IN EACH OTHER'S EMBRACES IN A LITTLE SUNNY VALLEY AMID THE CHIPS." What does this mean?

Writer: Like, you know, on a tree, the little leaves that are at the bottom.

Tutor: Okay.

Writer: They were underneath it.

Tutor: Okay, why does he say it like that? Why doesn't he say "on that frightful day with the pouring rain"?

Writer: Because he wants you to see that everything was hunky dory, everything was just perfect.

Tutor: Or, at least he wants to make it seem, maybe not perfect but . . .

Writer: There's no conflict.

Tutor: Okay, or, what else? That's the way things go. You fight. Survival of the fittest, right? That's life. The sun is shining. Those ants are amid the chips. Why are you shaking your head?

Writer: I don't know how you come up with these things.

Tutor: Does it make sense though?

Writer: Yeah, it doesn't matter whether people are still . . . , you know, is that what you're trying to say?

Tutor: Well, I want you to see it.

Notice that the tutor is primarily trying to lead the writer to *her* interpretation by asking questions (evidence perhaps that questions aren't necessarily a nondirective form of tutoring). The writer is certainly aware of this, asking, "Is that what you're trying to say?" after she somewhat unsuccessfully puts the tutor's words into her own. Here's one more passage from later in the session, an even more directive attempt by the tutor to have the writer guess the interpretation that the tutor sees:

Tutor: So now you have "NOW AT NOON THEY PREPARED TO FIGHT TILL THE SUN WENT DOWN OR LIFE WENT OUT." What does that mean? You're an expert now, so you have to tell me.

Writer: That I'd talk about how they're going to fight until the end of the day or till one person there is a victor or they're going to fight until the fight is over.

Tutor: Okay, excellent. Now you've gotten that far, now we're going to push it even further. Why noon? Why not 1 or 3 or 5 or 7 o'clock? Why did he pick noon?

Writer: I don't know.

Tutor: When you look at a clock, noon's up here. What does noon also represent?

Writer: 12?

Tutor: Good answer. What else does 12 represent? Or let me be more specific, what does 12 o'clock represent?

Writer: p.m.

Tutor: Or?

Writer: The night.

Tutor: What else?

Writer: When is the sun going to set in a few hours.

Tutor: Okay, actually at 12 p.m. what is it going to do?

Writer: The sun is going to go down in a few hours.

Tutor: Okay, it seems like the sun has been setting at 3 in the afternoon, but we'll just say, okay, we're going to go around the clock, around the clock 11:59, what is it now?

Writer: One minute to 12.

Tutor: Okay, now it's 12. Is it . . . ?

Writer: It's the day.

Tutor: Right so what 12 o'clock is that?

Writer: What do you mean?

Tutor: It's not p.m. it's . . .

Writer: a.m.

Tutor: Right, so the sun is going to rise. Twelve is kind of that point where the day changes, right?

Writer: Okay.

Tutor: Does that make sense?

Writer: That makes sense, but I can't see how it relates.

This extended lesson in clock reading once again has the tutor leading the student toward the tutor's interpretation of the passage. In its fits and starts, its reinforcing phrases by the tutor ("Okay," "Good answer"), it's difficult to characterize what seems to be going on here as learning. Rather than engaging the writer in a discussion of her interpretation of the passage and an analysis of the strategies she's using to make that interpretation, the tutor instead pulls the student ever closer to guessing what's in the tutor's head. It would seem far more efficient (though certainly not a positive model of tutoring) for the tutor to tell the writer her interpretation up front and cut out all of the guessing! In many ways this technique is an example of the power of expectation, as we presented in Chapter 4. Perhaps the tutor expects the writer to have the same interpretation as she does—and that the tutor's interpretation of the passage's meaning is the right one! We urge you to be careful if you find yourself practicing similar techniques and ask yourself if you are serving the best interests of the writer.

Example 3—Co-constructing Meaning

Our third example focuses on the writer's reading of poetry. However, in this instance the tutor and the writer were much more closely aligned than in the previous examples. Both are familiar with the task of literary analysis, the tutor as a graduate English student and the writer as an undergraduate English major. They have also met several times before, and the writer comes to this session primarily to talk about how to begin his analysis before he's done any writing. Here's how this session starts:

Writer: I have to write a five-page paper on sonnet 144.

Tutor: Okay, now tell me what they want you to do. Do they give you any direction or none at all?

Writer: He gives no direction at all. He said "four to five pages."

Tutor: So he said, what, just analyze the sonnet?

Writer: Yeah.

Tutor: Okay. And can you talk about anything?

Writer: Yeah.

Tutor: Okay, so that's really open-ended. Okay, so where do we start?

Writer: It's kind of scary. I mean I can pick any sonnet. I chose 144.

Tutor: Okay, I guess, good and that was going to be my next question. Why did you choose it? And start from that. What strikes you about it, either in terms of content or style? Ideally you'll talk about both. See it's such an open-ended assignment, I'm wondering if you want to talk about, like, a thematic thing and talk about content or if you want to do some sort of stylistic analysis.

In this opening, the tutor first clarifies the assignment and then immediately shares her knowledge of the task of poetry analysis. Notice that her language isn't delivered as commands; instead, she uses phrases such as "I'm wondering if you want to" and "I think you should," indicating that the writer must ultimately make these decisions.

This session proceeds as a co-reading of this particular sonnet and a co-construction of its interpretation. Quite often, the tutor is simply reading lines from the sonnet and thinking aloud as she models her reading and analysis processes:

Tutor: "And whether that my angel be turned fiend suspect I may, yet not directly tell." I'd have to mull on that line for a bit.

Writer: Yeah.

Tutor: " . . . suspect I may yet not directly tell." I think I get it. "But being both from me, both to each friend, I guess one angel in another's hell." I'd mull on that line, too.

Writer: Yeah.

Tutor: What does that mean "I guess one angel in another's hell"? "Yet this shall I ne'er know now, but live in doubt, to my bad angel fire my good one out."

Writer: To me it sounds like . . .

Tutor: Why don't we just put down, [she writes] talk about what intrigued you about it.

Writer: And it's kind of like the crux of his struggle with the sonnet. I mean in his sonnets because this is the one where . . .

Tutor: Good, talk about that, relate it to the other sonnets.

Writer: He is more drawn to the male lover throughout the whole series of the sonnets, but there's that side of him that gets the woman, too, and here the woman takes his male lover away, so he loses both, and now he has nothing. I think that it's just kind of the high and the low.

In this exchange, the tutor moves from a close reading that makes her thinking visible, to supporting the student's analysis ("Good, talk about that, relate it to the other sonnets") from the perspective of an insider to the discipline. These kinds of interactions are not merely an expert *telling* a novice the correct interpretation of this sonnet. Instead, the tutor models the ways of thinking about poetry, asks questions of the student, and gives commentary about those questions to reveal the foundation upon which analysis—and close reading—is built.

These three examples come from the kinds of tasks writers in English classes might face (though not all of the tutors had expertise as writers of these sorts of tasks). In the writing center you'll work with writers who are reading many more sorts of texts, some of which you might be familiar with and many with which you won't. If you are familiar with the specific discipline, as in our third example, you'll have opportunity to model and discuss the ways your discipline organizes and presents knowledge (for example, the presentation of primary research in the sciences). But if you and the writer do not share disciplines, no matter. As tutor, your goal is for the writer to teach *you* the content of the reading material. And you can help the writer do that by sharing what you know about successful reading and by helping writers become strategic readers—in control of specific reading strategies and flexible about when and how to use those strategies. There's a good chance that your sessions might not even address the writer's paper itself, but that's what subsequent appointments can be for. Your *immediate* concern, in a somewhat ironic sense, is the writer's long-term development. The strategies, habits, and thought processes of successful readers are all a vital part of that development.

9

WORKING WITH ESL WRITERS

We have often found that a large source of anxiety for new tutors surrounds the work they will do with ESL writers. "Will my knowledge of grammatical terms and rules be adequate?" they wonder. "Will my session get bogged down in line-by-line identification and correction of error?" they fear. "Will I emerge from a session spent and bleary eyed, hoping to find someone to talk about big ideas and not the minutia of English mechanics?" they ask. "Will I be pushed into the role of editor instead of being a tutor?" they fear. Certainly, these concerns are understandable; after all, many of you have had little contact up to this point with ESL writers.

In this chapter we want to address your concerns by confronting several misguided ideas about ESL writers. One of the first comes from the label *ESL* or *English as a Second Language*. More likely, many of the nonnative English speaking writers you'll work with have English as a third or fourth language or grew up in bilingual (or trilingual) households. Thus, for the purposes of this chapter we'll use the acronym NNS for nonnative English speakers.

Along with countering some persistent myths, we want to give you practical advice for working with NNS writers and call on the thoughts and words of Marquette's tutor trainees to help you on your path to becoming secure in your abilities as a tutor. Nevertheless, the worries that you might have are those shared by many beginning tutors, and we'll attempt to address those concerns.

MYTH #1—NNS WRITERS HAVE WEAK COMMAND
OF STANDARD WRITTEN ENGLISH

Like many generalizations, this one doesn't hold up well in the face of concrete evidence. As classroom teachers we know that some of our strongest and most gifted writers did not speak or write English as their first language. In the writing center, we see a wide range of preparation and skill among NNS writers. Certainly, some had a great deal of work to do to master certain aspects of English grammar and usage, particularly those aspects that do not exist or are in very different forms in their native languages (for instance, articles and subject-verb-object sentence order for many Japanese and Korean speakers). And many simply haven't had extended exposure to idioms and culturally specific usage.

However, even those NNS students with a weak grasp of mechanics are working to express and share meaning and have meaningful things to say. Your work with them will often be some of the most rewarding sessions you'll conduct, as you guide them to express their ideas in clear and coherent ways. As Sara, a tutor trainee at Marquette, wrote, working with NNS writers is "a great way to meet a person from a different culture with a different take on the world." And Angela added, "I think the great part of working with [NNS] students is that they are so much happier when they get it. There is such a contagious enthusiasm when students who struggle more than average have a breakthrough."

MYTH #2—NNS WRITERS THINK DIFFERENTLY
FROM NATIVE ENGLISH SPEAKERS

One of the more influential pieces of early research on NNS writers was done by Robert Kaplan, and in his research he described culturally based rhetorical patterns, ones he expressed in graphic form (and thus his article is often referred to as "the doodles article"!). For instance, in many Western countries, linear and direct argument is favored. In Asian countries, much of the writing is indirect and is sensitive to the writer's status vis-à-vis his audience, and in some Arabic countries, the rhetorical approach is more circular, approaching the main point only after a certain amount of preliminary negotiation. While these broad generalities, based on examinations of texts written in various cultures, have some truth, they are unfortunately extended to the idea that a pattern in writing necessarily means a pattern in thinking (see Severino "The Doodles in Context" for a critique of Kaplan). However, consider the impression you would make if everything you wrote consisted of the five-paragraph essay: would you want people to think that was the way you actually *thought* about each topic? Formats and rhetorical styles are certainly products of cultures and conventions we often are only barely aware of and value highly without really knowing why. But don't pigeonhole an NNS writer into a particular mode of thinking because of the rhetorical style to which he or she is accustomed. In fact, some of those NNS writers might be eager to break away from those at-times rigid structures. As one Japanese writer told us, "Before I came [to the United States], I tried to make my papers difficult; I tried to get some difficult phrase, you know, some old proverb across. . . . So very philosophical . . . but now I think it's a waste of time."

Nevertheless, we don't want to dismiss the role that cultural practices and expectations will play in your sessions with NNS writers, as we discussed in Chapter 4. Some writers will come from cultures that have gender expectations that you don't share (for example, men who are uncomfortable being tutored by a woman), some will have different notions than you do about personal space (and will sit closer or farther away than is comfortable for you), some will position you as an authority in ways that you don't expect and will be surprised either by your informality or by your preference to keep that tutoring door open or closed. And, as we have seen repeatedly, many NNS writers will have a very different view about plagiarism than is probably the policy at your school; notions of intellectual property and attribution are quite culturally specific. However, given all these differences, you shouldn't assume that NNS writers have cultural expectations that are fixed. NNS writers will often be open to learning about our expectations for matters ranging from personal space to gender roles to plagiarism. They will look to tutors to be what Judith Powers calls "cultural informants." What is most important is to try to open up these issues for discussion. In terms of tutor and writer behavior, talk about what tutor and writer responsibilities should be in a session. For cultural issues that have to do with what's in a writer's text, discuss your expectations for what accurate use of sources should look like and why you believe this to be the case. You will surely encounter sessions where a clash of cultures seems to be interfering with the work of tutoring; however, if you open up these topics for discussion and examination, you will be helping NNS writers a great deal.

MYTH #3—NNS WRITERS COME TO THE WRITING CENTER TO GET THEIR GRAMMAR CHECKED

Several parts of this myth need scrutiny. First, the request from an NNS student for you to "check my grammar" doesn't necessarily mean she wants line-by-line editing or for you to proofread her work. It's often a matter of vocabulary that results in such requests. In our experience, "check my grammar" can mean a whole range of requests, from "give me feedback on structure and organization," to "react as a reader to my argument," to "help me interpret this assignment." Many students, native and nonnative English speakers, simply aren't well versed in the vocabulary of writing tutoring. However, for many, the association between correcting grammar and tutoring writing is pervasive. But as a tutor, you'll have the opportunity to teach NNS writers that language of tutoring, and what once was a grammar check can next time be a request to "tell me if my evidence supports my thesis."

Furthermore, in the previous schooling of many NNS writers, good writing has often meant correct writing, and a focus on grammar is simply transferring what many of their instructors have requested. We know too well the instructor who just sends NNS students to the writing center, telling students, "Have the writing center fix that paper and come back to me so that I can grade your content." So often you won't be dealing only with a writer's request for a grammar check, but also a classroom instructor's. As Aesha, a Marquette tutor trainee, said, "For [NNS] students, grammar *is* a higher-order concern. It is emphasized in class, they are downgraded for improper use, and it is hard to understand and remember all the funny little rules about it. In fact, most native students wouldn't be able to recite all the rules about commas; we just use them."

To counter this myth, we recommend that you start a session by asking about the assignment and the class. If you do so, you will be able to uncover a great deal about who determined the writer's agenda. It's also essential that you be patient, working carefully to clarify the NNS writer's needs. Here's an observation from Paul, a Marquette peer tutor, that demonstrates what we mean:

> I found that the session went very smoothly because both Maria and the tutee were patient. I saw that it was important for the tutor to make sure the student understood what she was explaining. I also saw the importance of the tutee questioning anything confusing. But this is something I feel should be in any session we observe/tutor. Patience and understanding are two key factors to tutoring anyone. Just because someone does not use English as their native tongue should not change that.

Finally, we offer some fine strategies from Niki, another peer tutor: "Ask [NNS] students questions in order for us to better understand them: 'What do you feel like you have the most trouble with?' 'What was a concern that your professor brought up in your last paper?' 'What is difficult for you about writing this paper?' I think if we dig more in that direction, we can understand what an [NNS] student feels like when they are having problems with their work."

MYTH #4—NNS WRITERS JUST NEED MORE OF THE BASICS BEFORE THEY CAN MOVE ON TO MORE SUBSTANTIAL WRITING TASKS

This is a persistent and dangerous myth, one that surrounds not just NNS writers, but any writer whose previous schooling left him or her underprepared for the level now attained, as composition researcher Mike Rose has shown. Many NNS writers have had years and years of the basics, which usually means grammar drill-and-practice worksheets. Whether in their native countries or in NNS classes in the American public school system, approaches to remediating underprepared students are little cure for the "problem." Instead, they offer students sentence work that's removed from any meaningful context. And NNS students often master that sentence work quite readily, easily conjugating those verbs and matching up pronouns and antecedents. However, once they're called on to write—to express themselves in meaningful ways—cultural and cognitive overload can result. Writing is hard, complex work. Filling in blanks in a workbook is often not.

Myth #4 also assumes a writer's development to be based on a building-block approach; that is, first master sentences, then paragraphs, then controlled essays. But think about how you would react if you were restricted to only a sentence to express a complex idea or to persuade someone to agree with a position about which you feel strongly. Or imagine that you only had a paragraph to do that expression or persuasion. NNS writers need opportunities to work with complex forms that fit their complex ideas, not to plug thesis and evidence into five-paragraph templates. In the writing center, you'll have great opportunities to enable NNS writers to transcend their previous schooling and express themselves in sophisticated ways.

MYTH #5—I NEED TO CLEAN UP THE GRAMMAR IN NNS WRITERS' PAPERS BEFORE WE CAN GET TO HIGHER-ORDER CONCERNS

Closely related to Myth #4 and the idea of a building-block approach to writing development, this myth contradicts the advice we gave you on HOCs (higher-order concerns) and LOCs (later-order concerns) in Chapter 3. NNS writers will still be seeking feedback on meaning, structure, and evidence; unlike some native English writers, they will also be seeking feedback and instruction on English grammar and usage. However, we urge you not to give in to the easy inclination to tackle LOCs before HOCs. And we have found that NNS writers, while concerned about grammar and usage, will also be concerned about higher-order matters. They might need to make a second or third appointment to have all of their concerns addressed, but most will be amenable to that suggestion. Even in sessions in which writers report that they need help just with grammar and usage, our approach is first to talk about the assignment, the writers' approach to the assignment, and the gist of what the writers are trying to say in their papers. These conversations in and of themselves will often lead to the writers expressing concern about higher-order matters and dictate a session less focused on later-order concerns.

In the following example, note how the tutor acknowledges the writer's request for a language-level focus in the session (one essentially dictated by the classroom instructor), but still takes the time to ask about higher-order matters, one that he can discuss first with the writer and then focus on when examining her paper:

Tutor: Let's see, you're a sophomore in [liberal arts]. What can I do for you?

Writer: I am writing this paper for [an international relations] class.

Tutor: Okay.

Writer: The teacher's got us all freaked out about it already.

Tutor: That explains it.

Writer: He read over this yesterday for me. The contents is basically all set as far as all that. I just basically need to know if my grammar is . . .

Tutor: The language-level stuff.

Writer: Exactly. I think the organization is fine; I don't think there's a problem with that because he read over it, and he thinks it's okay, and he doesn't want to do it again, I guess.

Tutor: Okay, give me the sort of two-sentence overview of what the paper is about. Give me some context, or at least what the assignment is.

Quite often, even if NNS writers have a language-centered agenda, we ask them to read their whole texts aloud. This approach not only gives NNS writers practice in English pronunciation (and many will ask you how to pronounce certain words), but gives you a chance to assess the text as a whole and address those higher-order concerns that you feel need scrutiny. You'll find yourself saying things like, "Yes, there were some problems I heard with subject-verb agreement, but since we might end up changing those sections anyway, let me first ask you about what you were trying to say in this section of your paper."

However, you will also encounter some writers whose problems with English pronunciation and reading are severe enough to interfere with your session: they'll be struggling, and you won't be able to understand. When you have a student like that, we recommend you feel out the situation by asking him or her to read the assignment sheet aloud or just the opening paragraph. If you feel the work of the session will be better accomplished if *you* read the text aloud, try that technique, and ask the writers to stop you when they want to mark something for revision. You can read over the errors, as they would, and come back to them later so that you can focus on content and support first.

MYTH #6—I NEED TO BE WELL VERSED IN THE TERMINOLOGY OF ENGLISH GRAMMAR AND USAGE IF I'M TO TUTOR NNS WRITERS

Well, this is one myth that has some element of truth. We advise you to spend time with your favorite grammar handbook and become familiar with explanations to common grammatical problems. Most of the NNS writers you encounter will have quite complete grasps of terminology; they'll know their parts of speech and the rules of sentence construction. Endless filling in of those drill-and-practice worksheets imparted many of the rules and terms. In fact, we probably have gained much of our knowledge of English grammar from the inquiries of NNS writers about the difference between *might* and *may* or *that* and *which*. Rather than spout these answers off the tops of our heads and act as living grammar handbooks, we co-consulted those handbooks with NNS writers, reading together those sometimes arcane explanations and examples and applying that knowledge to NNS writers' texts.

Nevertheless, it is worth your while to be able to ask an NNS writer to identify the subject and the verb of a sentence to check if they agree in number or to ask if a word is functioning as a noun or an adjective. Grammar terminology can give you and the NNS writer a common vocabulary and greatly help your tutoring. But we want to reinforce that you don't have to be the source of all grammar knowledge; as we said, many NNS students will have quite advanced knowledge of the rules. As Jamie, a Marquette trainee, said, "Most [NNS] students will not need someone to tell them all the answers. From talking with tutors, and through our staff meetings, I've gathered that by merely asking questions about problematic areas in a paper, a tutor can focus an [NNS] student to analyze the problem area(s), and most times the student will be able to see and correct the error(s)."

MYTH #7—SO MUCH OF THE ENGLISH LANGUAGE IS IDIOMATIC AND THUS CAN NEVER BE TAUGHT

Certainly a great deal of what native speakers take for granted comes from growing up in an English-speaking culture. Our immersion in the English language makes it second nature to use the correct preposition or to know that we can "talk about" but not "discuss about" some topic. And even what might seem like rules in English often have bewildering exceptions. For instance, we know that we use the definite article *the* before concrete nouns, particularly those that are old information or have already appeared in the text ("A boy approached. The boy seemed friendly enough"). However, how come we use the definite article before certain bodies of water and not others (e.g., for "the Caspian Sea," "the Mississippi River," and "the Atlantic Ocean," but not for "Lake Ontario" or "Walden Pond")?

Many NNS writers will not be versed in these idioms or will use vocabulary in ways that defy our native connotations (one student who offered to "eradicate" the blackboard is an example). However, they will also be looking toward you, if you are a native speaker of English, to help them with idioms, to share some of your cultural knowledge. As Sarah, one of our tutors, observed, "If she didn't know that it was a mistake in the first place, then she couldn't identify it on her own." It's important for you to identify those problems in an NNS writer's text that deal with some fairly hard and fast rules of English usage and those that demand native competency. For the latter, you'll often need to let the NNS writer in on those little secrets that we hold dear.

MYTH #8—I'LL NEED TO BE A MUCH MORE DIRECTIVE TUTOR WITH NNS WRITERS

There are few bigger controversies in the writing center literature (and, we suppose, in actual practice) than the question of how directive to be with writers, particularly those least prepared for college writing (Clark). Most of these authors generally call for a more directive approach with NNS writers, arguing, as Susan Blau and John Hall do, that "a more directive approach, as well as an initial focus on sentence-level errors that affect the clarity and meaning of an entire paper, can be effective tutoring practice in a session with [NNS] students" (43).

The contrast to the directive approach is perhaps best characterized by the minimalist approach championed by Jeff Brooks, who argues that "When you 'improve' a student's paper, you haven't been a tutor at all; you've been an editor" (2). So what's a new tutor to do in the face of this directive/nondirective contrast, particularly when you're sitting with an NNS writer whose paper is filled with errors in grammar and usage?

Well, we do hope that you won't succumb to Brooks's fear and clean the writer's text, while she passively sits by, nodding politely. However, we suspect that many new tutors are coming to learn that, when focusing on language with NNS writers, the approach of allowing the writer to spot his or her own errors doesn't always work; it's difficult to apply knowledge that one doesn't necessarily have in the first place. Whether the following strategy we offer is directive or nondirective, we're not entirely sure; we prefer to believe, as Irene Clark does, that these terms represent two ends of a continuum, that neither is absolute and that as an effective tutor you'll need to respond to a writer's preparation and needs, the context of the assignment, and your sense of sound tutoring practice in order to best help the writer improve.

When you think of the processes of error correction, you can imagine that it consists of at least three stages: (1) spotting the error, (2) identifying the appropriate fix, and (3) applying that fix (Flower et al.). Many writers, NNS and native speakers, will be quite skilled in #2 and #3, but for a variety of reasons won't be so strong in spotting their own errors (this is the reason that it's easier to proofread someone else's paper than your own). For instance, you'll probably work with writers who tell you that they always have problems with comma splices and who can engage you in an extensive discussion of how they can use a semicolon to separate those independent clauses or pop in a coordinating conjunction after the comma or break those clauses into two sentences with a full stop between them. However, when you look at their papers, you'll find a whole host of comma splices! In these cases, you can perform what composition researchers call a "governing" function, but what we like to refer to as "the power of the index finger." You will find that all it takes for NNS writers to supply a correction is for you to point with your index finger at the problem. Often, you won't even need to say anything like "comma splice" or "subject-verb agreement." Your isolation of a problem will often be enough for the writer to focus on the error and then call up his or her knowledge of how to fix that error.

Generally, for approaching the language-level concerns of NNS writers (after you've dealt with higher-order concerns), we urge you to keep in mind the advice we gave in Chapter 3 when we talked about error analysis. Often, NNS writers will have patterns of errors, as well as fairly complete logic behind the error. It is your task to identify those patterns and prioritize. Don't overwhelm the writer by focusing on many different errors at once; instead, rely on single passes through a paper or a paragraph with a fairly specific focus. For instance, if you see that the writer has a problem with subject-verb agreement, focus on a single paragraph first and ask the writer why he or she conjugated the verbs in a specific way. Then, you can point out some of the instances when the subjects and verb didn't agree and explain why. You'll often find that the writer will make the correction himself or herself. Next, have the writer apply this knowledge to his or her text, examining the next paragraph and noting subject-verb agreement errors and making corrections where needed.

Research in error analysis has shown that NNS writers can more easily identify problems with verbs, rather than something for which there are many idiomatic exceptions, such as articles (Chappell and Rodby). In the case of articles, it's also important that you ask the writer for the logic behind his or her choices. By asking about this reasoning, you'll often find that the writer has misapplied a rule or created a rule where one doesn't necessarily exist. However, with so many exceptions to the rules, when it comes to articles, the ear plays a large role, and correct use of articles seems to come only with time.

Obviously, this is slow (and some feel tedious) work, but what you are doing is teaching the writer, not correcting texts or claiming ownership. You can then perform this same strategy with one or two more errors, if time permits. If not, sign the writer up for another session with you in which you can work on additional aspects of his or her language (signing the writer up with another tutor isn't particularly efficient since you've established a relationship and have broken important ground). Sara, a Marquette tutor trainee, reinforces our point based on her observation of NNS sessions: "I think that it would benefit [NNS] students a lot if they would find a tutor that they were comfortable with and see that person on a regular basis throughout the semester. Part of the frustration I felt when I observed was that it seemed like we had only just begun when the hour was over."

We want to end this chapter by offering some reminders of how to work with NNS writers. Keep in mind the following.

- Higher-order concerns still come first.
- Error analysis is essential and can be a slow process. It's important that you be patient.
- Ask the writer about the logic behind an error in order to understand fully why the mistake occurred.
- Most NNS writers can figure out their own verb tenses and agreement, particularly if you begin by pointing to the specific problem.
- If NNS writers need direct or indirect articles or American idioms, you can give them those. This is not dishonest—they simply have nowhere else to get this information.
- Remember to point out those occasions when they get their grammar and usage right; NNS writers can learn from those models.
- If they use good sentence structure or are effective with such things as subordination and coordination, tell them so.
- You might not finish in the allotted time, so urge the NNS writer to make multiple appointments.
- Try to get the writer to keep working with the same tutor.
- Urge NNS writers to do as much reading as they can and to make American friends.
- For additional strategies for working with NNS writers, see Blau, Hall, Davis, and Gravitz; Cogie, Strain, and Lorinskas; Harris and Silva; Leki; Ritter; Severino "Serving ESL Students."

10

WRITING CENTER RESEARCH

Another in our long list of the contrasts in tutoring writing is that of tutor versus researcher. A persistent belief is that research is done by a certain group of people and that tutoring is done by another group, and never the twain shall meet. We instead believe that everyone involved in writing center work is a researcher—from directors, to tutors, to writers. The most important purpose of this research is to better understand what we do so that we can then improve it. However, we also generate knowledge as researchers; we analyze patterns in our own sessions, then discuss that analysis with other tutors—noting similarities and differences—and work toward what's generally true and what's specific to our tutoring. These are the ways that we create knowledge that the writing center field as a whole values (and you can then share this knowledge in the form of conference presentations or articles). Thus, we believe that tutors *are* researchers.

Writing center research can mean many things that fit the complex array of questions that can be asked about our work. Some of these questions might include the following.

- What's the history of my writing center?
- What's the history of my practice as a tutor?
- What models or theories explain how students learn in writing center settings?
- Is my tutoring effective?
- How does the writing center affect student writers?
- How does on-line tutoring compare with face-to-face tutoring?

In this chapter, we will give you an overview of writing center research and then focus on one particular research method—using the tools of discourse analysis to study the language that you and writers will use. After all, in tutoring sessions, you can experience powerful acts of teaching and learning (and one of the wonderful things about tutoring is that either participant, tutor or writer, can be doing the learning and the teaching). This learning comes about through language, through talk about such things as words, ideas, and assignments. This fact makes studying the language of a tutorial one of the best ways to acquire an understanding of what happens and why. By applying the techniques of discourse analysis, you will be well equipped to analyze and learn from your tutoring: you'll be doing research!

RESEARCH 101: STARTING WITH QUESTIONS

One essential tenet of any type of research is that the driving force should be the questions you ask. In other words, it isn't a matter of choosing statistical methods or case studies or interviews and then compiling data. Instead, you need to start with questions, whether those questions are about your practice, about the writing center itself, or about larger issues of theory or politics. From whatever you ask, you then choose the research methods most likely to generate answers. For example, if your question was "Do student writers benefit from coming to the writing center?" you'd have to do several things. First, you'd need to define *benefit* or decide what that benefit might look like. Some possibilities might include students' higher paper grades, improved attitudes about themselves as writers, and changes in how students view themselves in relationship to the college or university (in other words, do they develop a sense of belonging as a result of their writing center experiences?). Next, you'd have to figure out a way of measuring these benefits, whether through surveys of writing center clients, examination of grades or other data, or interviews with student writers. Each of these methods has both value and limits, and, ideally, you would try to answer your initial question in as many ways as you could in order to provide lots of evidence for your conclusions. In whatever way you attempt to answer your initial question, you'll quickly discover that research of this sort is a complicated task, but one with intriguing outcomes (for examples of research on writing center effectiveness, see Bell; Lerner, "Counting"; Lerner, "Choosing"; Newmann; Waldo).

Writing center research is an exciting topic with a growing body of literature (see our appendix of Recommended Readings), but most important, in our view, is that all writing center workers—including directors and tutors, whether undergraduate, graduate, or professional—see themselves as engaging in an ongoing process of research. In this view, writing center research is akin to the teacher-research movement, whose advocates propose that teachers (or tutors) are best suited to study, understand, and change their work (Cochran-Smith and Lytle). In the remainder of this chapter, we describe how the methods of discourse analysis can provide one way of engaging in writing center research.

RESEARCH ON TUTORIAL INTERACTION

At Marquette, a regular part of the training is to have tutors tape-record one of their sessions (first gaining the writer's permission, of course) and then analyze what they see occurring. This analysis can be challenging, however. How can you make sense of what you hear? How do you know if something worked or not? How can you best understand the way you and the writer communicated?

Writing center researchers have devoted a considerable amount of time trying to answer these questions and to characterize just what tutorial interaction or discourse is like (e.g., Davis et al.; MacDonald; Walker and Elias). Is it a conversation akin to what peers would have with each other? Is it more like the interaction between students and classroom teachers? Some combination or unique hybrid? Addressing these questions is important for many reasons. For instance, if we want to characterize a session as effective, we need to figure out what effectiveness looks like. Certainly, a session that primarily featured a tutor doing all of the talking wouldn't be effective in most people's views, but most sessions are much more complex than that (in fact, Walker and Elias found that who dominates the talk was not a factor in how effective tutor and writer perceived their sessions to be). Examining the features of the interaction lets us make some headway toward understanding—and thus improving on—what we do.

Once we start looking at the interaction, we need to use some techniques to help sort things out. For example, imagine that you're reading a transcribed tape of your session and want to find out how controlling you were. You could do several things. You could count up the number of words both you and the writer spoke and see who said more (assuming that dominating the interaction is a measure of control). Or you could try to characterize the function of what you said to the writer—did you ask questions? Make statements? Issue orders? Or you could examine how you followed up each time the writer said something—did you cut the writer off before he could complete his statement or question? Did you offer the writer a paraphrase of what he said or asked in order to verify your understanding?

These particular ways of examining the transcript are just a few of many methods. Most important, what you look for depends on the questions you pose. In other words, in the examples above, we were mainly trying to determine what control looks like. You might also ask, "Were the questions I asked open-ended, and how did the writer answer them?" "How did I approach the teaching of grammar?" "How did I make my goals and responsibilities known to the writer and my expectations for his responsibilities in the session?" Over all, when analyzing your sessions, you need to come to the analysis with fairly specific goals. Perhaps these goals will come from your training class or perhaps from your own personal analysis of what you want your tutoring to be like.

To give you an idea of one tutor's analysis of a session, we turn to the following excerpt that involved Paige, a graduate student in theology. The writer in this session was analyzing an article on agricultural methods of developing nations.

Writer: This sounds weird. . . . It doesn't seem right, where here "is this a need for" and down here "is this a necessity" because it changes from the eighteenth century, which is like this, to the twentieth century, which is this. I mean, is that too close together?

Paige: You mean close together because you don't talk about the nineteenth century or close together because you use that phrase?

Writer: No, because it's talking about . . . yeah, because it's like this is saying, "it's needed," and this is saying, "it's not needed," and it's just such a quick . . . I mean does it make any difference?

Paige: Well, if you want because you're . . .

Writer: I mean I could make a separate sentence about it but . . .

Paige: You have made a separate sentence. If what you're trying to do is contrast these two, you could contrast it with "however" or "on the other hand" or something like that that would show this is different.

Writer: Do you think that's really needed or am I being really particular?

Paige: It couldn't hurt just to go ahead and emphasize the difference between the two eras.

Writer: Okay let's see . . . so should I add in the sentence or just restructure this part of it?

Paige: You can do either; it's up to you.

Writer: Okay.

Note that the writer is focusing on a particular phrase, essentially seeking Paige's correction; Paige, however, deflects making the correction outright, but instead investigates why the writer feels the correction is needed. When Paige does offer a possible change, strengthening a contrast with a transition word, she still leaves the final choice up to the writer with: "You can do either; it's up to you."

In an interview, Paige listened to this sequence and then commented upon what she was hearing: "Typical pastoral counseling techniques coming out." Expanding on this technique, Paige described it as "laissez-faire tutoring" and added:

> The student is saying, "Tell me what to do." You can picture them coming in here and pulling a knife and demanding to know what to do. "What do you think would happen if you put your knife away?" It is nuts. Sometimes they get totally frustrated because they want the answer, and you tell them they can find the answer. There are many different answers and many options and not necessarily a "best" option, so you need to find the option that's going to fit what you want to do.

Thus, this brief sequence reveals Paige's underlying philosophy of tutoring—to reveal potential options for the writer but to have the writer decide what will ultimately work best. And for Paige, this philosophy emerges from her experience in pastoral counseling.

Will all brief sequences from your sessions be as indicative of your approach and experience? Probably not, but analyzing your sessions will begin to make clear what you're doing and how you might change some of your tutoring techniques.

THE SPEAKING MODEL OF DISCOURSE ANALYSIS

For our first more-structured method of analyzing your tutorials, we need to introduce some terminology from sociolinguistics. Dell Hymes has described several concepts that are helpful in thinking about tutor/writer interaction, particularly in uncovering the underlying social rules that govern our behavior. The first of those is a "Speech Situation" or "situations associated with (or marked by the absence of) speech" (56). Hymes gives the examples of ceremonies, meals, or fights. Speech situations do not have broad rules that govern them, but are a broad boundary under which we can examine the next term—"speech events." In Hymes's words, a speech event refers to "activities, or aspects of activities, that are directly governed by rules or norms for the use of speech" (56).

So how do these terms apply to tutoring? Well, you can consider the whole range of tutor (or teacher) interaction as speech situations and within that broad class, many types of speech events: classroom lectures, class discussions, student-teacher conferences, and, of course, writing center sessions. Each of these has rules that participants follow; sometimes those rules are explicit but usually not (think about those times when someone violated the social rules and how people reacted: someone talking during a lecture, one person dominating a group discussion, a writer showing a bad attitude during your tutoring session). Hymes's interest is in uncovering these social rules that we largely adhere to unconsciously. By exposing these rules, we can begin to see the logic behind our behavior and particularly why miscommunication can occur. Did that writer really have a bad attitude, or did he simply have an entirely different sense of the social rules of tutoring than you did?

To perform this analysis, Hymes introduces the acronym SPEAKING. We'll briefly define each of these terms and then give an example.

> **S—Setting and Scene:** For tutoring sessions, the setting is, of course, where the session is held, but as you think about this aspect of the analysis, think about particulars of your locale. Are you and the writer sitting across from each other or next to each other? Are you at a rectangular table, on a couch, or around a circular table? Do you have harsh fluorescent lighting or incandescent lamps? Each of these components plays a role in creating an atmosphere and sending strong messages about the rules to be played in the session itself.

> **P—Participants:** Most often this will be you and the writer (and perhaps an observer), but certainly, the classroom teacher can also be a visible participant.

> **E—End:** Sociolinguist Peter Farb says that "when people speak, they do so in the expectation that a certain outcome—an exchange of information, the obtaining of something, an expression of their status, and so on—will result" (38). For tutoring writing, both you and the writer come to a session with certain goals or ends, both long and short term. Try to identify these ends as well as you can when analyzing your sessions.

> **A—Act Sequence:** This term refers to the actual dialogue that you will be analyzing. As we'll show in the example, start with something short and seemingly routine, such as the opening of a session. It is in the ordinariness that you can often find the greatest unstated expectations and agendas.

> **K—Key:** This term refers to what is often the mood of the interaction. Some examples of key are ironic or serious or playful. Often nonverbal clues can give you an indication of an interaction's key, such as whether the participants laugh or smile or how closely they are sitting.

I—Instrumentalities: While we'll assume that your sessions are conducted in English, the specific vernacular will probably vary depending on the relationship you feel with the writer—formal, informal, or specific vernaculars such as Black English. Thus, instrumentalities re-fers to the "forms of speech" (Hymes, 63) that are used.

N—Norms: This term refers to the rules that apply in a given speech event. We usually don't shout questions during a lecture; we expect to get our turn during a conversation; when we ask a question, we expect the other participant to offer an answer. Sequences within tutoring sessions will often have separate norms, for example openings of sessions, where it's usually the tutor who starts things off with a question, and closings of sessions, where the writer is often expected to give some indication of the usefulness of what occurred.

G—Genre: Hymes refers to genre as "categories such as poem, myth, tale, proverb, riddle, curse, prayer, oration, lecture, commercial, form letter, editorial, etc." (65). Certainly, different sequences within tutoring sessions will resemble different genres, for example, a lecture or counseling session or a conversation between peers.

Now that we've outlined the SPEAKING model, we want to show you how it can be applied to a sequence from an actual session. We'll use an excerpt that comes from the very beginning of a session and walk you through the analysis. Much of the inside knowledge of our analysis comes from interviews with the tutor and writer involved, but you should be able to perform an analysis without that additional insight.

Setting

The writing center where this session occurred is housed in an Academic Resource Center that's part of a large, private urban university in the Northeast. The room where tutoring occurs is small, windowless with a rectangular table and a couple of orange-covered, straight-backed chairs. Tutors and writers usually sit side-by-side, choose to leave the door open or closed, and face a bulletin board with the writing center rules posted (e.g., "We do not proofread!"), as well as articles for tutors to read on various aspects of tutoring.

Participants

The tutor in this excerpt is Paige, the graduate student in theology we introduced you to earlier. The writer is Leslie, a senior international relations major. Leslie has never been to the writing center before and is coming this time at the urging of her classroom teacher. Leslie is a bit frustrated by her grades in this class and figures that visiting the writing center might send the message to her instructor that she'll do what it takes to improve her grade. Thus, in many ways, Leslie's instructor is also a participant in this exchange (and figures prominently in the act below).

Ends

For Paige, any tutoring session should result in the writer emerging better equipped to go about her writing tasks. In a more immediate sense, she also wants the writer's paper to improve, but the improvement should largely be as a result of what the writer does, not necessarily what Paige might do. In the beginning of a session, Paige wants to get an idea of the writer's goals and begin to formulate a plan for how she might help the writer achieve those goals.

Leslie, as we said, is largely driven in this session by a desire to improve her grade in her international relations course. However, as a major in that field, Leslie also wants to master the material and communicate the discipline's ideas in a way that shows she belongs. After graduation, she plans on joining the Peace Corps and thus has a strong commitment to her major and field.

Act

The following exchange opens the session:

Paige: So what class are we working on today?

Leslie: EE 510.

Paige: Oh, my goodness. I think my roommate was in this class at one point. Who's the teacher?

Leslie: Professor R _____ .

Paige: Mm, hmm.

Leslie: Great.

Paige: [says something unintelligible]

Leslie: Okay, well this is the assignment I'm working on, and I have typed, printed this out and I brought the . . . I don't know how this works, so you should tell me how it works, and then I'll just follow your lead because I've never been here before. Actually Professor R _____ says he sends his students here all the time. So he thinks this is a good thing.

Paige: Okay. As soon as I have a chance to look over this we can look at your paper. In the meantime, could you fill this out for me? [hands her the writing center new-client form]

Leslie: Sure.

Paige: Because you've never been here before. So it's project number 2?

Leslie: Project number 2, and then this, and here's the article that I read, this, for the assignment.

Paige: Okay.

Key

In the opening of this sequence, you can see the informal, peer-to-peer bond that Paige creates by showing some knowledge of the class and instructor ("Oh, my goodness. I think my roommate was in this class at one point. Who's the teacher?"). Also, note how Leslie reveals that she's never been to the writing center before and asks Paige to "tell me how it works"; she wants an explicit understanding of the rules of interaction. Thus, the key here is friendly and cooperative, while at the same time quite focused on the task at hand; they set ground rules and get right down to business.

Instrumentalities

The English here is fairly informal (e.g., "Oh, my goodness") and in many ways resembles a conversation between peers. Note that Leslie asks Paige to take the lead in structuring this session ("I'll just follow your lead"), deferring to her expertise and showing that while the language used might be informal, the participants' roles aren't necessarily equal.

Norms

While Leslie acknowledges that she's never been to the writing center before, she does come to this session with some sense of the rules in that she defers to Paige's expertise to structure the session, as we noted, and Leslie also comes quite prepared with an assignment sheet, the article she was responding to, and her paper itself. Note also that Leslie invokes her classroom teacher's endorsement of the writing center ("Professor R_____ says he sends his students here all the time, so he thinks this is a good thing"), thus endorsing Paige's work herself and affirming Paige's expertise as a tutor. So the norms in this sequence are that Paige will set an agenda and help Leslie as the writing center has done for Professor R_____'s other students and that Leslie will come to this session prepared.

Genre

In the broadest sense, the genre is a tutoring session. In a more narrow sense, the genre is the opening to a tutoring session, one in which tutor and writer establish agendas, create or maintain relationships, and indicate what their specific responsibilities will be.

This analysis covers just a snippet of a tutoring session, but reveals a great deal of the underlying meaning. As you apply the SPEAKING model to your own sessions, you'll gain insight into not only the ways you act to achieve your goals, but also the ways in which writers respond to your actions. By looking deeply at even a small part of your tutoring, you can reveal the essential factors that often mean success or failure.

FEEDBACK SEQUENCES

Our second structured method of analysis addresses one of the challenges of analyzing tutorial discourse: deciding on what constitutes a unit of analysis. You could just look at questions and answers as several researchers have done in examining teacher-student interaction in the classroom (e.g., Mehan). In classrooms, a typical pattern of interaction is for the teacher to ask a question or initiate a sequence ("What's the capital of Mississippi?"), then for students to offer an answer in response, perhaps with some teacher prodding ("Biloxi?" says Johnny), and finally for the teacher to evaluate that response ("No, Johnny, that's not correct"). This sequence is known as the IRE (initiation, response, evaluation) pattern of classroom discourse, one quite dominant in classrooms (Cazden). Also, notice how teacher-centered and controlling this pattern can be, as the teacher plays a guess-what's-in-my-head game with her students.

Several researchers (e.g., MacDonald, Davis et al.) have applied this framework to their examination of writing center sessions, and it is a useful one to consider yourself, particularly if you believe that asking questions isn't necessarily directive. However, the question–and–answer mode is only one of the ways that tutors and writers will interact. For the others, we need some way of setting a boundary and describing a unit, which we can then analyze. By closely examining these units, you can learn a great deal about your approach to tutoring and the writer's reactions to your approach. For this purpose, we'll use a concept we call a *feedback sequence*.

In our study of tutoring, we often see how a writer seeks the tutor's feedback on how best to proceed with the text, whether this advice is on a word, paragraph, or whole-text level. Thus, most tutoring sessions can be seen as chains of requests for feedback. Some are started by writers, some by tutors, and some by the ever-present but invisible classroom teacher. Some focus on small bits of text and others on paragraphs, pages, or whole essays. And still others are more process-oriented and focus on the writer's approach to the paper. Whatever the focus and whoever begins the sequence, either the tutor or writer closes the sequence by giving an evaluation or offering a correction, and then the other participant indicates it's time to move on to the next section of text or writing problem.

In many ways, entire tutoring sessions can be seen as one large feedback sequence, particularly in terms of how writers often start sessions with agenda-setting statements, such as, "I wanted you to give me an idea whether or not my paper makes sense." Certainly, in the ideal case, a tutor doesn't simply say, "Yeah, this paper is fine," and end the session there. Instead, we urge our tutors to turn the evaluation back onto the writer, sometimes saying such things as, "Well, tell me what it is you're trying to say in your paper, and I'll tell you what I understood after you've read it aloud." Nevertheless, because most of the writers you'll encounter come in with a specific paper for which they're seeking specific feedback, you'll find yourself engaged in many rounds of evaluation and, oftentimes, correction as you point out some feature of the writer's text that doesn't work for you or for the writer. To help you identify these units in your own sessions, we next offer several examples of feedback sequences drawn from our research.

As we noted, either writer or tutor starts a feedback sequence, seeking some sort of reply from the other participant, and then the sequence is closed when the person who starts the sequence indicates it's time to move on to another concern. In the following example, the writer begins the sequence, one focused on her requests for evaluation of her whole paper. Once she receives a response from the tutor, she follows up with some commentary, in a sense reaffirming her initial request.

Writer: So like what do you think? I mean, I guess if I changed it around, do you think the paper has hope?

Tutor: Yeah, definitely. I like your format.

Writer: I like people to be hard on me.

Queries about specific chunks of text are common subjects for feedback sequences. In the following example, the writer seeks a paragraph-level evaluation on his application to law school:

Writer: Do you think this is all right, this paragraph, to leave in there?

Tutor: That's up to you.

Writer: Is it too personal? Again it said personal statement and I'm thinking they might want to know a little bit more about me other than my experiences, maybe to give them a little bit of a sense of who I am.

Common feedback sequences are those started by writers seeking the "right" word or a grammar/usage correction. In the following example, the tutor has just suggested a correction that would include the word *thus*. Note that this sequence lasts more than just a single turn, as the writer continues to inquire about wording until he seems satisfied:

Writer: When do you use *thus* normally?

Tutor: When you're concluding. Right? You're giving premises; thus, you have a conclusion.

Writer: But does it start a sentence or does it have to be in the middle of a sentence or it doesn't really matter?

Tutor: It doesn't matter. It's not a word that requires you to have it only in one place.

Writer: Is *thus* like a form of another word?

Tutor: No. It's its own word.

Writer: So it's a word itself. Okay.

In the previous examples, the writers started the sequence, directly seeking some evaluation of their texts. However, as a tutor, you will also begin these sequences, offering unsolicited feedback. This advice can range from suggested words to ideas for reorganizing text to tips on potential topics for a writer's text. At times, the sequence can veer closely to the classroom technique of "guess what's in my head," as in the following example where the writer is working on a paper on "Traumatic Brain Injury" or TBI:

Tutor: When you say something like traumatic brain injury, what do you suppose you need to do for your reader?

Writer: Define TBI?

Tutor: Yup. What is it? Right? So where do you think we could put that?

Writer: I'd put it in the first paragraph?

Tutor: Okay you can talk about what it is, and then you're going to talk about the problems, introduce the problems and what this paper's about. How about the second paragraph?

Writer: Okay. The definition, wait, want me to tell you about the definition in the second paragraph?

Tutor: Yeah, just like the general idea.

In the best of circumstances, your feedback will be more of a shared effort between you and the writer. While you might start a sequence, the writer will use that opportunity to start a sequence of his or her own and take some role in the correction of the text. In the following example, the writer has been reading aloud his text when the tutor stops him:

Tutor: Okay, it's a tiny, tiny thing . . . with *led* you just need a preposition with that, "led . . . "

Writer: "to"?

Tutor: Yes, exactly, "led to opportunistic feelings."

Writer: Do I need "the Middle East and the West" or I don't need the article?

Tutor: Oh, actually, yes, you do, I didn't notice it. Sure, yeah, "the West," exactly.

Finally, at times, it won't necessarily be you or the writer who begins a sequence of feedback; it will be the omnipresent classroom teacher, the ultimate evaluator of the texts in most writing center sessions. In the example below, the writer initiates the sequence, but it is in response to a criticism by the instructor, who is simply referred to with the pronoun *she:*

Writer: Yeah, but I want to cross out some stuff because on my last paper that she gave back, she made a comment on the back that I don't have to summarize what the book is about. I should just stick to analyzing. So I was thinking, should I cross out this first paragraph?

Tutor: Okay, let's see. Okay, does this have anything to do directly with what you want to talk about?

Writer: No, just this part right here has something to do with it.

Tutor: This second half right? So why don't, just for now, why don't we just say that we can cut this out.

Writer: Okay.

Overall, a tutoring session is made up of many feedback sequences that often overlap. The language that tutors and writers use to start, participate in, and close these sequences lends much evidence toward understanding the responsibilities they assume in a tutoring session and the responsibilities they expect the person sitting across the table from them to assume. Do you believe that feedback on a writer's text should be triggered by the tutor's views of what works, the writer's stated agenda, the classroom teacher's stated criteria, or some combination of these influences? Examining feedback sequences in your sessions can reveal not merely your beliefs, but the specifics of your practice.

In an even larger way, the feedback sequence as a unit of analysis also holds promise in our understanding the underlying processes of learning in a writing center session. Some researchers believe that the conversation between writers and tutors is an explicit dialogue that, eventually, will become an internalized dialogue, as writers develop their writing skills (Flynn). If this is true, then your feedback sequences might be the overt structure of this dialogue. In other words, if writers are learning how to think about their writing based upon the conversations we have with them in writing center sessions, then our examination of those conversations can reveal the issues and challenges of learning to write in college and how writers learn to overcome them.

Whatever method you use to analyze the discourse of your sessions, you will be contributing to improving your practice, as well as gaining insight that you can share with your fellow tutors or with the large writing center community. Tutors *are* researchers, and our hope is that this chapter has given you some ways of taking on that identity.

11

WRITING CENTERS: HISTORICAL AND THEORETICAL CONTEXTS

"Where do writing centers come from, and why do we do what we do?" So far our book has dealt with fairly practical matters. Now we want to anticipate those questions you may eventually ask about the way you fit into a rich history of tutoring writing. Neal wrote his dissertation on this topic, and it is near and dear to his heart. Paula lived through some of it and saw major changes in writing centers during her professional involvement. The voices of tutors are not as present in this material, except as echoes along college hallways throughout the country over time, echoes of the same sort of work we do today.

As we write the second edition of this book, writing centers are thriving, exciting places to work at many colleges and universities, many secondary schools, and even some elementary schools. This relative success has come about after a certain amount of struggle, a struggle that is part of higher education's longtime unease with and sometimes outright prejudice against students who come to college underprepared. That is not to say that writing centers have always been created to remediate ineffective writers, but the stigma of remediation has been a powerful influence to shape the identity of contemporary writing centers.

The essential questions of history, theory, and practice (and, ultimately, of politics and authority) powerfully inform what happens in our writing centers, coloring our practice without our knowledge. Our goal in this chapter is to help you gain an understanding of writing center foundations, an understanding we hope will provide an important context for the work you do.

WRITING CENTER HISTORY:
WHERE DO WRITING CENTERS COME FROM?

A persistent belief for many who work in writing centers is that the field is relatively young, most likely arising in the supposed literacy crisis of the 1970s when more and more underprepared students were coming to the nation's campuses. In fact, Paula's writing center at Marquette was founded in the late 1970s with funds from a federal grant to assist the education of underrepresented groups. The writing center where you work might only be a few years old and the result of long-standing efforts to enlighten administrators about the best ways to teach students to write. This belief in the newness of writing centers might also come from the relative newness of composition studies as an academic discipline or the recognition of teaching writing as a process, rather than with a focus solely on written products.

However, writing centers in various forms have been around for quite a long time, perhaps as long as the 125 years or so that composition has been a required course. That history has had its high and low periods, depending on enrollments, preparedness of students, local and national politics, funding, and dominant approaches to teaching writing, but, overall, the history of writing centers is a rich topic, one just beginning to be uncovered (see, for instance, Boquet, "'Our Little Secret'"; Carino, "Early Writing Centers"; Carino, "Open Admissions"; Lerner).

It's likely not a surprise that teaching writing has long been seen as laboratory work or an activity best learned through one-to-one practice, guidance, and feedback. As early as 1895, two influential English faculty members, John Franklin Genung of Amherst College and Fred Newton Scott of the University of Michigan, described the importance of laboratory methods in the teaching of writing. Newton Scott, in fact, argued that teaching composition should be thought of like teaching in any scientific laboratory so that "the instructor can again meet his students as individuals and can again have leisure for deliberate consultation and personal criticism" (180).

The student-teacher conference that we take for granted in our schools today has a long history and is a strong influence in the development of stand-alone writing centers. In 1913, Samuel Chandler Earle of Tufts noted that in the teaching of composition, "the 'heavy guns' should always be individual conferences. In no other way can the work be made personal; in no other way can the pupil be interested to give his [or her] best" (486). At Princeton, Charles Osgood recommended in 1915 a pedagogical technique that sounds distinctly modern: "It is often best to seek a private talk with a student who should be writing, to enable him [or her] to find his subject, and, if practicable, to have another talk while the composition is in process" (234). By 1929, in a survey of 225 institutions, Warner Taylor found that 66 percent required conferencing. This finding led Taylor to conclude that "no aspect of the first-year course is more vital than the fifteen or twenty minutes apart customarily assigned to personal conference with each student twice or more a semester" (26). Occasionally, calls were made to abolish freshman composition courses as a whole and replace them with a system of tutorials (e.g., Campbell). Such reports led E. C. Beck of Nebraska State Teachers College to claim in 1939, "Perhaps it is not too much to say that the conference method has established itself as the most successful method of teaching English composition" (594).

Another instructional trend evident in the early literature and influential in the development of the contemporary writing center was the use of peer feedback. For example, in 1897 Samuel Thurber, a high school teacher in Boston, noted that "the writer must not be cheated of his reward, the plaudits of his mates" (13), and in 1901 Robert Valentine of MIT cited the advantages of efficiency and sharpened critical skills when "the student takes home the theme of another, and writes his criticism upon it in red ink" (459). In 1939, Beck described "the use of student readers, or conference leaders, in the conference plan of teaching" (595). These readers were assigned students with whom they would conference once per week for fifteen minutes, where "using the student's composition as the basis for the conference, the reader helped the student toward more accurate, more fluent, and more interesting composition" (595).

The need for one-to-one teaching and learning for any student was evident to these early scholars; however, a powerful influence on the development of writing centers—and of composition as a required course—was the presence of students underprepared for higher education, particularly as college enrollments rapidly grew, tripling between 1910 and 1930 (Willey). If you've heard of complaints by faculty members in your schools that students don't write well, they might be surprised to know that this situation has a long history. Students in Victorian white blouses around the turn of the century, co-eds in bobbed hair during World War I, young men whose families felt the pinch of the Great Depression, bobbie soxers, beatniks, and hippies all came under that familiar criticism. For example, in 1914 C. S. Duncan of Ohio State wrote, "The complaint is heard year after year that boys and girls are coming to college more and more poorly prepared in [English composition]" (154), and in 1920 Florence Livingston Joy of Oberlin College noted that "I had never met an instructor in Freshman English who was satisfied with the preparation of a very large percentage of the students in his classes" (201). In the early twentieth century, many institutions followed the lead established by Harvard in 1874 when required English was created in response to the problem of poorly prepared upperclassmen (Rose). At many places along with required composition came basic writing or "sub-freshman" composition courses to remediate underprepared students (for accounts from this period, see, for example, Boynton; Reeves and Russell; Woolley). Early writing laboratories and clinics often became aligned with these remedial courses and at times stressed a building-block approach or a focus on the mastery of words, sentences, paragraphs, and of the rules of grammar and usage before allowing students to move on to college-level tasks. In this view, students needing more of the basics were sent to the writing center for remediation where they and their texts were "prescribe[d] treatment, administered by a staff member or tutor" (Russell 296). The result was a marginalization of writing centers, those who staffed or directed them, and the generations of students who visited them. In the words of Mike Rose, "to be remedial is to be substandard, inadequate, and, because of the origins of the term, the inadequacy is met-aphorically connected to disease and mental defect" (349).

Nevertheless, early writing laboratories were not all akin to sick wards of quarantined students (Carino, "Early Writing Centers"). Some, even early on, were closer in philosophy and attitude to our contemporary centers. Consider, for example, the writing laboratory at the University of Minnesota General College, which was created in 1932 "to replace the usual composition course," according to Francis Appel, its director ("English Studies" 280). Appel noted that at the General College, "we have no 'remedial' English because we feel that if there be such a thing, then from the common-sense point of view people from the most illiterate to industrial or university administrators and many authors would need some so-called 'remedial' English" ("A Writing Laboratory" 75–76). While students would receive feedback on papers from their courses, the general purpose of the laboratory, according to Appel, was to offer help "only when the student runs into difficulty writing things which he wishes to write in answer to natural demands" ("A Writing Laboratory" 71).

Students who came to the General College Writing Laboratory did so voluntarily, and, once there, would not find drill-and-practice grammar worksheets. As Appel described,

> At first, feeling that good writing depended largely upon a knowledge of grammar, we assigned a self-instructing, self-testing manual of grammar; but when it became apparent that there was but little demonstrable correlation between a knowledge of grammar and the ability to write, the manual was discarded. ("English Studies" 281)

This is not to say that the General College Writing Laboratory was a utopia. Working conditions for Appel and his one assistant seemed to be a consistent problem. Considering that in 1935 nearly 300 students elected to take the Writing Laboratory (Appel, "A Writing Laboratory" 77), the workload must have been overwhelming at times. As Fred Newton Scott had argued 40 years earlier, the recognition of composition as a laboratory subject should come with the necessary resources to enable such teaching. The history of writing centers, however, is fraught with institutions trying to make do with scant resources, resulting in overworked staff and frustrated students.

Additional reports of writing laboratories and clinics appeared regularly in the composition literature throughout the early twentieth century. Surveys of composition programs nationwide often revealed their presence, including the 1929 survey in which Warren Taylor reported that six institutions had created "English clinics" and commented that "in theory the project is excellent; in practice it may prove of little value through the lack of cooperation accorded by departments other than English" (31). A 1940–41 NCTE survey of 292 institutions on "the organization of composition courses" reported that 34 used a writing "laboratory" and 58 reported an English "clinic" (Grey et al.). By 1950, the writing center seemed to be an established presence at many institutions, taking advantage of the large increase in college enrollments following World War II and the communications movement in composition in which attention to students' "social dimensions and the affective domain" became a feature of many composition programs (Carino, "Early Writing Centers" 107). Seven of the first nine meetings of the Conference on College Composition and Communication (from 1949 to 1958) included workshops on the creation and sustenance of writing centers. However, by the late 1950s and early 1960s, writing centers seemed to pull a disappearing act. The reason for this disappearance has largely to do with the continuing association between remediation and writing centers. By the late 1950s, many institutions abandoned remedial writing courses, taking advantage of the growth of the junior-college system and funneling less-prepared students into those less-expensive options. Thomas Wilcox, in his 1973 book on the landscape of college English teaching in the 1960s, noted that

> a 1960 survey conducted by the NCTE found that 55.6 percent of all four-year colleges and universities provided special instructions for students who were "deficient in their use of English." By 1967 that number had decreased dramatically: only 27 percent, or less than half the previous number, continued to offer remedial English. (67)

As remedial writing classes disappeared, so did writing centers.

Writing centers were reborn in the Open Admissions era of the early 1970s (Boquet, "'Our Little Secret'"; Carino, "Early Writing Centers") when many campuses, particularly urban colleges, opened their doors to any student who wanted the opportunities that higher education promised. Once again, writing centers were called on to remediate the underprepared; however, by this time composition itself was gaining ground as an academic discipline, and writing center work could experience some trickle-down of professional status. This trickle has become a steady flow in many places, as writing center directors are increasingly occupying faculty or administrative positions within institutions that ensure stability for them and future for their writing centers.

In the last 25 years, the writing center field has grown tremendously and can now claim two academic journals, an affiliated publisher, an international professional association, and a network of regional associations. As we write this chapter, the visibility and security of writing centers seem fairly solid. Writing center history, however, teaches us that the formula of *crisis in student preparedness + influx of enrollments = more writing center resources* doesn't always add up. Our system's conflicted attitude toward the promise of college versus the opportunity of college (or the need for remediation versus the obligation to remediate) is far from resolved. In 1996, *The Boston Globe* warned that "an epidemic of remedial learning stretches from the Ivy League to public community colleges" (Dembner 1), and the "disease" of poor writing figured prominently in that "epidemic." The contemporary writing center is greatly shaped by these attitudes, and the result for many writing center directors is a constant struggle for adequate resources and professional standing.

The legacies of this history aren't always apparent to the writing center director busily attending to the myriad daily details of her work or to the tutor focused on the next student writer about to come through that door. Nevertheless, writing center history has a powerful influence on our contemporary situations and provides a guide for future actions. Two areas that have been particularly influenced by our history with remediation and institutional politics are writing center theory and practice, the focus of the rest of this chapter.

WRITING CENTER THEORY AND PRACTICE: WHY DO WE DO WHAT WE DO?

Writing Center Theory

While our subtitle of this section uses the word *theory*, more accurate would be to say "theories," for writing centers draw on a wide range of models in order both to understand their daily work and to guide the application of those practices. In fact, we argue that the theory-practice contrast is yet another false one; theory and practice are impossible to separate in writing centers settings, for one informs the other and is, in turn, shaped by its counterpart. In this way, writing center work can often be best characterized as *praxis,* or what literacy theorist Ira Shor describes as "action relating theory to practice, in a specific context that challenges limiting situations" (3).

Nevertheless, the work in our writing centers does not exist in a vacuum and has had a variety of theoretical influences. These influences have, at times, come from research into specific writing centers, from theories that have dominated composition studies or the understanding of how students learn to write, and from such diverse fields as family-systems therapy (Grimm) and acoustics (Boquet, "Noise"). In a sense the writing center has achieved its original designation as laboratory; however, this time our work has become a laboratory for gaining a better understanding of a wide range of phenomena, from peer collaboration, to composing, to institutional politics, to academic acculturation, to acquisition of English as a second (or third or fourth) language, to instructional technology, to basic literacy.

Writing center theory is most heavily influenced by theories guiding composition studies. Faigley et al. define the theoretical foundations of composing in terms of three "views": (1) "the literary view" and its focus on "a deeply mysterious process" (14) in which writers compose alone to discover "truth"; (2) the "cognitive view" and "its primary assumptions that the goal of composing is to communicate, that writing abilities follow a developmental sequence, that composing is an orderly process from which general principles can be abstracted, and that these general principles can be used to teach writing" (15); and (3) the "social view" and its belief in "the writer as a member of a larger literate community" and that each act of composing is "a socially determined action" (17).

Those who have theorized about writing centers usually align themselves with the "social view" (e.g., Bruffee; Ede; Hawkins). The underlying assumptions of this view are that learning and writing are essentially social acts and that conversation and collaboration are essential elements to promote critical thinking and good writing. Andrea Lunsford offers three models for what writing centers can be: "The Center as Storehouse," as "Garret Centers," and as "Burkean Parlors." The Storehouse metaphor is most closely aligned with Faigley et al.'s "cognitive view" of composing: the writing center "operates as information stations or storehouses, prescribing and handing out skills and strategies to individual learners" (4), a model that assumes that knowledge is to be primarily transmitted or "banked" (Freire) from expert teacher to willing student and that development is the mastering of discrete parts (e.g., the rules of grammar and usage or words and sentences) before approaching essay-sized tasks. As we noted earlier, this view perhaps best describes the historical legacy of writing centers as medical clinics for the disease of poor writing. Early documents in the Marquette writing center show that though work on grammar was by no means the only work that went on, it was the major emphasis for some students who were assigned to the lab; however, a close analysis of the documents shows that this emphasis might not have been grounded in theory but a method adopted by an extremely small staff to handle large numbers of students who came asking for help.

Garret Centers, Lunsford's second classification, "are informed by a deep-seated belief in individual 'genius'"(4), akin to Faigley et al.'s "literary view." These centers "see knowledge as interior, as inside the student, and the writing center's job as helping students get in touch with this knowledge, as a way to find their unique voices, their individual and unique powers" (5). Lunsford, however, rejects this view because it positions collaboration as a side activity rather than a central premise of learning to write. She instead calls for the "need to embrace the idea of writing centers as Burkean Parlors, as centers for collaboration," aligned with Faigley et al.'s "social view" of composing, and fulfilling Hannah Arendt's claim that "for excellence, the presence of others is always required" (Lunsford 8). Lunsford sees this ideal as embracing "the notion of knowledge as always contextually bound, as always socially constructed" (Lunsford 8).

In response to the pure social-constructionist views of Lunsford and others, several theorists have described problems with this position. For example, Eric Hobson, drawing on James Berlin's work in *Rhetoric and Reality*, also presents three categories of writing centers similar to Lunsford's metaphors—a positivist, an expressionistic, and a social-constructionist basis. Hobson, however, points out the shortcomings of each and warns against "the trap of dualist thought" (73). Instead, the writing center community needs to "acknowledge that each of these three epistemologies is actively present in the theory and practice of the writing center, that together they create a system that is more able to adequately describe the writing center than any of the three can in isolation" (74). According to Hobson, what is most important is for writing centers to maintain an "equilibrium."

These questions of knowledge making or epistemology become essential questions of how writing centers actually help student writers (and to ask how we know if and when they do help). From this critical point of view, many givens in our work have come under scrutiny, including the ideas of *peerness* as a sort of equality (Trimbur), nondirective tutoring as nonauthoritative (Shamoon and Burns), and the writing center itself as an alternative to dominant academic literacy practices (Grimm). The overall result can be a bit mind-bending for a new tutor searching for a solid strategy to open her first session, but this reflexivity and rich theoretical debate are indications of the scholarly potential of the field itself.

More recently, writing center scholarship has relied on a wide range of theoretical lenses with which to view our work. In trying to explain this phenomenon, James H. Bell, in a message to the WCenter listserv, offered the following:

Although a quarter century ago there was little theory or research on writing centers, from the mid-80s to the late 90s, the field followed an orthodoxy of student-centered methods to facilitate better writers, until recently [when] people became dissatisfied with what seemed a simplistic view and opened up the field to a flurry of new perspectives on just about any topic to do with writing centers.

Examples of these new perspectives abound. Relatively recent collections of writing center scholarship such as *Intersections: Theory-Practice in the Writing Center* (Mullin and Wallace) and *Writing Center Perspectives* (Stay, Murphy, and Hobson) include chapters on a wide range of theoretical approaches.

One particular framework that has attracted many writing center scholars (see, for example, Wolff) is to think of the center as a "contact zone," following Mary Louise Pratt's idea of "social spaces where cultures meet, clash, and grapple with each other, often in contexts of highly asymmetrical relations of power" (35). Given the commonality of a writing center session between a relatively privileged tutor and a remedialized student writer, Pratt's concept offers a powerful lens. The goal for many in our field is to make our writing centers into what Pratt calls "safe houses" or the "social and intellectual spaces where groups can constitute themselves as horizontal, homogeneous, sovereign communities with high degrees of trust, shared understandings, [and] temporary protection from legacies of oppression" (38). The notion of writing center as "safe house" is comforting for many writers. As Diana George and Nancy Grimm ask, "Where else on campus can a student simply walk in and ask for help? Where else on campus can a student rely on instruction without evaluation? Where else on campus is collaboration more valued or taken more seriously than in the writing center?" (62).

Both Nancy Grimm and Beth Boquet have offered recent book-length applications of theory to critically examine writing center work. Grimm, in her book *Good Intentions: Writing Center Work for Postmodern Times*, writes, "I use theory like I use fertilizer, to grow ideas and to enrich the context for decision making" (xi). Grimm challenges her readers to "theorize their practice" in order to come to a more complete understanding of what they do—both good and bad:

> Once a writing center achieves stability, the greater challenge is to ask if the writing center constructs a space for acknowledging the arbitrariness of academic practices and the possibility that these practices unintentionally oppress some students. Postmodernity has made us aware of the inadequacies of universalizing logic and perspective. Because it undermines belief in good intentions and academic practices based on modernist principles, it confronts us with the need to ask how writing centers maintain the status quo, thereby oppressing the very students most dependent on writing center assistance. (xvii)

In her book *Noise from the Writing Center,* Beth Boquet also draws on postmodern, feminist, and critical theory. However, Boquet also invokes Jimi Hendrix, music, and acoustic theory to work toward a "performative pedagogy" for writing centers. Near the end of her book, Boquet cites a description of a guitar exhibition in which the author describes the guitar as "no longer merely a machine that makes sounds," but, "without playing a note, it is already a bundle of meaning and possibilities" (Pareles qtd. in Boquet 149). She goes on to comment:

> The last several decades of scholarship on writing centers have provided us with rich description of the skills and strategies of writing center practitioners. We have not so self-consciously considered, however, the ways in which the writing center is no longer (was it ever?) merely a machine that makes writers (much less *writing*). How, without sounding a note, the writing center is already a bundle of meaning and possibilities hinted at, if not entirely contained, in the product. (149)

This "bundle of meaning and possibilities" exists on many levels, and the exploration of theories to help us understand and improve on our work in writing centers is just one. As you go about your daily tutoring life, it is sometimes difficult to think about the theories you are enacting, as you respond to a writer, think about a writing assignment, or offer a cup of coffee or a tissue to a crying writer. The reasons for our actions are complex, but trying to uncover and understand these reasons is essential to the kind of informed practice we call for in this book. As we show in the next section, writing center practice is shaped by these various theories and a large number of other competing influences.

Writing Center Practice

Writing center practice has had a variety of historical influences—including theoretical and political ones—and is by no means a simple matter to unravel. However, one long-standing theme among the various theories offered to explain writing center work has been the placement of tutoring in the writing center in contrast to teaching of writing in the classroom, and that contrast has powerfully shaped beliefs about writing center practice. While writing centers were often created to supplement classroom instruction, their existence as stand-alone entities, what Beth Boquet calls the shift from "method to site" ("'Our Little Secret'" 464) brought with it a struggle for identity. The struggle to escape the stigma of remediation further contributed to this identity formation, but what became comforting to many writing center workers was the idea that their work was superior to what was happening in composition classrooms. As the participants in a workshop at the 1950 meeting of the Conference on College Composition and Communication concluded: "The writing laboratory should be what the classroom often is not—natural, realistic, and friendly" ("Organization and Use of a Writing Laboratory" 18). In a 1980 article, Thom Hawkins, whose work provides an important influence on the contemporary writing center, drew a clear distinction between the perceived process-orientation of the writing center and the product-orientation of the classroom:

> A tutor . . . uses informal, congenial dialogue to guide students through the writing process, from pre-writing to revision to editing. Instructors rarely observe this entire process, let alone evaluate it. The nature of the classroom teacher's job is generally such that [she/]he can only examine and judge the product of a student's work, not the process the student uses to achieve that product. (67)

From descriptions such as this one come inklings of the writing center as alternative or a place where the often isolating teaching in the composition classroom is replaced with a collaborative, one-to-one or small group environment. Tutors' responsibility is to become "facilitators" (Reigstad 32), and a hierarchy of mastering discrete skills in order to move on to substantive work is "replaced with quite a different hierarchy, one that [is] broadly cognitive, stressing process and purpose rather than structure and correctness, the larger potentialities of style and form rather than grammar and usage" (Hartwell 68).

The rallying cry for many in the writing center field came from Stephen North in a 1984 *College English* article titled "The Idea of a Writing Center." North's purpose was to refute the long-held perception that "a writing center can only be some sort of skills center, a fix-it shop" (435), and he was able to reduce the writing center mission to a single slogan: "In a writing center the object is to make sure that writers, and not necessarily their texts, are what get changed by instruction. In axiom form it goes like this: Our job is to produce better writers, not better writing" (438).

North aligned writing centers with ideas of teaching writing as a process, what two years earlier Maxine Hairston, borrowing from Thomas Kuhn, had labeled a "paradigm shift" in the pedagogy of college composition. North positioned writing centers as central in the teaching of writing, "student-centered" places where students seek help when they need it, giving tutors the advantages of "timing and motivation" (442), and where tutors assess dynamically a student's needs through talk and feedback, reacting as genuine readers. Finally, North offered an ideal:

> Writing centers [can be] the centers of consciousness about writing on campuses, a kind of physical locus for the ideas and ideals of college or university or high school commitment to writing—a status to which

they might well aspire and which, judging by results on a few campuses already, they can achieve. (446)

The central tenets of North's argument—writing centers as essentially collaborative places where tutors develop students' processes of writing in order to improve a written product—have greatly shaped writing center discussions since 1984. Central to North's idea is the notion of writing centers' challenging established notions of instructional practice in higher education, whether in the composition classroom or other locations. For many writing center scholars, learning to compose in a writing center can also offer a challenge to larger notions of authority in the university (e.g., Joyner; Kail; Kail and Trimbur). As Mary King writes, "Writing conferences which simply reproduce the interpersonal relationships of conventional schooling intensify teacher-centeredness, magnifying the teacher's authority and more powerfully denying the student any access to control" (17).

The field's mistrust of teacher authority and the nonauthoritarian identity of writing centers have led to frequent warnings in the writing center literature against a tutor exerting too much control. For example, Evelyn Ashton-Jones cautions that "tutors often find it too easy to lapse into a 'directive' mode of tutoring: silently reading students' papers, identifying defect, and issuing tutorial 'commands' usually couched in non-threatening, nurturing language, but commands nonetheless" (31). Mistrust of "directive modes" and negatively labeling tutors as "little teachers" are common. For example, John Trimbur questions the effectiveness of undergraduate peer tutors who "are most familiar with . . . a hierarchical structure in which the teacher passes down knowledge to the students and then measures how much the students receive" (22).

Based on this alignment with process-oriented approaches and the rejection of classroom-based and product-oriented approaches, the writing center literature often has prescribed a set of rigid responsibilities for tutors to assume. A dominant rule is that tutors should be "nondirective" or "minimalist" (Brooks). As Peggy Broder writes, "The tutor's role is not to tell the student what to do with his paper but to help him to discover what it is that he himself wishes to do" (38). At the same time, tutors are told that they should be a "nonjudgmental, non-evaluative helper—a collaborator in whom the writer can confide" (Harris 376), who engages in "individualized, student-centered pedagogies" (Ashton-Jones 30). The problem, of course, is that these prescriptions do not take into account the great variability of each writing center session and the need for tutors to maintain a certain amount of control *and* flexibility, as we've argued in this book.

The backlash to fairly rigid ideas of how tutors should work is perhaps best characterized by Linda Shamoon and Deb Burns, who call these prescriptions a writing center bible. Shamoon and Burns write that "these codes and appeals seem less the product of research or examined practice and more like articles of faith to serve to validate a tutoring approach which 'feels right'" (135). This reaction to prescribed notions of tutor identity can be seen as part of a larger discussion of what a tutor's role should be. The literature on writing centers is filled with attempts to define metaphorically the roles of tutors, including "listener, teacher, coach, counselor, fellow writer, editor, and critic" (Leahy 44), psychological counselor (Marx), physician (Morrow), and midwife (Rabuck). However, until recently many of these characterizations have left out the powerful influence that student writers have on a tutoring session. As Dave Healy describes, goals and expectations of students and tutors might come into conflict: "For tutors, role conflict may result when tutees' expectations conflict with their own preferred style or with their assessment of the best role to adopt in a given tutorial session or at a given tutorial moment" (43). Similarly, John Mayher notes that the conflict between tutor and writer goals "gives rise to a certain amount of tension between the writer who has—in the main—come for a short-term cosmetic repair, and the tutor who believes that a more long-term solution is needed" (53–54). Thus, for a new tutor who opens her session by asking the writer, "What would you like to work on today?" followed by the student's "I want you to check my grammar," this tension between process and product goals is all too real.

In the writing center literature, this tension was most visibly revealed when Stephen North—the architect of the idea that for writing centers, "Our job is to produce better writers, not better writing" (North, "The Idea" 438)—revisited his original article ten years later and pointed out the realities of his ideal in terms of student writers' expectations:

> [Students will] be motivated to (say) finish writing; to be finished with writing; to have their writing be finished. They will be motivated to have the writing they submit for a class win them a good grade, whatever they imagine that will take: for it to be mechanically correct, or thoroughly documented, or to follow the instructor's directions to the letter. (10)

As a result, North sees potential conflict in the tutorial, what he describes as a "shock":

> It does come as a shock when, having been led by your training to expect some deep, unalloyed, genuine engagement—some eager wrestler-of-texts—you meet instead a frightened freshman who seems only to want a super proofreader; a sophomore who seems preoccupied

by her fear that the instructor doesn't like her; a senior who seems concerned with doing just enough to pass an S/U course, but not a whit more; or any of the other very complicated, very human creatures who find their way to writing centers. (11)

Further highlighting these tensions in practice have been a variety of factors: how best to tutor nonnative English speakers, questions about whether writing centers should be in the business of promoting standard written English at the expense of writers' native idioms, what the role of explicit grammar teaching is in a writing center that eschews remedial instruction, and whether nondirective tutoring can be effective in all situations. Instructional technology, whether in the form of on-line writing centers or simply computers in the center, has also given rise to a number of practice contradictions, particularly when writers can drop off papers and potentially avoid the process-orientated conversations that are essential to learning.

Overall, the tensions in writing center practices show how intertwined our work is with theoretical positions that have particular currency at a given moment, with institutional and extramural politics, with current technology, and with an adequate supply of resources. As an example of the last, consider whether the length of time allotted to a tutoring session in your writing center—whether 30 minutes or 60 or some other configuration—is a result of what we know about best practices or the result of a limited number of resources stretched as widely as possible. That situation, of course, is the reality for most contemporary writing centers. The added presence of peer tutors (whether undergraduate or graduate students) makes the writing center field unique, as it enacts every day the conflicts, theories, and passions of what learning is all about. What is most important is to understand where our practices come from and to unravel the various influences on those practices. The result of such an understanding is, we hope, a recognition of writing centers as essential academic entities, ones worthy of resources and stability. We are a *laboratory* in the exploratory sense of the word, and it is in that space that we hope your tutoring practices will flourish.

12

INTERDISCIPLINARY
AND ON-LINE TUTORING

The secret is out: Writing isn't just for students in freshman composition or English classes any more! Well, you likely knew this bit of news, particularly if you are not an English major or if you have taken writing-intensive courses in the wide variety of social or natural science classes in which students will be writing essays, lab reports, and scientific articles, among other tasks. The recognition of writing as an essential means of learning—what is known as *writing-to-learn*—is fast taking hold at many institutions, whether informally among a core group of faculty or formally as a course requirement for graduation.

While the basic structure of many colleges can be antithetical to cross-disciplinary cooperation—split into departments, each with its own sources of expertise and knowledge bases, each with funding to protect and space to guard—writing is often the element that can bridge these gaps. After all, every discipline has the need to communicate its content knowledge, and every discipline struggles with the question of how to integrate its majors into the profession itself. How do you get sociology majors to write and think like sociologists? Biology majors to write and think like biologists? And what does it mean to write and think like a sociologist or a biologist? These are the sorts of questions that the writing-across-the-curriculum (WAC) movement has taken up over the last several decades.

In this chapter, we offer some background and advice for any tutor who will encounter writers from disciplines other than hers, as well as for the increasingly large numbers of tutors who are working specifically in WAC programs. While we stress overall the basic principles of tutoring that we have described throughout this book—strong listening and questioning, supportive feedback, colearning with the student writer—we also recognize the unique features of interdisciplinary tutoring. In fact, since the first edition of this book appeared, Neal has taken a position teaching and tutoring in a WAC program at MIT, so we also bring to the topic a certain amount of personal experience and professional identity.

While we were writing this chapter, we also realized that the advice we wanted to offer for disciplinary tutors who are primarily responding to students' papers also applies to tutors in on-line environments. Thus, we'll include some specific thoughts for on-line tutoring, an increasing area of interest for many writing centers.

WRITE-TO-LEARN

The recognition of writing as an essential means of learning any course content has been fundamental to the WAC movement. We have all had the experience of feeling as though we really didn't know something—whether it was a literary interpretation, a historical analysis, or a biological process—until we had to communicate that knowledge in some way. However, this concept is actually much more powerful than it would seem at first glance. Most of what individual disciplines accept as the facts of their fields only come about through an intense process of knowledge presentation, negotiation, and persuasion. In other words, Gregor Mendel could not simply claim that he understood the fundamentals of genetics in the mid–nineteenth century. He had to demonstrate to his peers his approach to the questions of inherited traits and the evidence he had gathered to support the claims he was making. He then had to argue based upon his evidence, thus convincing his peers to accept his reasons. In fact, according to John Swales, this socially mediated process of creating knowledge within a discipline is just as fundamental to the natural sciences as to any field in the humanities. Swales recounts the pneumatic experiments of Robert Boyle, experiments conducted in public at the Royal Society of London in the mid–seventeenth century. This public display was meant to ensure that Boyle's claim would be credible, that his methods were replicable, and that his results had witnesses. These public rhetorical acts established the foundation for the modern scientific research article (Swales 112).

Thus, all disciplines have a body of facts that have only come about through a long period of negotiation. Writing-to-learn scholar Paul Connolly contrasts the presentation of facts in a formal, product-oriented "repertoire" with an informal, process-oriented one that is the heart of knowledge production in any discipline:

Every "community of discourse," not just the community of bio-chemists or astrophysicists but also the community of Marxist historians and of Keynesian economists, has these same two repertoires or linguistic registers, one to bolster the best possible public claim that can be made to having constructed new knowledge; and the other to deconstruct and reconstitute knowledge that is in the process of being re-made. (8–9)

Of course, the oral or written give-and-take is often lost on the sophomore who has to memorize the causes of the Peloponnesian War for Friday's quiz. But for historians (or chemists or economists), that knowledge has only come about through a social process of presentation and persuasion. Furthermore, students in many classes only get to see the finished products of these debates and miss out on all of the informal talk that led up to them. Connolly argues that it is essential for students to benefit from both kinds of knowledge making:

Allowing more oral, colloquial, contingent speech and more informal, tentative writing into the classroom allows students to think for themselves—however imprecisely and haltingly at first—as opposed to only knowing secondhand what others have thought before them. If the latter is all a student gets from a class, in any field, the end is less than a complete education. (9)

So what does this mean for the freshman confronted with a thick textbook of facts for a particular class? Well, at many colleges, students will need to write about those facts in a variety of provocative ways. Perhaps a student will come to the writing center with an assignment to put himself in the position of a general making an argument to launch or to abort the Peloponnesian War. Or perhaps the writer will be faced with the task of rewriting Mendel's original scientific article, but updating the language for a modern audience. Or perhaps the writer will have been asked to write a brief essay to accompany her calculus problem set, in which she details the steps she has taken to solve the problem. These are all examples of write-to-learn exercises, and all take the approach of putting students in a position to see how the facts fundamental to a discipline only come about through communicating them in meaningful ways.

We would like to say that every teacher, regardless of the field, employs such a dynamic approach to learning, but that would be naïve. Write-to-learn activities face tremendous hurdles, primarily financial and time constraints. The faculty member facing a class of two or three hundred students is hard pressed to employ anything other than assigned textbook readings, lectures, and multiple-choice exams that can be graded by a

computer machine (though, of course, there are many informal writing assignments that even this teacher can use—for lots of terrific ideas, see John
Bean's book *Engaging Ideas*). What is most pedagogically sound isn't always most economical, particularly for cash-strapped institutions or
schools where the research tradition far overwhelms any incentive to devote time to teaching. However, one reason we tell you this background on
write-to-learn is so you can become an advocate for these activities. The
fact is that most faculty members we have encountered genuinely care
about student learning and love to engage their students in meaningful
discussion of course content. Writing is a terrific way to accomplish that
goal, and your position in the writing center (or as a writing tutor attached
to a particular class or department) is a terrific venue from which to influence this kind of teaching.

TUTORING WRITING IN A
DISCIPLINE OUTSIDE OF YOUR OWN

For many new tutors, one common fear is to be confronted with a student
writing on some topic that is far outside their area of expertise. In her e-mail
tutoring journal, Stephanie voices many of the concerns that new tutors often have:

> Since I am a writing-intensive English major, if, for instance, the paper
> was very science-y or an engineering paper, what would happen if I got
> so lost in the terminology that I couldn't comprehend whether the paper
> made sense? What if the writer was so used to the complex terminology
> that he/she just flew through it aloud expecting me to understand and I
> got really lost? In any of those circumstances, what would I say to the
> student during that scary expectant silence after he/she was finished
> reading it aloud? What if the writer expected me to know what he/she
> was discussing in the paper? What if the writer needed to discuss the
> scientific theory/practice behind the paper as a way of clarifying
> his/her thinking/writing? How could I help him/her clarify the think-
> ing/writing without understanding what was being said? What if I
> asked a dumb question and the writer became frustrated with the
> whole process of having "to educate" me? What if he/she gave up on
> the writing center all because I couldn't understand the paper?

Now, in the ideal world, we could just tell Stephanie not to worry, that
the writers' expectations aren't that she be a disciplinary expert; however,
we have experienced many instances where this expertise was what the
writer wanted from the tutor, and it is an expertise that's difficult for many

writing centers to provide. From a logistical point of view, writing center directors couldn't hire enough staff to represent each discipline at the college and then ensure that each tutor be available when a student with an electrical engineering paper shows up or another with an architectural history paper appears. And at high levels, many disciplines become increasingly specialized in terms of language and theory, and a "generalist" biology tutor might not have the background knowledge to understand clearly a paper on advanced genetics. Whew! It makes our administrator heads spin!

Overall, though, the assumption underlying the effort to match disciplinary or "specialist" tutors and students writing for particular disciplines accepts the idea that these tutors have something "special" to offer. This idea has had a relatively long debate in the writing center field. Two articles, appearing five years apart in *The Writing Center Journal*, perhaps best characterize the two sides—which are better, "generalist" or "subject expert" tutors? Susan Hubbuch worries that the "expert" or "knowledgeable tutor" will be more likely to take an "authoritative stance" and that students will perceive this stance (similar to the teacher's) as "being told what to do—and welcome that fact" (26). In other words, Hubbuch claims that faced with this "expert," student writers can become quite passive (27). On the other hand, the generalist or "ignorant" tutor has the following advantage: "Because the ignorant tutor has no expertise in the subject matter, the tutor has no choice but to focus on the intrinsic logic of the student's ideas" (27).

Jean Kiedaisch and Sue Dinitz, on the other hand, were originally in favor of the generalist role: "We felt pretty confident that if we trained our tutors to be good facilitators, to use questioning to help students clarify their ideas, and to guide students through the writing process, they could help almost any student working on almost any paper" (63). However, they examined this assumption through research on specific tutoring sessions and concluded that "the 'ignorant' or generalist tutor sometimes has limitations" (64). In fact, the knowledgeable tutors they studied were able to address global concerns in their sessions and did not simply steam roll student writers. Nevertheless, being knowledgeable was no guarantee of a tutor's success. The authors include an example of a tutor who was familiar with disciplinary conventions but conducted the session as little more than a guided proofreading of the student's text with little involvement on the student's part. As a result, Kiedaisch and Dinitz conclude that "looking closely at these sessions suggested that tutors who don't know how to go through the process of writing a paper in a discipline may be limited in what they can accomplish, and that tutors who do know this process may be tempted to appropriate the student's paper" (72).

Quite a conundrum! Too much disciplinary expertise can be harmful, and not enough won't be particularly helpful. Well, rather than have you become semi-ignorant, we propose that experienced tutors can work well with students from any discipline, even if that role sometimes means urging students to seek out disciplinary experts in order to get multiple sources of feedback. Former Marquette tutor Mykl Novak, now a university web development manager and webmaster, reflects back on his experience as a tutor: "The writer should see the writing center tutor as *one* reader of her text." Writing center and WAC program director Anne Ellen Geller describes several advantages of nonexpert tutors:

> Working outside of their discipline is part of what helps tutors be better "writing tutors." And I think another advantage of working outside one's discipline is helping students be more invested students in that discipline. What I mean is that it's a great opportunity to help the student writer take responsibility for knowledge, genre, content, etc., and for the tutor to learn something about relying on/working from the student's knowledge. As we know, students can often say more about what they know (from class, from the assignment, from the prof., etc.) than they might seem as if they can say, or than they might seem as if they know, if the tutor really asks about all of that well.

The idea here is that facing these uncomfortable situations pushes a tutor into the role of colearner with the writer. The tutor will need to ask questions about a wide variety of matters, including the specifics of the task or of the content; the discipline's writing conventions, such as whether a piece of writing must be in third person or the passive voice; and the style manual that discipline expects, such as *The Chicago Manual of Style* (CMS), as used in this book and in many interdisciplinary texts, American Psychological Association (APA), often used in the social sciences, Modern Language Association (MLA), common in the humanities, or Council of Science Editors (CSE), frequently found in the natural sciences. Then, the writer will be put into the position of teaching the tutor these elements (or of having to go out and learn them from disciplinary experts). Thus, generalist tutors have far more to offer any writer than simply a grammar check. Here's how Craig, a student in the Marquette tutor training class, describes his approach:

> If I were tutoring, say, a nursing student, or a biochemist, on a paper, I would not feel the pressure to critique the content, as much as I would just pay closer attention to the organization, flow, and lower-order concerns. My only problem with tutoring English papers, is that I always want to talk about the idea, and how they can make it better, which can be good in its place, but sometimes focusing on the thesis can take time away from looking at organization, etc. I think tutoring outside of your discipline is a good challenge, and like any challenge it is difficult, but it can also be rewarding.

Still, we don't necessarily want to pitch our tent entirely in the camp of the generalist tutor. The questions that Stephanie raises at the start of this section are not easy to answer. We have increasingly seen writing centers being created for particular disciplines or fields, whether for engineering colleges or health-science programs. Tutors in these places have disciplinary expertise or will quickly gain that expertise when they work primarily with particular classes and particular assignments. The models that place tutors within particular disciplines or departments count on a certain amount of tutor expertise, and even the most generalist writing center will often have tutors from a fairly wide range of disciplines in order to match student writers' needs in even some small way. Thus, to the question of which is better, generalist or specialist tutors, we answer, "Yes!" It's likely that you will at some point work with a writer who has brought in a paper that looks like it is written in some secret code. Our hope is that you are a specialist in sound tutoring techniques and will help this student in the best way you can, even if that means giving a call to your friend the math major to lend a hand.

RESPONDING TO STUDENT WRITING: OFF- AND ON-LINE

In some writing programs, one of the responsibilities of tutors is to provide only written feedback to students' drafts, an activity often done via on-line conferencing. The limitations of this practice might, at first, seem quite a contrast to the careful listening, questioning, and suggesting that you would do in a face-to-face writing center session, and perhaps akin to the notion of "writing center as dry cleaner" (where writers drop off their texts and pick them up when clean). However, we like to think that you can successfully employ many sound tutoring strategies even if your primary means of interacting with a writer is through comments on his or her text. We offer advice specific to on-line environments in the next section, but in what follows we want to give you some ideas to keep in mind as you respond in writing to student work in any context. We'll specifically address the multiple purposes for responding and the various forms your response might take:

Why Respond?

It might seem simple enough—you give written feedback to writers so that they can improve those texts. But take a look at that statement for a moment: Where's the attention to the process of writing? How will students learn from your feedback? Responding to student writers is, we believe, quite complicated and extremely important. In a distance-learning situation in which face-to-face contact with a writer might be minimal or nonexistent, response to writing takes on a variety of purposes. You might respond as a way of starting a discussion with the writer about his or her paper content. You might respond as a way of building a relationship with the writer. You might respond to share your reactions as a reader. You might respond in the role of disciplinary expert to provide specific knowledge and feedback about the writer's approach. However, whatever your specific purpose, the bigger picture to keep in mind is that your response should enable the writer to learn, whether that learning will show up in subsequent drafts or future papers. Now, contrast that goal with the comments that we've unfortunately seen hastily written across student writers' papers: "Awk!!" "TAKE THIS PAPER TO THE WRITING CENTER!" "FRAG!" It's actually quite easy to make a list of poor written response, befitting the long tradition of student bashing that seems to come across in response to student writing. Good written response is not easy to do. In what follows we offer several strategies for both summary response (commentary that sums up your feedback to a writer's draft) and in-text comments (the feedback that you place throughout the draft).

Summary Response—Make It Personal
It might seem simple enough, but we always try to start our overall response to a writer by addressing him or her by name. This individual touch has a powerful meaning; it conveys sincerity and acknowledgment of the writer as a person. For those writers you might have little contact with beyond your response, it is an attempt to create a relationship that will make your comments more meaningful than a generic-sounding note. And who of us doesn't pay more attention to what we read when it starts with addressing us by name?

Summary Response—Start with the Positive
No matter how much of a mess a writer's paper might be, we find it important to begin our response with anything he or she did well. If a goal is to have writers learn from your comments, an initial focus on what works allows for a smoother transition to what needs work. Leading with what writers did well, whether it be a strong sense of purpose, a vivid detail, or a focused controlling sentence, allows messages of concern to be more readily accepted and translated into improvement.

Summary and In-Text Response—Stop at Three
You don't have to ask very many writers (and perhaps you were one of them as we were) to find someone who's had the experience of getting back a draft that was bleeding in red ink. Some instructors' imperative to be comprehensive in their responses often can end up overwhelming and intimidating writers. We have found that three is a useful number to keep in

mind: Focus on three areas of concern in the writer's paper or three specific suggestions for revision. More than that won't necessarily be productive.

Summary Response—Think Big to Little

One of our preferred methods of offering summary response is to start with the positive (as we suggested previously) and then, when discussing the areas of concern in a writer's draft, address higher-order concerns first followed by later-order concerns. In other words, we talk about general issues first and then focus on specifics in the text. Sound familiar? Well, this preferred practice in writing center work also holds in response to drafts. Keep in mind that you are responding to both sets of issues here, but that you want to foreground these big concerns of focus, detail, evidence, and structure before you respond to how the sentences were put together.

In-Text Response—Respond as a Reader

It is awfully easy to read student writing with a pen ready to mark, correcting those grammar errors, cutting out those excess words, or offering alternatives. This act of editing (as we discussed in Chapter 3) can be effective in small doses (for instance, one or two paragraphs) as a way of modeling one way to rewrite the student's words, but in large doses it is largely ineffective as a means of teaching (and it largely leaves student writers dispirited and unmotivated). When we work with teachers who complain about the time they spend responding to student writers' drafts, we ask how long they spend on each. Their answers usually suggest that they spend far longer than need be. Often this time consumption is a result of the instructors' excessive editing. If student learning is the goal (and we sure think it is), then excessive editing won't bring much of that about. As an alternative, we suggest you respond to the writer's draft as a reader, and that means primarily asking questions or indicating something that works well or some things that need clarification: "I don't know what you mean here." "I expected you to tell me your focus at this point." "Great detail!" "What do you mean by this?" "What happened next?" "I needed a transition between these two ideas."

Summary and In-Text Response—Use a Tape Recorder

An effective (though potentially time-consuming) method for response is to record your comments as you read the writer's paper aloud. In this way, the writer hears you reacting as a reader (and this reaction will often be questions or comments as you go along: "Hmm, that sentence didn't sound right," or "Wow, that was a compelling anecdote!"). This type of response can often go against the orthodoxy of higher-order concerns before later-order concerns, but we think its effectiveness can be found in the honest reading that you're giving the writer. When the writer plays back the recording (whether taped on a cassette or recorded on a computer file), she will hear you saying her words (we think that's a terrific way for the writer to get some distance from her text) and your reactions to those words and ideas. With this method, we also provide summary comments, following the advice we described previously.

In-Text Response—Utilize Technology

In wired environments where writers might be sending you their papers electronically, technology provides us with a variety of useful tools for response. Many word processing programs include features such as "Track Changes," which will highlight or otherwise identify any changes made to a draft. You could use that feature to provide specific comments within a writer's draft or ask the writer to turn on that feature as she revises, so that you can see the changes she's made for the next version of the paper. You could also embed your comments into the electronic draft with footnotes, endnotes, or pop-up boxes, features readily available in word-processing programs. Finally, you can embed your comments throughout the draft by choosing a different font or color from that of the body text (if the writer will be reading your comments electronically).

Whatever your technological route (and we imagine that many more will be available by the time you're reading this chapter), keep in mind the strategies we've outlined in this section. It is important, of course, not to overwhelm the writer as we noted above, but we feel that if writers get a sense of a reader on the other end of their writing, they'll feel more connected to their texts and invest more time and effort in the revision process.

ON-LINE TUTORING

While much of the advice we offer applies to tutoring in on-line environments, we also want to address some of the specifics of that context. Since our first edition, on-line tutoring has become far more technologically sophisticated. In practice, it has become more common. Each on-line tutoring program has its own stamp: some take place in real time, some through asynchronous e-mail, and others in chat rooms in real time. These programs will also have their own ways of proceeding: if you will be expected to tutor on-line, you will be given guidelines by your director. Chances are you will read some of the excellent sources now in print: *Wiring the Writing Center* (ed. Eric Hobson) or *Taking Flight with Owls* (ed. James A. Inman and Donna M. Sewell). If you are interested in the administration of OWLs (on-line writing labs), you can consult *The OWL Construction and Maintenance Guide*, a CD, edited by James A. Inman and Clinton Gardner.

Our experience with on-line sessions teaches us several things, and the following advice is informed by the belief that learning should come first and should not be driven by the technology.

- Establish a friendly tone. This will establish that writers are not working with some kind of automated service, but with a peer. If you have a website with a picture of you or a brief bio, this might help the writer to know you and to feel more involved in the tutoring process.
- Establish the context. Ask about the assignment, the writer's goals for the paper, and the writer's concerns.
- On-line tutoring is tutoring. Higher-order concerns should still come first.
- Make sure you have some way of letting the writer know what to expect and what not to expect from an on-line conference: they won't be dropping off a paper they'll pick up later, all corrected.
- Asking questions is the way to go. But take care:
    Questions on-line can seem even more like commands than they do in person.
    Too many questions can overwhelm the writer; ask the most important question or two, and hope for an interaction.
- The more you can make this conference interactive the better. Ask if the writer can be reached by phone; ask the writer to meet you in a chat room.
- It's hard to do an error analysis on-line. The temptation will be to edit. Consider the patterns of error, if you can find them, point out one example and the way to edit for it, link to an on-line handout on the subject (such as those at http://owl.english.purdue.edu), and encourage the writer to use the computer's search feature to look at problem areas, such as all commas.
- Papers with lots of errors are best handled in a face-to-face session. Don't hesitate to say that.

Some controversies surround on-line tutoring. How much tampering with a writer's text is too much? If a writer sends you an electronic copy of a draft, is it all right to type on it? Perhaps in another color? In most face-to-face sessions we would make a point not to mark up a writer's draft. It would put us in roles we don't want: teacher or editor. How much response is too much? Our feeling is that the best on-line sessions are those that allow dialogue of some sort to take place and provide opportunity for questions to be asked separately from the text. Even adding questions to the end of the text makes them seem like teacher's comments.

Some researchers feel that on-line tutoring makes some fundamental changes in how we perceive our work with writers (e.g., Coogan). The lack of visual cues and the need to make expectations and rules clear—this clarity must come through written text—are fascinating elements of on-line tutoring. We believe that the ultimate goal is the development of the writer; we're hopeful that technology will help us to achieve this.

How Do I Close the Loop?

One of the pitfalls of only providing written response (and not seeing the writer face-to-face) is that you won't get much of a sense of a writer's reactions to your feedback. In some writing programs, you might even be grading those essays you provided response to. In others, your sole interaction with a writer might be via that one draft. The feedback you need to find out if your comments were effective might never arrive. If you are in this situation, we urge you to seek feedback as actively as you can. That might mean showing your comments to your peers or your supervisor before you send them out (in a sense, getting feedback on your feedback). Or you might offer the writer your e-mail address or contact information so that he or she can come to you with questions or concerns. Or, if you have the writer's e-mail address, you can drop a note to break the ice and get some feedback on your work. Whatever your strategy, you need some form of feedback in order to improve as a tutor. We often wish that those instructors who scrawl a quick "AWK!!" had sought that feedback a long, long time ago!

WRITING CENTERS AND WAC

We want to end this chapter by offering some background on the relationship between writing centers and WAC programs. Whether your college has a formal WAC program with required writing-intensive classes or an informal network of faculty committed to having their students write, the relationship between these efforts and the writing center is important. In some programs, WAC will be administratively housed in the writing center (and the Writing Center Director will also wear the hat of WAC Director). In others, the two might be simply physically close or share tutoring space. Whatever the configuration, we want to provide you with some context for these possibilities and give you some grounding in the politics and power involved.

Like most innovations in teaching, attempts to use writing as a means of teaching any subject have a long history (Russell). That history is also often closely tied to the history of writing centers as Warner Taylor illustrated in 1929 upon learning about the existence of several writing clinics in his survey of composition practices nationwide: "In theory the project is excellent; in practice it may prove of little value through the lack of cooperation accorded by departments other than English" (31). Taylor was prescient, for the cooperation of other departments is a key factor in the success of any WAC program and usually for any writing center. Modern WAC-pioneers Art Young and Toby Fulwiler note that the organizational structure of most institutions can be antithetical to a successful WAC program. In a description that can be easily applied to writing centers, they note that "many newly formed comprehensive writing programs do not fit comfortably into the academic structure. They are often given special status outside of academic departments, but not equal to them. Such programs are created by the immediate perceived need of faculty, administrators, or legislators, but they remain vulnerable to the budget axe in ways that academic departments do not" (289–290).

While one would expect a strong alliance between writing centers and WAC programs as a way of countering this lack of fit into the institutional hierarchy, it is not always the case. In fact, historian David Russell sees the creation of writing centers as potentially a more symbolic move that an institution is doing *something* about student writing rather than a move with any substance or potential for change:

> Some WAC programs never progress beyond (or may revert to) remedial labs, outside the curricular structure. Today many universities carry on the tradition of writing police and remedial labs; faculty prescribe treatment (often using computers), administered by a staff member or tutor—but rarely a tenure-line faculty member. Responsibility remains outside the disciplinary communities, dropout rates are high, and the status quo is preserved. . . . Some campuses have even attempted to overcome the stigma by separating a writing center from a remedial lab—further marginalizing the students who most need intellectual contact with students and faculty who use language in the approved ways. (296)

Despite this grim picture, the relationship between writing centers and WAC programs can often be quite strong and both entities highly valued by the institution. The book *Writing Centers and Writing Across the Curriculum Programs: Building Interdisciplinary Partnerships* (Barnett and Blumner) describes many of these relationships and many provide important models for future efforts.

What we believe is most important for the writing center tutor, whether formally part of a WAC program or not, is to think of him- or herself in that bigger picture. That means creating and maintaining relationships with students *and* faculty, knowing writing center and institutional missions, and becoming politically savvy and resourceful. While these might describe the qualities of effective writing center directors, they also apply to tutors in effective programs. It's easy enough to think that once the door to that tutoring room is closed, it's only you and the writer, but the many forces swirling outside of that room have not gone away. Keeping tabs on those elements, if not putting as many of them into your favor as possible, is a sound strategy.

13

WHAT IF . . .

We've tried our best to help you develop techniques that will take you through smooth sessions. But what about those times when they don't go smoothly? The more you observe, the more you will see that not all sessions are ideal. Over the years, our staffs have encountered many troublesome situations, and we have found that it helps to be prepared. The staff of tutors you will be working with will have encountered these situations, too, and will have come up with approaches of their own, so you don't have to figure all these situations out yourself; ask the experienced tutors for their advice.

Here are some scenarios that we've run into, and we make suggestions for ways to cope. These are *only* suggestions, though. In some cases they will work, and in others they could be awful. Use your best judgment in these difficult situations, and ask for advice. What if . . .

YOU SUSPECT THE WRITER MIGHT HAVE A LEARNING DISABILITY (LD)

Perhaps a writer is hesitant to read a draft to you. He asks you to read it, and when you do, you find it is full of errors, particularly reversed letters, too many for a student at his educational level. Or perhaps you have him read aloud, and his reading is labored and full of errors that might not be on the page. You begin to wonder if he has a learning disability (LD).

Learning disabilities manifest themselves in many forms and have a wide range of severity. So it's hard to make generalizations about a single

way to proceed. Nevertheless, the basic tutoring principles of careful listening and observing and being sensitive to the writer's specific needs apply
with LD writers, just as they do with all. Still, it's good to keep a few things in
mind before you start, particularly for newly diagnosed LD writers, who will
be experiencing the most difficulty with coping and will need the most help.

To ask or not to ask: We think it's better for LD writers to self-identify.
Some of them will send a letter to the writing center via the school's LD specialist. Some will just volunteer that they are LD. But some will prefer just to
work on their writing in their own terms. If you wonder if it's appropriate to
ask, check with your director first to see what your writing center's policy is.

Confidentiality: Suppose the writer has identified herself as having a
learning disability. She has a right to her privacy on this matter and might
prefer not to have friends and casual acquaintances know all about her, so
don't discuss this writer's problems with friends or colleagues. It may be
appropriate to discuss strategies for working with LD writers in staff meetings, but keep your discussion private and professional.

Dealing with difference: The written page might not look the same to the
LD writer as it does to you. He might not be able to see spelling errors at all
(a spell checker does a lot, but leaves a lot undone, too, as we all know). He
might not be able to spot grammatical errors, either, and might need help
finding them. Also, LD writers are generally of average or above-average
intelligence; poor spelling is certainly not an indication of low intelligence!

Talk about strategies: You'll discover that some LD writers evolve very in-
genious ways of getting around their disability and are themselves your
best resource in the tutorial. The writer has had a long time to adjust to his
disability and probably knows very well what kinds of help he needs.
Listen to him and take lots of cues from him. Work to help him refine his
strategic repertoire by asking about his methods for success in a variety of
tasks, even nonwritten ones. You will need to be flexible, patient, and cre-
ative in your sessions.

Be positive: Your tone of friendly acceptance will help writers to feel
more comfortable with a task they probably find formidable.

Finding a topic and getting started: Sometimes the LD writer will need
your help brainstorming. Many LD writers know a great deal about the subjects they must write about, but come to sessions thinking they have no ideas
to work with. For many LD writers, the typical brainstorming techniques we
use—freewriting, for example—might not lead to useful writing ideas.
Instead, your questions will help them develop their ideas. Some will need
you to write down key terms or take notes as you ask them questions about
the subject matter. Some may need you to help them organize their ideas
into an outline. If you suggest a technique and the writer resists it, trust her.

Working with error: The LD writer might not be able to see an error until
it is pointed out. Expect her to be well acquainted with the spell-check feature on her computer. But don't necessarily expect her to be able to see the

misspelled word the way you do. Help her to find it, and then help her to correct it. She'll probably have a very good memory, and hearing the word spelled correctly might be all she needs. If you read a sentence aloud, the LD writer is likely to be able to catch and correct the error. You can help the writer make a list of words to have the computer search for, if she is able to see and correct her errors once they are pointed out.

Leave extra time: You might need to schedule an extra-long session or multiple sessions with the LD writer.

Finding space: Some LD writers need a quiet, uncluttered space. Some writers will have attention-deficit disorder (ADD) and will find a noisy room a huge distraction. See if you can find a quiet space to work.

Seek out expertise: Most schools will have a learning-disabled student specialist or an office of disabled students, which has access to this expertise. Talk with your director about bringing in an LD specialist to better inform the writing center staff.

THE PAPER IS ALL MARKED UP

An instructor has scribbled all over the draft, corrected errors, and written so many comments in the margin that it's hard to see the writer's text. The writer needs to revise. In many cases, the writer will want to do only what he has been commanded in red ink to do, and it makes the session difficult, since you and the writer, if allowed to use his own judgment, might come to different revision strategies, not the ones suggested by the teacher. The decision is whether to give the instructor exactly what she wants or to go for a different revision strategy. It might help to ask the writer if he has the document on disk. You could run off a clean copy and see what the two of you come up with and then compare notes with what the teacher has suggested. If that isn't practical, it might be good to ignore, at first, what the instructor has said and make the revisions the writer thinks are important. Try to keep in mind that whatever chaos the situation creates for you, the instructor meant well and may well have done this marking out of exasperation. Try, at all costs, to keep your feelings or biases toward minimal marking out of a session such as this.

THE GRADE ON A WRITER'S PAPER SEEMS UNFAIR

Case A—The Grade Seems Unfairly Low to You

First, remember that it's not our function to whip the teaching staff into shape. It's our job to help the writer deal with his writing contexts, including the instructor. Any remarks we might pass about a grade could very well get exaggerated and repeated to that person. Second, remember that we don't know about all the verbal contracts the teacher and the writer have. A paper that looks fine to us might be off the topic, or the writer might have forgotten or ignored some verbal instruction the teacher set up in class, instructions that might not appear in print. It's best not to betray to the writer any reaction you might have about the fairness of the grade. If she asks your opinion point blank, tell her you are not in a position to make such a judgment. If the situation disturbs you, bring it up at a staff meeting (without mentioning the name of the instructor) or talk to your director. Every center will have its own way of dealing with such situations.

Case B—The Grade Seems Unfairly Low to the Writer

If you've ever been in this kind of situation, you know what kind of stress the writer is bringing to this conference, so it will be hard to find the right balance between making him feel all right about himself and taking his side. Don't let yourself be called in as an expert on what grade a paper deserves. You can read the paper over and try to help the writer understand the instructor's comments, if this seems appropriate, but avoid taking sides. If, after you've gone over the comments, the writer is convinced that the grade is truly unfair, he can appeal the grade and deserves to know what the process is. The question is whether you should suggest such a course of action. The first and best suggestion is to have the writer discuss the grade with the instructor. If the writer were to initiate a grade appeal, this would be his first step, anyway, in most schools, and nothing would be done until this was initiated. Often the instructor is able to explain the grade in a way that satisfies the writer. If the writer has spoken to the instructor and hasn't been given any help in understanding the grade, he can pursue the grade appeal process. Ask your director about this. But regardless of how you feel about the grade's fairness, this is one of those times when you'll need to keep your opinions to yourself. We rely a great deal on the goodwill and open communication and cooperation we have established with the teaching staff. They trust us, and this is the reason we see so many of their writers. Criticizing them to their writers in any way will erode that trust pretty quickly.

THE WRITER DEMANDS A LETTER GRADE

Tell the writer that to guess at a grade is absolutely against your policy and that you will get into trouble if you do it. Refer her to the director if she insists.

THE WRITER IS USING A FORMAT YOU ARE NOT FAMILIAR WITH

Ask the writer to explain to you, briefly, what the disciplinary conventions are. That will make you both feel more comfortable and will put the writer in the good position of being the one with the expertise. If he is unsure of the conventions, now is a good time to find out what they are. The instructor is the best source for this; the writer may have written guidelines that will clarify questions that you have.

THE WRITER IS NOT FAMILIAR WITH A FORMAT THAT YOU ARE FAMILIAR WITH

What if the writer has started a lab report with a narrative to get the reader's interest? What if she is inappropriately using first person and you are sure it's going to cause problems? Now is no time to withhold important disciplinary information. Ask the writer what she knows about the format, ask to see any written guidelines or examples she might have, and if those are not available, share with her your concerns, based on your understanding of the genre. If you're both unsure, urge the writer to consult with the instructor. We're not asking you to be the voice of the institution here or to stifle the writer's creativity, but to let her know, realistically, that the format calls for a certain set of writing standards. Then it's up to her if she still wants to start her lab report with a story about her first chemistry set.

THE WRITER COMES IN AND ASKS YOU TO PROOFREAD

There's no need to tip your hand too early. Don't say, "We don't proofread," or the writer may just leave. Tell the writer that you'll begin the session by listening to the paper and looking at larger issues first. Then, if there's no time to get to proofreading after you've discussed higher-order concerns, point out one or two things you noticed (if you noticed anything at all) for the writer to work on, and urge her to come back to look at surface errors. And remember, you can't *hear* certain errors—you'll have to *see* them, so don't be too quick to reassure the writer that the paper is free of errors. But it makes no sense to correct the errors in a paper that needs revision, and some writers will not change or move or strike out a section, no matter how badly it fits into a paper, once it's been corrected for errors.

THE WRITER HAS PLAGIARIZED

There are many variations on this scenario. Most commonly, writers will unintentionally plagiarize, whether that means not citing someone else's words or ideas or not paraphrasing well and instead presenting nearly word-for-word what someone else wrote. For these writers, it's important that you probe their knowledge of plagiarism. Most often, you'll find that they just haven't learned the correct method for citing sources or they've come from a culture with a very different sense of intellectual property. A brief tour of the handbook or some exercise in accurate paraphrasing will fix matters.

Less often, we hope, you'll encounter a writer who has deliberately plagiarized. The writer might admit this act to you (as has happened to us, pulling us in as co-conspirators in the activity), or the writer will deny something you know to be true (because you know the original essay or you saw another writer earlier in the day with the same exact paper). What do you do? What's your responsibility for enforcing what is in almost all places a serious violation, one that could result in failure, suspension, or dismissal?

Most important is to know your writing center's and director's policy in such matters. Most writing center directors will take on the responsibility of deciding whether or not to contact the writer's class instructor. But this is an important topic to bring up in your staff meetings or in a training class— better to know policy before the problem occurs.

At some schools and colleges, all students are held to an honor code, and that often includes the responsibility for reporting on violations, as well as upholding the code yourself. If you're using this type of system, the procedures should be clear cut, but again this is an important topic to bring up in class or meetings before you're called on to take action.

YOU FIND THE WRITER'S POINT OF VIEW OFFENSIVE

There's nothing to challenge our sense of writer empowerment and ownership like one whose views we find utterly offensive. Certainly, there will be writers who take stands with which we disagree, but in this scenario we're talking about views you find reprehensible or personally troubling. Is it your ethical responsibility to set this writer straight? Perhaps you have been advised to say, "Well, any argument is strengthened by acknowledging the views of the opposing side. So what are some of the counterarguments that you've considered?" But instead your mind races with personal insults (which you suppress) and then with a list of logical points in opposition to the writer's viewpoint. In the following excerpt from her reflective essay, Stephanie Wankum encountered just this dilemma:

During my fifth tutoring session, I had a head on collision with a paper that struck me in a personal manner. The student's assignment was to present a common and widely accepted view about a particular issue and then present "bad news" that would cause the audience to question the common view. The tutee's paper was about chemotherapy and the common view was supposed to be that chemotherapy is considered a great treatment. I thought "chemotherapy is NOT considered good." Then I thought "wait—maybe people do think it's good." How could I *not* know?

Chemotherapy is a personal issue for me. My mother was on chemotherapy while I was growing up. When the student started to reveal all the bad things about chemotherapy, I found that I wasn't able to concentrate. I was back at the question about the common view. Was the common view he presented valid and I couldn't see it because I take for granted that everyone knows that chemotherapy is a horrible treatment? Perhaps I only know this because I have dealt with it personally. I had to confront this issue quickly and began searching for a way to do it. I mentally started to reflect on class discussions and preparation that dealt directly with the issue of personal disagreement. I realized that I may be opposed to the student's thesis statement because I have personal knowledge about the subject, but more importantly, because it makes me emotional. I also knew that I should be able to step back and consider the paper in an objective manner.

When I began to consider the paper objectively, I realized that my initial reaction was not as personal as I originally thought. I simply considered what my peers might think about chemotherapy. Most of them did not grow up directly involved with the treatment and surely would not claim that the common view of chemotherapy was that it was a good treatment.

The student had finished reading his paper and was silently waiting for me to say something. I was still mentally playing tennis with the idea of common view when I realized that I had to go on with the session. I procrastinated by asking him to outline his thesis statement. I started asking more questions and eventually my mental limbo began to work itself out. The nondirective tutoring style of questioning helped me to do this.

Tutor training taught my class that nondirective tutoring was the preferred method of tutoring because it allowed the student to figure things out for themselves. I would not have guessed that it would help me figure things out as well. The more I questioned the student the more I was aware that this assumption of the common view was incorrect. Question-oriented tutoring eased the confusion of my personal dilemma. This tutoring style shaped the session and began to give it direction. The student finally came to a point where he admitted that he never thought that chemotherapy was a great treatment. When he left he said that he didn't plan to change the paper but was going to re-model how he presented the common view. As I wished him good luck, I felt relief and consciously realized that I had made a connection between two concepts discussed in training.

When I began tutoring, I was aware of directive and nondirective tutoring styles, how to be professional in the face of opposition, and even where the tissues are located. I did not know then that circum-stance would weave some of these concepts together. In this particular circumstance, I realized that nondirective tutoring can help the tutor as much as the student. I needed to muddle through the process of sev-ering personal and professional views. Class discussion created an awareness of the need for such severing. The discussions also taught my class how to help the student wade through issues of clarity by uti-lizing nondirective methods and forms of questioning. I have discov-ered that the tutoring techniques that help students understand what to do in a session are the same ones that help the tutor understand what direction to take.

As Stephanie shows, she was committed to an ethical view of tutoring. She was challenged by the desire to directly counter the writer's expressed point of view, but ultimately she relied upon what she felt to be responsible conduct—with this or any other writer.[1] You will be challenged by writers who don't—at least initially—share your sense of responsibilities or stan-dards of ethical behavior. But it is in that challenge that you can strengthen your beliefs, as Stephanie did, and help the writer more fully explore her point of view.

THE PAPER IS DUE SOON!

It makes a huge difference whether the paper is due in a day or an hour. If the writer has a day to work on it, proceed as usual, looking at higher-order concerns. But urge the writer to make an appointment for earlier in the writing process. If the paper is due in an hour, then don't ask the writer to read aloud; help her look for errors, but don't hesitate to point out struc-tural elements that need revision. There might be time for her to make some significant revisions while correcting errors. Be tactful as you urge these

---

[1]For another example of how to work with a writer who has objectionable views, see Sloan, Jay D. "Closet Consulting." *The Writing Lab Newsletter* 21.10 (June 1997): 9–10.

writers to come earlier. Surely some of them will have tried to, but will not have been able to get an earlier appointment.

THE WRITER IS CRYING

Get to know where to find a box of tissues. Leaving for a minute to get a few will give the writer a chance to regain his composure and give you a chance to work out a strategy. When you get back with the tissues (bring plenty; this may be a long session), ask the writer if he would like to be alone for a minute. If not, it wouldn't hurt to try some Rogerian techniques, repeating to the writer or paraphrasing what he has said to you. He says, "I'm so stressed." You say, "You seem pretty upset." This helps the writer get things out. Remember, though, that we are not the counseling center, and if the writer's upset seems serious, or if the writer is crying for what doesn't seem to you to be anything serious, or if he comes in and cries at more than one session, ask if he has heard of the counseling center or student support service on your campus. Sometimes we are the first to see a student's true stress or depression, because writing on sensitive topics or getting a bad grade can trigger these outward signs of upset. Sometimes the cause is time management and grade pressure, and then your student retention counselor will be able to help. The important thing is to let the writer have space and time to regain composure and to suggest some people he can contact. Look up the numbers if he seems interested in getting help, or call and hand the phone over to him. It wouldn't hurt to follow up on this writer, either, perhaps with a call the next day to make sure he's all right.

THE WRITER WON'T REVISE

A few years ago we had a writer who would come in for regular appointments, as many a week as we would give him, work with the same tutor, but expect to make all his revisions during the session. He would come in with his paper unchanged for the next session. Now this can happen to the most conscientious of writers: they run out of time before their next appointment. But this writer developed a pattern of never revising outside of the appointment. The tutor felt that she was doing too much and that he had to take responsibility for his work. Eventually she told him that he would have to make revisions if he wanted to have another appointment. It turned out that he lacked the confidence to make the changes himself, but his confidence grew as he observed the revision process taking place during the sessions. It just took him a while to get the hang of revising papers.

THE WRITER WON'T LISTEN

You recognize that a paper is deeply flawed, and you've tried to get the writer to see what you see by asking questions about it. The writer insists that she likes everything in the paper, sometimes the very things that make the paper weak. Your well-intentioned questions don't work. Finally you might try saying, "Such and such just doesn't work for me." The writer still likes the entire thing. One of our staff members once said, "You can lead a horse to water, but you can't make him freewrite." After suggesting that the writer show the draft to the instructor, give up gracefully. Not everyone is meant to be helped. But be comforted: maybe after the writer leaves, she will rethink her decisions or see her instructor.

THE WRITER IS DEPENDENT

If we have plenty of open time in our schedule, we let writers schedule multiple appointments in a week. A few years ago we had an absolutely delightful writer from India. She had a standing appointment to improve her writing (though she was a very good writer), but before papers were due, she would schedule a number of appointments with various tutors. Yet we never considered her dependent. Why? Because between sessions she revised and improved her papers. She took our questions to heart and did excellent revisions, then wanted more feedback, often from another reader. Late in the semester she mentioned that the tutors in the writing center were her only friends. We asked her if she knew about the international student associations, and to our surprise, she said she had never heard of them. The turnaround was immediate and dramatic. She called that day, found that there was going to be a celebration of Diwali, the Indian festival of lights, and she signed on and became involved. She still came in for tutoring, but less often, and she invited us to the celebrations and came in one day to paint the tutors' hands with henna. So coming to get help often doesn't necessarily imply dependence. She had just found a friendly place where she got good work done.

But we've had writers who were completely dependent, such as the previous example of the writer who wouldn't revise. One of our tutors became frustrated with him at one point and asked if he could schedule this writer with another tutor. We encourage tutors to ask for this if they need to.

THE WRITER IS TUTOR SURFING

You have an appointment with a writer. You notice as you glance over the schedule that she is also seeing two other tutors that day and two the next.

She is tutor surfing. Now, there are good reasons to do this. She may be looking for someone who has the right chemistry to work with her. We've seen this with writers who had worked regularly with a tutor who graduated. And once we had a very canny writer who liked to brainstorm with one tutor, show a first draft to another, polish a draft with a third, and look for errors with a fourth. He was a true writing center connoisseur. We all looked forward to working with him and enjoyed his expertise in writing center nuances. But there are bad and counterproductive reasons for tutor surfing. Sometimes writers are terrified of a paper assignment and want to get as many appointments as they can. Occasionally they are hoping that they'll find a tutor who actually will proofread for them, so they come in again and again and ask for the same thing. These writers will make much better progress with fewer appointments but with the same tutor, and usually all we have to do is point this out to them, and then they make a choice. And it's an informed choice, since by then they know us all.

THE WRITER IS NOT COOPERATING

Sometimes a writer will schedule an appointment and sit sullenly, say "I don't know" when you ask questions, or give monosyllabic and unenthusiastic replies. One of our writers, when asked to read her paper aloud, showed her rebellion by stuffing her mouth full of peanuts and mumbling as she chewed them. The members of our staff began to refer to these uncooperative types as "peanut people." Sometimes it's possible to find out what's bothering them and correct it.

Were they forced to come? Ask, "What made you decide to come here?" They'll tell you if they were required to attend. Some classes have a regular policy of making students use the writing center. Some instructors give extensions to writers who will seek tutoring. Sometimes these restrictions make the writers resentful, and they don't put much into the sessions. We try to let instructors know in our public relations material that requiring writing center sessions can backfire, and our policy is that when writers don't do their part, we tell them, quite courteously, that they can go. Sometimes just letting them off the hook makes them thaw out and want to be part of the session.

Did we fail to meet their expectations? Sometimes writers hear that we will proofread. We try hard to let them know what we do. We visit classes and spread the word, but sometimes writers get bad information anyway. By the time the writer is glaring and sullen, it may be too late, but if it's the writer's first session, it helps to sketch out what will happen, so she can say, "Whoa! I'm leaving. I wanted proofreading." Often, though, writers are convinced to stay.

Sometimes there are no reasons we can discern for what might seem like sullen, uncooperative behavior. If you ask a question and there's no answer, there's a good chance the writer is just mulling over the possibilities. Try not to jump to conclusions about a quiet writer. Some writers are more passive than others, and if you jump in and answer your own questions, they quickly catch on and wait you out. Turn the tables by waiting them out. If there is a long pause, you might ask them to jot down a few ideas while you take a short break. Sometimes writing can break a mental logjam.

THE WRITER FRIGHTENS YOU

We don't think it's a good idea to work with someone who scares you. Once a tutor of ours got a writer angry by insisting that he read his paper aloud. She felt that because it was our policy, she was required to do it. It really made this student feel uncomfortable and threatened, because he was struggling as a writer and was not a fluent reader. When he became angry, he frightened the tutor, because the writer was quite large and agitated. This would have been a good time to let go of our policy and do what the writer needed, but the tutor felt strongly that she was doing the right thing. Don't hesitate to ask someone else to take an angry or upsetting writer. This is what the tutor did. The writer began to work with a different tutor and came in for help for several years as he finished his degree. In the Marquette Writing Center, we have a very broadly worded conduct statement posted:

> The Norman H. Ott Memorial Writing Center expects those who use our services to respect the rights of others. Responsible conduct is expected and required. Individuals who engage in unacceptable behavior such as physical and/or verbal abuse may lose their writing center privileges and/or be subject to university disciplinary action.

If a writer is verbally or in some other way abusive, you have a right to ask him or her to leave, as long as you have posted some kind of notice. If there is no conduct statement in your center, we strongly suggest that you get one (see also Eric Hobson's article, "An Ounce of Prevention: Ensuring Safety in the Writing Center" in *The Writing Lab Newsletter,* June 1997).

THE WRITER HAS CHOSEN A REALLY BAD TOPIC

Case 1—The Topic Is Clichéd

Sometimes we'll hear what a writer is working on and groan, thinking that the topic is really bad, only to discover that she's worked wonders with it.

Recently, a writer came in and announced that her paper was about bees. The topic was to find something that most people view negatively and share some surprising good news about it. Two of the three sample essays from the textbook were about spiders, so when Kristin announced that she was writing about bees, Paula felt apprehensive. She had formed an ideal text, or rather formed a text, and it wasn't ideal at all. Paula was afraid that the writer's essay would be a close imitation of those samples in the book. But then the writer told Paula that her good news was that bee stings were being used as alternative medicine for such serious problems as arthritis and MS. When she told Paula that she'd gotten her information from her mother, who had MS, the topic seemed interesting, and Paula could see that the writer's topic, far from being weak, was interesting. Paula learned a lot as the writer read her drafts aloud.

But some topics truly are clichéd, and it's difficult to say new things about them. Most teachers will rattle off a list of topics they never want to see again, because the opposing sides have been discussed to death. We need to remember, though, that one person's cliché is another person's news flash. So it's important to be tactful when we help writers think more critically about topics that are new and vibrant to them. One way to get them to dig more deeply is to invite them to use what Peter Elbow and Pat Belanoff call the Loop Process. You begin by having the writer jot down all his first thoughts and preconceptions on a topic, and then urge him to go deeper, to find the corner of the topic that's meaningful for him. Ask him to think about the audience: What does the audience already know? What do they need to know? Sometimes, however, a conference with a teacher might be the only way to get a writer to choose a better topic.

Case 2—The Topic Doesn't Fit the Assignment

As much as we want to foster creativity and independent thinking, choosing a topic that doesn't meet the assignment is likely to get the writer a bad grade, regardless of how well he's written on it. He needs to be told that his assignment is off the topic, and you will be able to help him find another. This is hard for a writer. He's invested a lot of energy in his topic, and he might not seem glad to be told that his topic is off, but depending on his goals for the course, he will thank you later. Urge him to ask his instructor if the writer is in doubt about his topic.

Case 3—The Topic Is off the Wall

One of our trainees observed a session in which the writing topic was to describe a time when the writer had changed his mind. He chose to write about the experience of using a public bathroom in his residence hall. The details he included seemed inappropriate for the topic, and the trainee wondered how she'd get the writer to see this without being directive. But the tutor had had plenty of experience, and he knew what to do. He focused on the assignment and asked the writer how he had changed his mind. The writer agreed that he hadn't really written about a change of mind, so he changed his topic. It would be good to discuss this topic with your fellow tutors and your director to see how your center handles these kinds of situations.

THE WRITER IS EMOTIONALLY INVESTED IN THE PAPER AND CAN'T WRITE IT

You have several options. You can help the writer find a part of the assignment that isn't so close to home. Brainstorm with him about the topic in general, staying away from his personal story, but talking about the issues involved. As you brainstorm, you might find some topics that interest him in an intellectual way, that are distanced from an experience that might be painful for him. You can also help him talk through the difficulty so that he better understands his deep investment in the topic and so that he is able to write a version of the paper. You can also suggest a visit with the instructor, to talk things over.

THE WRITER'S PAPER IS FULL OF ERRORS

Persist in your policy of looking at the higher-order concerns first, but point out to the writer before the session is over that you saw a lot of errors, and show her a few. Urge her to come back with a revision, if possible, to work on them. If that is not possible, get her to ask a friend to help her spot them. Remember that some errors are a function of the writer's weak grasp of the subject matter. As she revises and rethinks her topic, sometimes those errors go away on their own, and the writing flows more smoothly and correctly. If there is time to do an error analysis with the writer, perhaps you can focus on one or two patterns of error.

THE WRITER CAN'T RECOGNIZE ERRORS

This writer needs help and lots of it. Urge him to make a standing appointment, weekly, to get this problem under control. It's best to work with his own writing rather than doing exercises from a handbook, so have him bring in his work or write on the spot.

YOU FEEL THE WRITER STILL HAS FAR TO GO

The session has ended, but there is still much to do. Some tutors like to give the writer three things to work on. If the writer has time before the assignment is due, urge her to come back. If possible, help her set up an appointment, with you if at all possible. If only proofreading is left to finish and the deadline is near, suggest that writers seek out classmates for help. Urge international writers to ask their American friends to help them proofread. Don't let writers take advantage of you. When your time is up, tell the writer so, and don't feel guilty. Keeping a watch or clock on your desk will help both you and the writer remember to stay within time limits.

THE WRITER WON'T QUIT

A good way to avoid this situation is this: about five minutes before the session ends, begin to ask the writer what her plans are for revision. This communicates that the session is coming to an end and helps the writer do some good work, consolidating her gains. If the writer persists, a tactful approach is for you to say, "Did the session help you?" If this doesn't work, stand up and say, "I enjoyed working with you. Another writer is waiting to see me," or whatever may be appropriate.

THE SESSION SEEMS ALL WRONG

In a reflection paper, Angela Jesik discusses two less-than-perfect sessions that she encountered as she was just beginning her training process:

Tapping my fingers impatiently on the desk in Room 489, I grew anxious and nervous about observing my first session. I didn't know what to expect. I only assumed that I was about to witness the "tutor's magic," that specialized knowledge where they know the perfect questions to ask at precisely the right time to make the students discuss and improve their papers. As my mind drifted into scenarios of myself actually having that "magic," the student walked in, and it was time to observe the expert tutor at work.

First, Maggie, the student, explained the objective of the paper. She was to write an essay illustrating a point in her life when she changed her mind. She decided to write about how she grew up in Asia, hated America when she first moved back, and eventually accepted the American way of life. This essay seemed to be interesting, but I noticed Stewart, the tutor, grow tense with every sentence read. He did not behave in this manner because he was nervous like myself, but because each statement was insulting and ridiculed Americans. However, Maggie did not view her statements as offensively as did Stewart and I. She felt that these were her first impressions and refused to tone down her strong sentiments. After a few moments of composing himself, Stewart began to ask questions to help improve her paper. But, no matter how many questions he asked, and how forward he tried to be without being "directive," he could not make her understand that this language might insult the reader. It was in watching this deadlock between the tutor and the tutee that my whole world came crashing down upon me.

I wondered to myself, "What was going on?" "Why isn't she responding to his questions like the way we practiced in class?" And most importantly, "Where was his special tutor insight that would help this girl with the paper?" Although I had many questions, none of them were answered for me at that time. I left the session feeling distressed because I had witnessed the transformation of a "super tutor" into an average student with struggles just like me.

So, observing this did not give me an overabundant amount of confidence for my first tutoring session. If a person employed at the tutoring center had difficulties, how in the world was I going to help students with their papers? This thought resonated in my head as I introduced myself to my first tutee. To my dismay, she was an ESL student. Now, I have absolutely no prejudice against these students, but I knew that this session would be extra challenging, and honestly, I did not know if I was prepared. As I expected, this session went nothing like the "ideal ones" we had read or practiced. The student, Tracy, didn't even have a rough draft of her paper. She simply came in and said she had to write a four-page paper on the poem "Laguna Blues," and wanted me to explain it to her. Desperately scanning my memory for tips from class, the only thing I remembered was *"Don't be directive."* So I told her I would assist her in interpreting the material herself.

As the session progressed, I again tried to think of all the practice tutorials we had in class and the sessions I had observed, searching for the exact questions to help Tracy understand the material. But even though I tried and tried and tried, I couldn't recall any examples from class that would help me in this situation. I realized I was on my own, and that it was not the textbook scenarios we practiced in class, but my own interpretation of the material that was going to lead me to the next question. So, hands clenched, gnawing on my pen cap, I continued to discuss the poem with her.

Although it was perturbing and tedious, the session actually ended on a positive note. And, as I sighed with relief, Tracy told me I had helped her tremendously. It was at that moment I began to reflect upon my experience at the writing center. I realized that, from the beginning of class to the present, my whole opinion had changed. I used to believe that the writing center tutors knew everything, and that every session would be ideal. But, through my observations and experiences, I now realize there is no "magic formula" for being a tutor. Every session is unique, and every student will have a different attitude regarding the session. The only way to truly be a successful tutor is through a whole-hearted attempt to understand the assignment and the student. It is this individualized assessment, and not writing book guidelines, that will provide the foundation for improvement.

As I continue to observe and tutor, I do so with a fresh consciousness. I am no longer confined by the ideal classroom simulations. I have too much experience to believe that, once we write our names down in the appointment book, we are given supernatural tutor powers. I realize these expert tutors are experts only because they have experienced similar tutoring situations. Their expectations have also been built up by hearing about perfect sessions, only to have them crash down in real life. But what makes them different from novices is they understand that the key to effective tutoring is being adaptable and flexible. And, most importantly, they know the only "secret formula" to tutoring is not to expect anything that is ideal or easy.

Angela is right. There may be no secret formula, and it's impossible to anticipate all the problems you might encounter. We spent some time in our weekly staff meeting discussing the session Stewart had with his writer, trying to figure out the best ways to deal with a student whose approach or tone we don't agree with. It helps to have a group discuss these situations, because we're able to try out different perspectives and draw on our various experiences as we come up with possible solutions. But Angela is also right that sensitivity, flexibility, and an open mind will make these sessions productive and maybe even enjoyable.

RECOMMENDED READINGS

WRITING CENTER HISTORY

Boquet, Elizabeth H. "'Our Little Secret': A History of Writing Centers, Pre- to Post-Open Admissions." *College Composition and Communication* 50 (February 1999): 463–82.

Carino, Peter. "Early Writing Centers: Toward a History." *The Writing Center Journal* 15 (spring 1995): 103–15.

———. "Open Admissions and the Construction of Writing Center History: A Tale of Three Models." *The Writing Center Journal* 17 (fall 1996): 30–48.

Lerner, Neal. "Drill Pads, Teaching Machines, and Programmed Texts: Origins of Instructional Technology in Writing Centers." In *Wiring the Writing Center*, ed. Eric H. Hobson, 119–36. Logan: Utah State University Press, 1998.

———. "Searching for Robert Moore." *The Writing Center Journal* 22 (fall/winter 2001): 9–32.

WRITING CENTER THEORY, RESEARCH, AND PRACTICE

Barnett, Robert W., and Jacob S. Blumner, eds. *The Allyn and Bacon Guide to Writing Center Theory and Practice*. Boston: Allyn & Bacon, 2001.

Boquet, Elizabeth H. *Noise from the Writing Center*. Logan: Utah State University Press, 2002.

Briggs, Lynn Craigue, and Meg Woolbright, eds. *Stories from the Center: Connecting Narrative and Theory in the Writing Center*. Urbana, IL: NCTE, 2000.

Bruffee, Kenneth A. "Collaborative Learning and the 'Conversation of Mankind.'" *College English* 46 (1984): 635–52.

Coogan, David. *Electronic Writing Centers: Computing the Field of Composition*. Stamford, CT: Ablex, 1999.

Ede, Lisa. "Writing as a Social Process: A Theoretical Foundation for Writing Centers?" *The Writing Center Journal* 9 (1989): 3–13.

Flynn, Thomas, and Mary King. *Dynamics of the Writing Conference: Social and Cognitive Interaction.* Urbana, IL: NCTE, 1993.

Gillespie, Paula, Alice Gillam, Lady Falls Brown, and Byron Stay, eds. *Writing Center Research: Extending the Conversation.* Mahwah, NJ: Lawrence Erlbaum, 2002.

Grimm, Nancy Maloney. *Good Intentions: Writing Center Work for Postmodern Times.* Portsmouth, NH: Boynton/Cook, 1999.

Harris, Muriel. "Collaboration Is Not Collaboration Is Not Collaboration: Writing Center Tutorials vs. Peer-Response Groups." *College Composition and Communication* 43 (1992): 369–83.

Harris, Muriel, and Tony Silva. "Tutoring ESL Students: Issues and Options." *College Composition and Communication* 44 (1993): 525–37.

Haviland, Carol Peterson, Maria Notarangelo, Lene Whitley-Putz, and Thia Wolf, eds. *Weaving Knowledge Together: Writing Centers and Collaboration.* Emmitsburg, MD: NWCA Press, 1998.

Hobson, Eric H. "Maintaining Our Balance: Walking the Tightrope of Competing Epistemologies." *The Writing Center Journal* 13 (1992): 65–75.

——, ed. *Wiring the Writing Center.* Logan: Utah State University Press, 1998.

Kail, Harvey. "Collaborative Learning in Context: The Problem with Peer Tutoring." *College English* 45 (1983): 594–99.

Lunsford, Andrea. "Collaboration, Control, and the Idea of a Writing Center." *The Writing Center Journal* 12 (1991): 3–10.

Mullin, Joan A., and Ray Wallace, eds. *Intersections: Theory-Practice in the Writing Center.* Urbana, IL: NCTE, 1994.

Murphy, Christina, and Joe Law, eds. *Landmark Essays on Writing Centers.* Davis, CA: Hermagoras Press, 1995.

Murphy, Christina, Joe Law, and Steve Sherwood. *Writing Centers: An Annotated Bibliography.* Westport, CT: Greenwood, 1996.

North, Stephen M. "The Idea of a Writing Center." *College English* 46 (1984): 433–46.

——. "Revisiting 'The Idea of a Writing Center.'" *The Writing Center Journal* 15 (1994): 7–18.

Podis, Leonard A., and JoAnne M. Podis, ed. *Working with Student Writers: Essays on Tutoring and Teaching.* New York: Peter Lang, 1999.

Silk, Bobbie Bayliss, ed. *The Writing Center Resource Manual,* 2d ed. Emmitsburg, MD: IWCA Press, 2002.

Stay, Bryon, Christina Murphy, and Eric H. Hobson, eds. *Writing Center Perspectives.* Emmitsburg, MD: IWCA Press, 1995.

Trimbur, John. "Peer Tutoring: A Contradiction in Terms?" *The Writing Center Journal* 7 (1987): 21–28.

WRITING CENTER ADMINISTRATION AND POLITICS

Barnett, Robert W., and Jacob S. Blumner, eds. *Writing Centers and Writing Across the Curriculum Programs: Building Interdisciplinary Partnerships.* Westport, CT: Greenwood, 1999.

Kinkead, Joyce A., and Jeanette G. Harris, eds. *Writing Centers in Context: Twelve Case Studies*. Urbana, IL: NCTE, 1993.

Nelson, Jane, and Kathy Evertz. *The Politics of Writing Centers*. Portsmouth, NH: Boynton/Cook, 2001.

Olson, Gary A., ed. *Writing Centers: Theory and Administration*. Urbana, IL: NCTE, 1984.

DISSERTATIONS ON WRITING CENTERS

Anglada, Liliana B. "On-Line Writing Center Responses and Advanced EFL Students' Writing: An Analysis of Comments, Students' Attitudes, and Textual Revisions." Ph.D. diss., Texas Tech University, 1999. Abstract in *Dissertation Abstracts International* 60 (1999): 1111.

Bauman, Gail A. "A Case Study Examination of the Development of the Writing Process Behaviors of Kindergarten Children as Demonstrated in an Informal Classroom Writing Center." Ph.D. diss., Florida State University, 1985. Abstract in *Dissertation Abstracts International* 46 (1985): 0889.

Bednarowicz, Eva K. "The Revisionary Writing Center: The Rhetoric of a MOO Tutorial." Ph.D. diss., University of Illinois at Chicago, 2002. Abstract in *Dissertation Abstracts International* 63 (2002): 927.

Bell, James H. "Tutoring in a Writing Center." Ph.D. diss., University of Texas at Austin, 1989. Abstract in *Dissertation Abstracts International* 50 (1989): 2763.

Blythe, Stuart R. "Technologies and Writing Center Practices: A Critical Approach." Ph.D. diss., Purdue University, 1997. Abstract in *Dissertation Abstracts International* 58 (1997): 4633.

Boquet, Elizabeth H. "Writing Centers: History, Theory, and Implications." Ph.D. diss., Indiana University of Pennsylvania, 1995. Abstract in *Dissertation Abstracts International* 56 (1995): 1671.

Boudreaux, Marjory A. "Toward Awareness: A Study of Nonverbal Behavior in the Writing Conference." Ph.D. diss., Indiana University of Pennsylvania, 1998. Abstract in *Dissertation Abstracts International* 59 (1998): 1145.

Bowen, Betsy Anne. "Talking About Writing: Collaborative Revision in the Peer Writing Conference." Ph.D. diss., Carnegie-Mellon University, 1988. Abstract in *Dissertation Abstracts International* 49 (1988): 2953.

Briggs, Lynn Craigue. "Writing Center Talk in a Long-Term Writer-Consultant Relationship." Ph.D. diss., Syracuse University, 1991. Abstract in *Dissertation Abstracts International* 52 (1991): 2846.

Brown, Alan N. "Writing Centers: How They Succeed and Fail." Ph.D. diss., Illinois State University, 1984. Abstract in *Dissertation Abstracts International* 46 (1984): 0091.

Callaway, Susan J. "Collaboration, Resistance, and the Authority of the Student Writer: A Case Study of Peer Tutoring." Ph.D. diss., University of Wisconsin–Milwaukee, 1993. Abstract in *Dissertation Abstracts International* 54 (1993): 2555.

Carter-Tod, Sheila Lorraine. "The Role of the Writing Center in the Writing Practices of L2 Students." Ph.D. diss., Virginia Polytechnic Institute and State University, 1995. Abstract in *Dissertation Abstracts International* 56 (1995): 4262.

Coogan, David. "Electronic Writing Centers." Ph.D. diss., State University of New York at Albany, 1995. Abstract in *Dissertation Abstracts International* 56 (1995): 3861.

Crawford, James E. "Writing Center Practices in Tennessee Community Colleges." Ph.D. diss., East Tennessee State University, 1998. Abstract in *Dissertation Abstracts International* 60 (1998): 0052.

D'Angelo, Lawrence M. "Writing Centers as Manifestations of Pedagogical Philosophy." Master's thesis, Eastern Michigan University, 1996. *Masters Abstracts International* 34 (1996): 1351.

Eckard, Sandra Jean. "The Ties That Bind: Storytelling in Composition Classrooms and Writing Centers." Ph.D. diss., Indiana University of Pennsylvania, 2001. Abstract in *Dissertation Abstracts International* 62 (2001): 3033.

Fischer, Fred H. "The Effect of the Tutorial Writing Center on Underprepared Community College Students." Ph.D. diss., Northern Arizona University, 1989. Abstract in *Dissertation Abstracts International* 50 (1989): 3833.

Geller, Anne Ellen. "A Big Tangled Mess: New Graduate Student Tutors Reflect on Their Experiences in the Writing Center." Ph.D. diss., New York University, 2001. Abstract in *Dissertation Abstracts International* 62 (2001): 2407.

Grimm, Nancy Maloney. "Making Writing Centers Work: Literacy, Institutional Change, and Student Agency." Ph.D. diss., Michigan Technological University, 1995. Abstract in *Dissertation Abstracts International* 56 (1995): 1693.

Henderson, Maurice M. "A Study of the Structure of the Writing Laboratory Programs in Two-Year Community Colleges." Ph.D. diss., Indiana University of Pennsylvania, 1980. Abstract in *Dissertation Abstracts International* 41 (1980): 3924.

Hobson, Eric H. "Where Theory and Practice Collide: Beyond Essentialist Descriptions of the Writing Center." Ph.D. diss., University of Tennessee, 1992. Abstract in *Dissertation Abstracts International* 53 (1992): 3828.

Hunt, Barbara Jean. "Establishing and Implementing a Writing Center on the College Level." Ph.D. diss., University of Michigan, 1980. Abstract in *Dissertation Abstracts International* 41 (1980): 2083.

Hunter, Kathleen R. "Tutor Talk: A Study of Selected Linguistic Factors Affecting Tutor-Writer Interaction in a University Writing Center." Ph.D. diss., Indiana University of Pennsylvania, 1993. Abstract in *Dissertation Abstracts International* 54 (1993): 3727.

Johnson, Tracey Jane C. "In Search of Status: An Empirical Study of Writing Centers in Four Academic Settings." Ph.D. diss., West Virginia University, 1997. Abstract in *Dissertation Abstracts International* 58 (1997): 0720.

Kearcher, Kurt P. "The Theory-Practice of Writing Center Ideology." Ph.D. diss., University of Toledo, 2000. Abstract in *Dissertation Abstracts International* 61 (2000): 4370.

Kim, Youn-Kyung. "Frame Analysis of NS-NS and NS-NNS Discourse in University Writing Center Tutorials: Volubility and Questions." Ph.D. diss., Oklahoma State University, 2000. Abstract in *Dissertation Abstracts International* 62 (2000): 145.

Laque, Carol F., and Phyllis A. Sherwood. "A Teaching Monograph: Co-Designed Laboratory Approach to Writing." Ph.D. diss., University of Cincinnati, 1975. Abstract in *Dissertation Abstracts International* 36 (1975): 4418.

Lerner, Neal. "Teaching and Learning in a University Writing Center." Ph.D. diss., Boston University School of Education, 1996. Abstract in *Dissertation Abstracts International* 57 (1996): 1060.

MacDonald, Ross Barclay. "Tutoring: A Descriptive Investigation of Four One-to-One Community College Tutorials." Ph.D. diss., University of California-Davis, 1988. Abstract in *Dissertation Abstracts International* 49 (1988): 1686.

Mackiewicz, Jo M. "The Co-Construction of Social Relationships in Writing Center Tutoring Interactions: An Analysis of Politeness Strategies in Discourse Activity Frames." Ph.D. diss., Georgetown University, 2001. Abstract in *Dissertation Abstracts International* 62 (2001): 4145.

Magnatto, Joyce Neff. "The Construction of College Writing in a Cross-Disciplinary, Community College Writing Center: An Analysis of Student, Tutor, and Faculty Representations." Ph.D. diss., University of Pennsylvania, 1991. Abstract in *Dissertation Abstracts International* 52 (1991): 2382.

McCall, William W. "Writing Center Theory and the Idea of Academic Discourse." Ph.D. diss., Michigan State University, 1996. Abstract in *Dissertation Abstracts International* 58 (1996): 0153.

McClure, Susan Harpham. "An Observational Study of the Behavior of First Semester College Students as Tutors in a Writing Center." Ph.D. diss., Indiana University of Pennsylvania, 1990. Abstract in *Dissertation Abstracts International* 51 (1990): 0771.

Mcinerney, Kathleen Hanley. "A Portrait of One Writing Center Through Undergraduate Tutors' Talk: Themes of Home, Heart and Head." Ph.D. diss., University of Iowa, 1998. Abstract in *Dissertation Abstracts International* 59 (1998): 2894.

Murphy, Susan Wolff. "Politeness and Self-Presentation in Writing Center Discourse." Ph.D. diss., Texas A&M University, 2001. Abstract in *Dissertation Abstracts International* 62 (2001): 3766.

Nordberg, Beverly. "Descriptive Case Studies of Basic Writers in Grades Four Through Eight in a Writing Center Setting." Ph.D. diss., University of Wisconsin–Milwaukee, 1986. Abstract in *Dissertation Abstracts International* 48 (1986): 0069.

North, Stephen M. "Writing Centers: A Sourcebook." Ph.D. diss., State University of New York at Albany, 1979. Abstract in *Dissertation Abstracts International* 40 (1979): 0816.

Peguesse, Chere L. "Writing Centers Professionalize: Visions and Versions of Legitimacy." Ph.D. diss., University of Arizona, 2000. Abstract in *Dissertation Abstracts International* 61 (2000): 3154.

Roswell, Barbara Sherr. "The Tutor's Audience Is Always a Fiction: The Construction of Authority in Writing Center Conferences." Ph.D. diss., University of Pennsylvania, 1992. Abstract in *Dissertation Abstracts International* 53 (1992): 3830.

Russell, Ann. "The University of Michigan-Flint Writing Center: A Case Study and a History." Ph.D. diss., Michigan State University, 1997. Abstract in *Dissertation Abstracts International* 58 (1997): 3442.

Ryan, A. Leigh K. "An Investigation and Description of Some Relationships Between Tutorial Assistance in a Writing Center and the Writing Apprehension of Freshman Composition Students." Ph.D. diss., University of Maryland College Park, 1986. Abstract in *Dissertation Abstracts International* 47 (1986): 2930.

Sadlon, John A. "The Effect of an Auxiliary Writing Skills Center Upon the Writing Improvement of Freshman Community College Composition Students." Ph.D. diss., Indiana University of Pennsylvania, 1978. Abstract in *Dissertation Abstracts International* 39 (1978): 4081.

Scanlon, Bettye Bene. "Future Priorities for College and University Writing Centers: A Delphi Study." Ph.D. diss., Peabody College for Teachers of Vanderbilt University, 1980. Abstract in *Dissertation Abstracts International* 42 (1980): 1889.

Seckendorf, Margaret Hess. "Writing Center Conferences: An Analysis." Ph.D. diss., State University of New York at Albany, 1986. Abstract in *Dissertation Abstracts International* 47 (1986): 3024.

Shakespeare, William O. "A Study of Writing Tutor Selection Instruments for College Writing Centers." Ph.D. diss., Brigham Young University, 1996. Abstract in *Dissertation Abstracts International* 57 (1996): 3350.

Shouse, Claude F. "The Writing Laboratory in Colleges and Universities." Ph.D. diss., University of Southern California, 1953. *ADD* W1953 (1953): 0220.

Simpson, Jeanne H. "A Rhetorical Defense of the Writing Center." Ph.D. diss., Illinois State University, 1982. Abstract in *Dissertation Abstracts International* 44 (1982): 0693.

Strand, Sharon E. "Reporting Writing Center Successes: Authentic Assessment in the Writing Center." Ph.D. diss., Bowling Green State University, 1997. Abstract in *Dissertation Abstracts International* 58 (1997): 3148.

Taylor-Escoffery, Bertha. "The Influences of the Writing Center on College Students' Perceptions of the Functions of Written Language." Ph.D. diss., Indiana University of Pennsylvania, 1992. Abstract in *Dissertation Abstracts International* 53 (1992): 3885.

Van Dam, Denis C. "Effects of Writing Center Usage and Motivation on Academic Writing." Ph.D. diss., University of Southern California, 1985. Abstract in *Dissertation Abstracts International* 46 (1985): 2590.

Walker, Kristin Wilds Davidson. "Assessing Students' Genre Knowledge in an Engineering Writing Center: An Analysis of Sophomore Lab Reports in Electrical and Computer Engineering." Ph.D. diss., University of South Carolina, 1997. Abstract in *Dissertation Abstracts International* 58 (1997): 0855.

Weaver, Margaret E. "Composition as Disciplinary, Postdisciplinary, Feminized and Comedic: Revisiting the Process/Product Dichotomy." Ph.D. diss., University of Texas at Arlington, 1997. Abstract in *Dissertation Abstracts International* 59 (1997): 0478.

Wiebers-Mitchell, Lissa Beth. "Technology and Writing Centers: Implementing Change." Master's thesis, Truman State University, 1999. *Masters Abstracts International* 37 (1999): 1305.

Wilson, Barbara Hurd. "Prewriting Behaviors of Field Dependent and Field Independent Remedial Writers in a College Writing Center." Ph.D. diss., University of Maryland College Park, 1984. Abstract in *Dissertation Abstracts International* 46 (1984): 0605.

Young, Virginia H. "Politeness Phenomena in the University Writing Conference." Ph.D. diss., University of Illinois at Chicago, 1992. Abstract in *Dissertation Abstracts International* 53 (1992): 4236.

LIST OF WORKS CITED

CHAPTER 1: WHY WE TUTOR

Harris, Muriel. "Talking in the Middle: Why Writers Need Writing Tutors." *College English* 57 (1995): 27–42.

CHAPTER 2: THE WRITING PROCESS

Beach, Richard. "Self-Evaluation Strategies of Extensive Revisers and Nonrevisers." *College Composition and Communication* 27 (1976): 160–64.

Berlin, James A. *Rhetoric and Reality: Writing Instruction in American Colleges, 1900–1985.* Carbondale, IL: SIUP, 1987.

Brannon, Lil, and C. H. Knoblauch, "On Students' Rights to Their Own Texts: A Model of Teacher Response." *College Composition and Communication* 33 (1982): 157–66.

Britton, James, Tony Burgess, Nancy Martin, Alex McLeod, and Harold Rosen. *The Development of Writing Abilities (11–18).* London: Macmillan, 1975.

Duncan, C. S. "A Rebellious Word on English Composition." *English Journal* 3 (1914): 154–60.

Elbow, Peter. *Writing Without Teachers.* New York: Oxford UP, 1973.

Emig, Janet. *The Composing Processes of Twelfth Graders.* Urbana, IL: NCTE, 1971.

Faigley, Lester, and Stephen Witte. "Analyzing Revision." *College Composition and Communication* 32 (1981): 400–14.

Flower, Linda, and John R. Hayes. "A Cognitive Process Theory of Writing." *College Composition and Communication* 32 (1981): 365–87.

Flower, Linda, John R. Hayes, Linda Carey, Karen Schriver, and James Stratman. "Detection, Diagnosis and the Strategies of Revision." *College Composition and Communication* 37 (1986): 16–55.

Freire, Paolo. *Pedagogy of the Oppressed.* New York: Herder & Herder, 1972.

Genung, John Franklin. "English at Amherst College." In *English in the American Universities,* ed. William Morton Payne. Boston: D.C. Heath, 1895. 110–15.

Grimm, Nancy M. "The Regulatory Role of the Writing Center: Coming to Terms with a Loss of Innocence." *The Writing Center Journal* 17 (1996): 5–29.

Hairston, Maxine. "The Winds of Change: Thomas Kuhn and the Revolution in the Teaching of Writing." *College Composition and Communication* 33 (1982): 76–88.

Lunsford, Andrea. "Collaboration, Control, and the Idea of a Writing Center." *The Writing Center Journal* 12 (1991): 3–10.

Macrorie, Ken. *Telling Writing.* Rochelle Park, NJ: Hayden, 1968.

Murray, Donald M. "The Listening Eye: Reflections on the Writing Conference." *College English* 41 (1979): 13–18.

Paris, Scott G., Margerie Y. Lipson, and Karen K. Wixson. "Becoming a Strategic Reader." *Contemporary Educational Psychology* 8 (1983): 293–316.

Perl, Sondra. "Understanding Composing." *College Composition and Communication* 31 (Dec. 1980): 363–69.

Reigstad, Thomas J., and Donald A. McAndrew. *Training Tutors for Writing Conferences.* Urbana, IL: NCTE, 1984.

Rico, Gabriel L. *Writing the Natural Way.* Los Angeles: J. P. Tarcher, 1983.

Sommers, Nancy. "Revision Strategies of Student Writers and Experienced Adult Writers." *College Composition and Communication* 31 (1980): 378–88.

CHAPTER 3: THE TUTORING PROCESS

Bartholomae, David. "The Study of Error." *College Composition and Communication* 31 (1980): 253–69.

Carbone, Nick. "Questions." WCenter Mailing List <wcenter@lyris.acs.ttu.edu> 22 October 2001.

Elbow, Peter, and Pat Belanoff. *A Community of Writers.* New York: Random House, 1989.

Harris, Muriel. *Teaching One-to-One: The Writing Conference.* Urbana, IL: NCTE, 1986.

North, Stephen M. "The Idea of a Writing Center." *College English* 46 (1984): 433–46.

Reigstad, Thomas J., and Donald A. McAndrew. *Training Tutors for Writing Conferences.* Urbana, IL: NCTE, 1984.

Shaughnessy, Mina P. *Errors and Expectations: A Guide for the Teacher of Basic Writing.* New York: Oxford UP, 1977.

CHAPTER 4: EXAMINING EXPECTATIONS

Gee, James Paul, Sarah Michaels, and Mary Catherine O'Connor. "The Multifaceted Nature of Discourse Analysis." *The Handbook of Qualitative Research in Education,* ed. M. D. LeCompte, W. L. Milory, and Judith Preissle. Orlando, FL: Academic Press, 1992. 228–291.

Lunsford, Andrea. "Collaboration, Control, and the Idea of a Writing Center." *The Writing Center Journal* 12 (1991): 3–10.

Mittendorf, Janet G. "Effective Writing Tutors/Advanced Training." Internet. WCenter <listproc@listserv.acs.ttu.edu> (March 8, 1996).

North, Stephen M. "The Idea of a Writing Center." *College English* 46 (1984): 433–46.

Tannen, Deborah. "What's in a Frame? Surface Evidence for Underlying Expectations." In *Framing in Discourse,* ed. Deborah Tannen, 14–56. New York: Oxford UP, 1993.

CHAPTER 5: OBSERVING IN THE WRITING CENTER

Sommers, Nancy. "Revision Strategies of Student Writers and Experienced Adult Writers." *College Composition and Communication* 31 (1980): 378–88.

CHAPTER 7: REFLECTING ON THE FIRST SESSION

Carino, Peter. "Posing Questions for Collaborative Evaluation of Audio Taped Tutorials." *The Writing Lab Newsletter* 14 (Sept. 1989): 11–13.

Murray, Donald M. "The Listening Eye: Reflections on the Writing Conference." *College English* 41 (1979): 13–18.

Gillespie, Paula, and Jon Olsen. "Tutor Training." In *The Writing Center Resource Manual,* ed. Bobbie Bayliss Silk, 3.1–12. NWCA Press, 1998.

Perl, Sondra. "Understanding Composing." *College Composition and Communication* 31 (December 1980): 363–69.

Ramage, John D., and John C. Bean. *The Allyn and Bacon Guide to Writing,* 2d ed. Boston: Allyn & Bacon, 2000.

CHAPTER 8: READING IN THE WRITING CENTER

Behrens, Laurence, and Leonard J. Rosen. *Writing and Reading Across the Curriculum,* 6th ed. New York: Harper Collins, 1997.

Cole, Michael, and Peg Griffin. "A Sociohistorical Approach to Remediation." In *Literacy, Society and Schooling,* ed. S. deCastell, A. Luke, and K. Egan, 110–31. Cambridge: Cambridge UP, 1986.

Garner, Ruth. *Metacognition and Reading Comprehension.* Norwood, NJ: Ablex, 1986.

North, Stephen M. "The Idea of a Writing Center." *College English* 46 (1984): 433–46.

Paris, Scott G., Margerie Y. Lipson, and Karen K. Wixson. "Becoming a Strategic Reader." *Contemporary Educational Psychology* 8 (1983): 293–316.

Tierney, Robert, and Timothy Shanahan. "Research on the Reading-Writing Relationship: Interactions, Transactions, and Outcomes." In *Handbook of Reading*

Research. Vol. 2, ed. Rebecca Barr, Michael L. Kamil, Peter Mosenthal, and R. David Pearson, 246–80. New York: Longman, 1991.

Vacca, Richard T., and JoAnne L. Vacca. *Content Area Reading,* 2d ed. Boston: Little, Brown & Co., 1986.

CHAPTER 9: WORKING WITH ESL WRITERS

Blau, Susan, and John Hall. "Guilt-Free Tutoring: Rethinking How We Tutor Non-Native–English-Speaking Students." *The Writing Center Journal* 23, (fall/winter 2002): 23–44.

Blau, Susan, John Hall, Jeff Davis, and Lauren Gravitz. "Tutoring ESL Students: A Different Kind of Session." *The Writing Lab Newsletter* 25 (June 2001): 1–4.

Brooks, Jeff. "Minimalist Tutoring: Making the Student Do All the Work." *The Writing Lab Newsletter* 15 (February 1991): 1–4.

Chappell, Virginia A., and Judith Rodby. "Verb Tense and ESL Composition: A Discourse Level Approach." *On TESOL '82: Pacific Perspectives on Language Learning and Teaching,* ed. Mark A. Clarke and Jean Handscombe, 309–320. Washington, D.C.: TESOL, 1983.

Clark, Irene. "Perspectives on the Directive/Non-Directive Continuum in the Writing Center." *The Writing Center Journal* 21 (fall/winter 2001): 33–58.

Cogie, Jane, Kim Strain, and Sharon Lorinskas. "Avoiding the Proofreading Trap: The Value of the Error Correction Process." *The Writing Center Journal* 19, (spring/summer 1999): 7–32.

Flower, Linda, John R. Hayes, Linda Carey, Karen Schriver, and James Stratman. "Detection, Diagnosis, and the Strategies of Revision." *College Composition and Communication* 37 (February 1986): 16–55.

Harris, Muriel, and Tony Silva. "Tutoring ESL Students: Issues and Options." *College Composition and Communication* 44 (December 1993): 525–37.

Kaplan, Robert. "Cultural Thought Patterns in Intercultural Education." *Language Learning* 16.1,2 (1966): 1–20.

Leki, Ilona. *Understanding ESL Writers: A Guide for Teachers.* Portsmouth, NH: Boynton/Cook, 1992.

Powers, Judith K. "Rethinking Writing Center Conferencing Strategies for the ESL Writer." *The Writing Center Journal* 13, no. 2 (spring 1993): 39–48.

Ritter, Jennifer J. "Recent Developments in Assisting ESL Writers." In *A Tutor's Guide: Helping Writers One to One,* ed. Ben Rafoth, 102–10. Portsmouth, NH: Boynton/Cook, 2000.

Rose, Mike. "Remedial Writing Courses: A Critique and a Proposal." *College English* 45 (1983): 109–28.

Severino, Carol. "The 'Doodles' in Context: Qualifying Claims About Contrastive Rhetoric." *The Writing Center Journal* 14 (fall/winter 1993): 44–63.

———. "Serving ESL Students." In *The Writing Center Resource Manual,* ed. Bobbie Bayliss Silk. Emmitsburg, MD: IWCA Press, 1998. IV2.1–IV2.7.

CHAPTER 10: WRITING CENTER RESEARCH

Bell, James H. "When Hard Questions Are Asked: Evaluating Writing Centers." *The Writing Center Journal* 21 (fall/winter 2000): 7–28.

Cazden, Courtney B. *Classroom Discourse: The Language of Teaching and Learning.* Portsmouth, NH: Heinemann, 1988.

Cochran-Smith, Marilyn, and Susan L. Lytle. *Inside/Outside: Teacher Research and Knowledge.* New York: Teachers College Press, 1993.

Davis, Kevin M., Nancy Hayward, Kathleen R. Hunter, and David L. Wallace. "The Function of Talk in the Writing Conference: A Study of Tutorial Conversation." *The Writing Center Journal* 9 (1986): 45–51.

Farb, Peter. *Word Play: What Happens When People Talk.* New York: Bantam, 1973.

Flynn, Thomas. "Promoting Higher-Order Thinking Skills in Writing Conferences." In *Dynamics of the Writing Conference: Social and Cognitive Interaction,* ed. Thomas Flynn and Mary King, 3–14. Urbana, IL: NCTE, 1993.

Hymes, Dell. "Models of the Interaction of Language and Social Life." In *Directions in Sociolinguistics: The Ethnography of Communication,* ed. John J. Gumperz and Dell Hymes, 35–71. Oxford: Basil Blackwell, 1986.

Lerner, Neal. "Counting Beans and Making Beans Count." *The Writing Lab Newsletter* 22, no. 1 (September 1997): 1–4.

———. "Choosing Beans Wisely." *The Writing Lab Newsletter* 26 (September 2001): 1–4.

MacDonald, Ross B. "An Analysis of Verbal Interactions in College Tutorials." *Journal of Developmental Education* 15 (1991): 2–4, 6, 8, 10, 12.

Mehan, Harold. *Learning Lessons: Social Organization in the Classroom.* Cambridge, MA: Harvard UP, 1979.

Newmann, Stephen. "Demonstrating Effectiveness." *The Writing Lab Newsletter* 23 (April 1999): 8–9.

Waldo, Mark L. "More Than 'First-Aid': A Report on the Effectiveness of Writing Center Intervention in the Writing Process." *Issues in College Learning Centers* 5 (1987): 12–22.

Walker, Carol P., and David Elias. "Writing Conference Talk: Factors Associated with High- and Low-Rated Writing Conferences." *Research in the Teaching of English* 21 (1987): 266–85.

CHAPTER 11: WRITING CENTERS: HISTORICAL AND THEORETICAL CONTEXTS

Appel, Francis S. "English Studies." In *The Effective General College Curriculum as Revealed by Examinations: A Report of the Committee on Educational Research of the University of Minnesota.* 274–300. Minneapolis: Univ. of Minn. Press, 1937.

———. "A Writing Laboratory." *Journal of Higher Education* 7 (1936): 71–77.

Ashton-Jones, Evelyn. "Asking the Right Questions: A Heuristic for Tutors." *The Writing Center Journal* 9 (1988): 29–36.

Beck, E. C. "Composition-Teaching in a State Teachers College." *English Journal* 28 (1939): 593–97.

Bell, James H. "Theory Talk in Historical Context." WCenter Mailing List <wcenter@lyris.acs.ttu.edu> 26 September 2002.

Berlin, James A. *Rhetoric and Reality: Writing Instruction in American Colleges, 1900–1985*. Carbondale: Southern Illinois University Press, 1987.

Boquet, Elizabeth. *Noise from the Writing Center*. Logan: Utah State University Press, 2002.

———. "'Our Little Secret': A History of Writing Centers, Pre- to Post-Open Admissions." *College Composition and Communication* 50, no. 3 (February 1999): 463–82.

Boynton, Percy H. "Sorting College Freshman." *English Journal* 2 (1913): 73–80.

Broder, Peggy F. "Writing Centers and Teacher Training." *WPA: Writing Program Administration* 13 (1990): 37–45.

Brooks, Jeff. "Minimalist Tutoring: Making the Student Do All the Work." *The Writing Lab Newsletter* 15 (1991): 1–3.

Bruffee, Kenneth A. "Collaborative Learning and The 'Conversation of Mankind.'" *College English* 46 (1984): 635–52.

Campbell, Oscar James. "The Failure of Freshman English." *English Journal* 28 (1939): 177–85.

Carino, Peter. "Early Writing Centers: Toward a History." *The Writing Center Journal* 15 (spring 1995): 103–15.

———. "Open Admissions and the Construction of Writing Center History: A Tale of Three Models." *The Writing Center Journal* 17 (fall 1996): 30–48.

Dembner, A. "Remedial Ed: Playing Catch-Up in College." *The Boston Globe,* 17 March 1996, 1, 26–27.

Duncan, C. S. "A Rebellious Word on English Composition." *English Journal* 3 (1914): 154–60.

Earle, Samuel Chandler. "The Organization of Instruction in English Composition." *English Journal* 2 (1913): 477–87.

Ede, Lisa. "Writing as a Social Process: A Theoretical Foundation for Writing Centers?" *The Writing Center Journal* 9 (1989): 3–13.

Faigley, Lester, Roger D. Cherry, David A. Jolliffe, and Anne M. Skinner. *Assessing Writers Knowledge and Processes of Composing*. Norwood, NJ: Ablex, 1985.

Freire, Paolo. *Pedagogy of the Oppressed*. New York: Herder and Herder, 1972.

Genung, John Franklin. "English at Amherst College." In *English in American Universities,* ed. William Morton Payne, 110–115. Boston: D.C. Heath, 1895.

George, Diana, and Nancy Grimm. "Expanded Roles/Expanded Responsibilities: The Changing Nature of Writing Centers Today." *The Writing Center Journal* 11 (fall/winter 1990): 59–67.

Grey, Lennox, Merritt Y. Hughes, Fred W. Lorch, and George B. Parks. "National Council of Teachers of English College Section." *College English* 3 (1942): 584–86.

Grimm, Nancy. *Good Intentions: Writing Center Work for Postmodern Times*. Portsmouth, NH: Boynton/Cook, 1999.

Hairston, Maxine. "Thomas Kuhn and the Revolution in the Teaching of Writing." *College Composition and Communication* 33 (1982): 76–88.

Harris, Muriel. "Collaboration Is Not Collaboration Is Not Collaboration: Writing Center Tutorials vs. Peer-Response Groups." *College Composition and Communication* 43 (1992): 369–83.

Hartwell, Patrick. "A Writing Laboratory Model." In *Basic Writing: Essays for Teachers, Researchers, and Administrators*, ed. Lawrence Kasden and Daniel R. Hoeber, 63–73. Urbana, IL: NCTE, 1980.

Hawkins, Thom. "Intimacy and Audience: The Relationship Between Revision and the Social Dimension of Peer Tutoring." *College English* 42 (1980): 64–68.

Healy, Dave. "Tutorial Role Conflict in the Writing Center." *The Writing Center Journal* 11 (1991): 41–50.

Hobson, Eric H. "Maintaining Our Balance: Walking the Tightrope of Competing Epistemologies." *The Writing Center Journal* 13 (1992): 65–75.

Joy, Florence Livingston. "Gleanings from the Class in Freshman English." *English Journal* 9 (1920): 201–09.

Joyner, Michael A. "The Writing Center Conference and the Textuality of Power." *The Writing Center Journal* 12 (1991): 80–89.

Kail, Harvey. "Collaborative Learning in Context: The Problem with Peer Tutoring." *College English* 45 (1983): 594–99.

Kail, Harvey, and John Trimbur. "The Politics of Peer Tutoring. *WPA: Writing Program Administration* 11 (1987): 5–12.

King, Mary. "Introduction to Section II." In *Dynamics of the Writing Conference: Social and Cognitive Interaction,* ed. Thomas Flynn and Mary King, 17–23. Urbana, IL: NCTE, 1993.

Leahy, Richard. "What the College Writing Center Is—and Isn't." *College Teaching* 38 (1990): 43–48.

Lerner, Neal. "Searching for Robert Moore." *The Writing Center Journal* 22 (fall/ winter 2001): 9–32.

Lunsford, Andrea A. "Collaboration, Control, and the Idea of a Writing Center." *The Writing Center Journal* 12 (1991): 3–10.

Marx, Michael Steven. "Bringing Tutorials to a Close: Counseling's Termination Process and the Writing Tutorial." *The Writing Center Journal* 11 (1991): 51–60.

Mayher, John S. "*Uncommon Sense* in the Writing Center." *Journal of Basic Writing* 11 (1992): 47–57.

Morrow, Diane Stelzer. "Tutoring Writing: Healing or What?" *College Composition and Communication* 42 (1991): 218–29.

Mullin, Joan A., and Ray Wallace, eds. *Intersections: Theory-Practice in the Writing Center*. Urbana, IL: NCTE, 1994.

North, Stephen M. "The Idea of a Writing Center." *College English* 46 (1984): 433–46.

———. "Revisiting 'The Idea of a Writing Center.'" *The Writing Center Journal* 15 (1994): 7–18.

"Organization and Use of a Writing Laboratory: Report of Workshop No. 9." *College Composition and Communication* 2 (1951): 17–18.

Osgood, Charles G. "No Set Requirement of English Composition in the Freshman Year." *English Journal* 4 (1915): 231–35.

Pratt, Mary Louise. "Arts of the Contact Zone." *Professions '91* (1991): 33–40.

Rabuck, Donna Fontanarose. "Giving Birth to Voice: The Professional Writing Tutor as Midwife." In *Writing Center Persepectives*, ed. Stay, Murphy, and Hobson. 112–19.

Reeves, Floyd Wesley, and John Dale Russell. *Some Aspects of Current Efforts to Improve College Instruction*. Bulletin of the Bureau of School Service, 1.2. Lexington: University of Kentucky, 1928.

Reigstad, Thomas. "The Writing Place at Buffalo: The First Years." *ADE Bulletin* 65 (1980): 31–33.

Rose, Mike. "The Language of Exclusion: Writing Instruction at the University." *College English* 47 (1985): 341–59.

Russell, David R. *Writing in the Academic Disciplines, 1870–1990: A Curricular History*. Carbondale: Southern Illinois University Press, 1991.

Scott, Fred Newton. "English at the University of Michigan." In *English in American Universities*, ed. William Morton Payne, 116–23. Boston: D.C. Heath, 1895.

Shamoon, Linda K., and Deborah H. Burns. "A Critique of Pure Tutoring." *The Writing Center Journal* 15 (1995): 134–51.

Shor, Ira. *When Students Have Power: Negotiating Authority in a Critical Pedagogy*. Chicago: Univ. of Chicago Press, 1996.

Stay, Bryon L., Christina Murphy, and Eric H. Hobson. *Writing Center Perspectives*. Emmitsburg, MD: NWCA Press, 1995.

Taylor, Warner. "A National Survey of Conditions in Freshman English." *University of Wisconsin Bureau of Education Research Bulletin* (May 1929).

Thurber, Samuel. "Five Axioms of Composition Teaching." *School Review* 5 (1897): 7–17.

Trimbur, John. "Peer Tutoring: A Contradiction in Terms?" *The Writing Center Journal* 7 (1987): 21–28.

Valentine, Robert G. "On Criticism of Themes by Students." *Technology Review* 4 (1901): 459–78.

Wilcox, Thomas W. *The Anatomy of College English*. San Francisco: Jossey-Bass, 1973.

Willey, Malcom Macdonald. *Depression, Recovery and Higher Education. A Report by Committee Y of The American Association of University Professors*. New York: McGraw-Hill, 1937.

Wolff, Janice M. "Tutoring in the 'Contact Zone.'" In *Stories from the Center: Connecting Narrative and Theory in the Writing Center*, ed. Lynn Craigue Briggs and Meg Woolbright, 43–50. Urbana, IL: NCTE, 2000.

Woolley, Edwin C. "Admission to Freshman English in the University." *English Journal* 3 (1914): 238–44.

CHAPTER 12: INTERDISCIPLINARY
AND ON-LINE TUTORING

Barnett, Robert W., and Jacon S. Blumner, eds. *Writing Centers and Writing Across the Curriculum Programs: Building Interdisciplinary Partnerships*. Westport, CT: Greenwood, 1999.

Bean, John C. *Engaging Ideas: The Professor's Guide to Integrating Writing, Critical Thinking, and Active Learning in the Classroom*. San Francisco: Jossey-Bass, 1996.

Connolly, Paul. "Writing and the Ecology of Learning." In *Writing to Learn Mathematics and Science*, ed. Paul Connolly and Teresa Vilardi, 1–14. New York: Teachers College Press, 1989.

Coogan, David. "E-mail Tutoring: A New Way to Do New Work." *Computers and Composition* 12 (1995): 171–81.

Geller, Anne Ellen. E-mail communication. 1 October 2002.

Hobson, Eric H., ed. *Wiring the Writing Center*. Logan: Utah State University Press, 1998.

Hubbuch, Susan M. "A Tutor Needs to Know the Subject Matter to Help a Student With a Paper: ___Agree ___Disagree ___Not Sure." *The Writing Center Journal* 8 (1988): 23–30.

Inman, James A., and Clinton Gardner. *The OWL Construction and Maintenance Guide*. Emmitsburg, MD: IWCA Press, 2002.

Inman, James A., and Donna M. Sewell. *Taking Flight with OWLs: Examining Electronic Writing Center Work*. Mahwah, NJ: Erlbaum, 2000.

Kiedaisch, Jean, and Sue Dinitz. "Look Back and Say 'So What': The Limitations of the Generalist Tutor." *The Writing Center Journal* 14 (1993): 63–74.

Novak, Mykl. Personal Communication. 16 October 2002.

Russell, David R. *Writing in the Academic Disciplines, 1870–1990: A Curricular History*. Carbondale: Southern Illinois University Press, 1991.

Swales, John M. *Genre Analysis: English in Academic and Research Settings*. Cambridge, UK: Cambridge UP, 1990.

Taylor, Warner. "A National Survey of Conditions in Freshman English." *University of Wisconsin Bureau of Education Research Bulletin* (May 1929).

Young, Art, and Toby Fulwiler. "The Enemies of Writing Across the Curriculum." In *Programs That Work: Models and Methods for Writing Across the Curriculum*, ed. Toby Fulwiler and Art Young, 287–94. Portsmouth, NH: Boynton/Cook, 1990.

CHAPTER 13: WHAT IF . . .

Elbow, Peter, and Pat Belanoff. *Sharing and Responding*. New York: Random House, 1989.

INDEX